Domination, Dependence, Denial and Despair

North American Studies in Nineteenth-Century German Literature

Jeffrey L. Sammons
General Editor

Vol. 12

PETER LANG
New York • San Francisco • Bern • Baltimore
Frankfurt am Main • Berlin • Wien • Paris

Charles F. Good

Domination, Dependence, Denial and Despair

Father-Daughter Relationships
in Grillparzer, Hebbel and Hauptmann

PETER LANG
New York • San Francisco • Bern • Baltimore
Frankfurt am Main • Berlin • Wien • Paris

Library of Congress Cataloging-in-Publication Data

Good, Charles F.
    Domination, dependence, denial and despair : father-daughter relationships in Grillparzer, Hebbel and Hauptmann / Charles F. Good.
        p. cm. — (North American studies in nineteenth-century German literature ; vol. 12)
        Includes bibliographical references.
        1. German drama—19th century—History and criticism.
2. Austrian drama—19th century—History and criticism.   3. Fathers and daughters in literature.   I. Title.   II. Series.
PT653.G66   1993   832'.709—dc20   92-26673
ISBN 0-8204-1696-7   CIP
ISSN 0891-4109

Die Deutsche Bibliothek-CIP-Einheitsaufnahme

Good, Charles F.:
Domination, dependence, denial and despair : father-daughter relationships in Grillparzer, Hebbel and Hauptmann / Charles F. Good.—New York; Berlin; Bern; Frankfurt/M.; Paris; Wien: Lang, 1993
    (North American studies in nineteenth-century German literature ; Vol. 12)
        ISBN 0-8204-1696-7
NE: GT

Table of Contents

Chapter I

Sociological and Psychological Considerations

"The knowledge of fundamental change in the past enables us to envisage the possibility of fundamental change in the present."[1] Applied to literature, this observation establishes the worth and necessity of literary study. Indeed, the literature of the nineteenth century tells the reader something of what was significant for that time. Furthermore, it provides insight into aspects of current life by expressing a basis of the present day and demonstrating patterns of human behavior. Within the context of the father-daughter relationship, situations from the past, depicted in dramas, show examples of familial interaction within the period in which the works are set, of the nineteenth century (as far as the works considered here are concerned) and for the present. Modern readers learn from these examples - we see both positive and negative depictions. Thus an analysis of these relationships can provide insights significant for any age.

This study of the father-daughter relationship focuses primarily on four dramas, Franz Grillparzer's *Das goldene Vlieβ* and *Des Meeres und der Liebe Wellen*, Friedrich Hebbel's *Maria Magdalene*, and Gerhart Hauptmann's *Rose Bernd*. This discussion is preceded by a brief investigation of four eighteenth-century works, G. E. Lessing's *Miβ Sara Sampson* and *Emilia Galotti*, H. L. Wagner's *Die Kindermörderin* and Friedrich Schiller's *Kabale und Liebe*, which act as important precursors to the other plays.

This examination demonstrates how these authors expressed key perspectives of the father-daughter relationship, including the father's concern for honor and reputation, objectification, domination, and possible rejection of the daughter by the father, the daughter's denial of her father's system of moral values, her isolation from family and society, and the degree of each daughter's individuation. Through close textual analyses of the dramas, each author's presentation of these patterns of familial interaction becomes apparent.

Works dealing with the father-daughter relationship depict family situations. The family has been a frequent, if not the primary, topic of literature from its very beginnings.[2] From the "Hildebrandslied" to modern plays, such as Kroetz's *Stallerhof* and Achternbusch's *Weihnachtstod*, families have played a central role. The current chapter focuses on general psychological and sociological aspects of the father-daughter relationship. An overview of pertinent literature summarizes significant issues surrounding the role of the father and the status of the daughter within the relationship. Important issues include the patriarchal role of the father and his responsibility vis-à-vis his children for sex-role evolution, moral development, and education. The status of the daughter as "property" and her actions to free herself from domination by the father as she seeks to establish herself as an independent entity will conclude the sociological study. This discussion seeks to draw together important perspectives of the father-daughter relationship both broadly for western society and specifically for nineteenth-century Germany. It is not the task here to question the validity of these aspects; rather, themes recurring in a variety of historical, sociological and psychological texts are summarized to demonstrate general patterns of familial interaction and personal development.

In general terms, the father's "occupational status"[3] determines the status of the family. The father thus acts as the family's representative in the community and as the representative of the community in the family.[4] According to Rose Laub Coser, this special position stems from the value system of religion which bestows on the father "well-defined privileges and rights" despite his status as a "'dependent personality'."[5] A religious value system may change from one age or civilization to another, but always reflects elements of the moral code generally accepted by a majority of the members of a society. Thus one cannot speak of a specific religious value system for eternity and all cultures, but rather of attitudes of morality shared by a common group. As Coser notes, the father may be thought of as a "dependent personality" because of his historically indirect relationship to his children. Whereas the mother concentrated on the daily life of the children - washing, clothing and feeding -, the father focused primarily on their attitudes.[6] This difference in child-care activities, which today is no longer as prevalent as it was 100 years ago, results from the phenomenon that "once a child leaves infancy, and the exclusive primary caretaking of the females, the males often begin to enter progressively more intrusively in that child's life."[7]

But certainly the father also plays a significant role in the life of the child while it is still in infancy. According to Malinowski, this role centers on establishing the child's legitimacy. Malinowski explains that biologically the father serves simply as the impregnator of the female. But socially he performs a vital role since "an unmarried mother is under a ban, a fatherless child is a bastard."[9] The role of "legitimizer" is indispensable, but nonetheless indirect. Michael Lewis and Marsha Weinraub explain that this indirect relationship to the child results in the father being "aloof, distant, authoritarian, and action oriented."[10] Indeed, the patriarchal and authoritarian aspects of the father figure are the perspectives of this parent to which reference is most often made.

Historically, as Michael Mitterauer and Reinhard Sieder point out, the "connection between rising absolutism and the increase in the father's authority" is quite evident.[11] Moreover, as serfdom disappeared, the average man began to assert himself at home and exercise power over his own house and family as had been exercised over him by his former master: he now truly became king in his personal realm. As Tannahill explains, with the increased development of agriculture came greater self-sufficiency through ownership of private property. This phenomenon resulted in more widely spread monogamy and the subordination of woman to man.[12] For children there was little, if any, change in their status as slaves into the nineteenth century.[13] Even after World War II, European family life has continued to revolve "around an omnipotent, omniscient, and omnipresent father."[14]

In short, the father demanded full and total reverence.[15] Thus the patriarchal father occupied a godlike position. The direct correlation of "father" with "God" dates back to pre-Christian times.   The proto Indo-European word *pater (father) forms a portion of the name of the supreme god of mythology, Jupiter. Emil Benveniste explains that the "Latin term *Jupiter* is taken from a formula of invocation: *dyeu pater* 'father Heaven', which corresponds exactly to the Greek vocative Zeû páter."[16]   Throughout Christian history the concept of a (sometimes vengeful) God the Father supported the earthly father's stern position.[17]

On a psychological level this powerful status is reflected by Freud, who maintained that "the ideal father was a somewhat threatening authoritarian."[18]   No matter where, the main function of the patriarchal head of the family was "to watch over the safety of his children, to provide for them and to guide them through life."[19] Lucy Gilbert and Paula Webster express the related notion that the father provides security for his offspring, in particular his daughter. In order to protect her "sexual purity," the father seeks to restrict her activities with males. His justification for this control is the claim of "parental duties and obligations."[20] In addition to protection of the child, the father's actions are an attempt to maintain "the patriarchal status quo."[21] This is most certainly not the case throughout the entire world, but, as Lynn observes, modern Germany still possesses a "powerful patriarchal structure" in which the father "still holds a strong role" when compared with his American counterpart.[22] Thus patriarchy was and continues to be a significant feature of the father figure and is deeply rooted in society and Western culture. It allows the father to exercise control over his family.

A second significant element is the father's responsibility for sex-role development in children. The sex-role is simply the degree to which males behave in traditional masculine ways (i.e., playing with guns, engaging in sports) and women in traditional female ways (i.e., playing with dolls, cooking, sewing). Whether or not such traditional sex-roles ought to be passed on to our children is not at issue here. Of interest is the effect the father has on establishing sex-roles.[23] Lamb explains that the father's "masculinity and his status in the family are correlated with the masculinity of his sons and the femininity of his daughters."[24] Robinson and Barret indirectly point to the importance of the father in sex-role development when they explain that, unlike traditional fathers, androgynous fathers "encourage their children to pursue their interests without regard to role appropriateness."[25] Lamb points out that the father is not only concerned with traditional sex-roles,[26] but also with the adoption of cultural values. The father acts as a mediator between society and family by helping the children become aware of what "society regards as gender-appropriate behavior," and through promoting "the adoption of the society's moral values."[27]

In numerous sociological studies the involvement of the father in the moral development of his children appears as the primary aspect of this parental figure in child rearing. Moral development concentrates on "a child's acquisition of the rules that guide moral actions."[28] Greif explains that it is necessary for children to learn these standards of behavior in order to fit into the society to which they belong. As stated above, the father represents the community in the family[29] and becomes the "link between the wider social system and the family system."[30] In previous centuries, the father was most frequently the only member of the family who had business dealings outside the family circle.[31] Furthermore, as "head of the household," a position established via adherence to patriarchy, the father's reputation became synonymous with his family's, and vice versa.[32]

The father's role as mediator between family and society is closely associated with the notion that the family unit as a whole provides the foundation for moral development. Whereas the father serves as the representative, the family setting functions as the "school house" where the mores emphasized by the community through the father are learned and internalized.[33] Although competition between the family and other social groups, such as a child's peers, has developed in this century regarding socialization, the family has continued to assert itself and its moral traditions. Clearly, the family's extreme influence is no longer characteristic of the modern world.[34] But, nevertheless, the family and, most importantly, the father continue to help individuals develop morally. The literature agrees that the father, rather than the mother, principally determines the development of social morality. This is true not only because the father represents the community, but also because he "is the more punitive parent and thus is relatively more effective in the inhibition of antisocial and undesirable behaviors."[35] Lynn reports that positive values are established when close father-child relationships, rather than mother-child relationships, are present.[36]

Between different social classes aspects of moral development vary. While middle-class parents emphasize a child's internalization of standards of conduct, working-class parents demand obedience.[37] No matter what elements of moral development a particular class deems most important, successful existence within society necessitates adherence to social mores. If one rejects this ethos, through socially improper behavior, one risks isolation.[38] Instruction and enforcement of social traditions guard against such isolation and even social censure, enabling the child to assume an active and accepted role within the social network. Thus the importance of social norms in the determination of an individual's existence becomes apparent.

Several authors assert that these norms were (and in some instances still are) rigid, unrelenting and harsh. In pre-industrial times, children were unable to free themselves from the few "tightly organized groups"[39] that comprised their social network and for this reason experienced a narrow spectrum of social attitudes. In present society, families themselves may establish rigid codes of behavior. As children grow older, relationships between parents and offspring change. At times parents refuse to admit that the relationship has altered and do not allow children to develop autonomously. Robinson and Barret report that in such cases fathers "become more strident in enforcing the family rules, almost as if they are determined to hold on to a relationship that they know is gone."[40]　Moreover, since the father (and in more recent history the mother, too) is separated from the family while at work, he judges his children according to his system of religious values.[41] These norms fit into the category of "rigid and unrelenting" since they may not correspond to the child's level of social and psychological maturation.　Furthermore, when the father seeks to impose such standards of behavior on children for whose care he is not primarily responsible (as was primarily the case in the nineteenth century), he demonstrates an impersonal approach to the issue of moral development.

Moral development results in the establishment of a reputation.　A family's reputation reflects the way the larger social network perceives separate familial entities since historically each house functioned as an individual unit.　Even in twentieth-century Germany, the reputation determined the ability of parents to find good mates for their children and to nurture necessary relations with the wider community.[42]　Thus concern for reputation has been and continues to be an important aspect of child development for Germans.

Sociologists have actively examined the role of the father in child development in recent years.　This reflects the changing attitudes about what the father can and should do in raising his children.　Patriarchy and moral development become the aspects of greatest importance for the subsequent literary study.　These issues complement one another since the strong, patriarchal father concerns himself with his reputation and that of his family.　As has been shown, reputation is a direct manifestation of the moral development of family members. In a society where the father carries the greatest responsibility for moral development, the reputation of the family reflects most significantly on him.　Thus he actively concerns himself with the behavior of his offspring in order to ensure that he and his family appear positive to the wider social community.

Having analyzed key perspectives of the father's role in child development, let us now consider the status of the daughter within the father-daughter relationship.　Historically, women's lives in general centered on obedience and humility.[43] Particularly in the nineteenth century, conditions worsened for women as the patriarch controlled all members of the household, including the wife and mother.[44] Gilbert and Webster emphasize that in such a patriarchal society, an unequal, duo-gender system, the woman had no social power.[45] Such social systems that repress women impede autonomous development because they leave women "unprepared to define or defend their own interests."[46] Indeed, the woman was long "confined" to the house, saddled with the responsibilities of caring for the children, the kitchen and livestock. Moreover, public affairs and membership in social and political associations were viewed as being beyond her grasp since she was closely identified with the home sphere.[47] Coupled with this external repression is the notion that even "in the face of cruelty and cold indifference, women are junkies for male approval and do almost anything to have it delivered to the door."[48] This statement by Gilbert and Webster might be refuted by other women, but these authors assert that the need for male approval in order to achieve success continues to haunt women today.[49]   Gilbert and Webster also maintain that the repressed role of woman develops when she is a daughter,[50] stating clearly that "it was the experience and institution of daughterhood that prepared us to know ourselves as women and victims."[51]   When describing the situation of nineteenth-century Europe, Tannahill concludes that women encouraged male domination as women found it "pleasant to be worshiped, cherished and deferred to, flattering to be considered vulnerable, virginal, and remote; pure angels to whom a man might turn for respite from the rough, cruel world of business realities."[52]

The daughter might see herself not only as a victim, as Gilbert and Webster maintain, but most certainly as a piece of her father's property. In past centuries, this notion applied to women in general - both daughters and wives.[53] Rather than being a union of love, marriage was equal to a business practice.[54] Even the etymology of the word *Ehe* itself reflects this association with law and business dealings. Originally the word denoted a business contract, but has become more specific in meaning. Kluge shows the connection between *Ehe* (Old High German *êwa*, Middle High German *ê*) and commerce when he maintains the current meaning "beruht auf Besonderung: unter den gesetzmäßigen Verträgen war der zur Ehe führende der wichtigste."[55] Daughters were long seen as burdens that at times had to be got rid of.[56] Reporting on nineteenth-century England, Tannahill explains that a "London court of law confirmed that a husband was justified in even kidnapping a refugee wife . . . and keeping her under lock and key because 'the happiness and honour of both parties place the wife under the guardianship of husband.'"[57]

As a bride, the daughter was a source of revenue for the parents as the groom had to pay a dowry. Business dealings were an important element of courtship. The size of the bride's *Mitgift*, comprised of towels, bedding and clothing, was also a significant issue. The father carried out all such "transactions" with the father of the groom. Theoretically, the daughter could refuse the choice made by her father, but this was not often the case as the father took great care in picking the best possible mate.[58] In the nineteenth century, social and religious customs forbid the daughter from initiating contact with a man.[59] Such behavior would place her in conflict with her father and the social order he represents. This topic will be addressed below in greater detail. For now it is sufficient to say that women did have some rights against unwanted marriage, but the practice of a marriage arranged by the father remained strongly in force during the nineteenth century.[60] Male control over the female in the areas of morals and sexuality enabled the male to determine the choice of partner for the woman.[61]

Thus the woman in general (and the daughter in particular) was repressed and treated like a piece of property - something to be bought and sold, not unlike a slave. As will be shown in the dramas, the daughters may reject domination by the father and begin to assert themselves as the process of self-realization[62] or individuation takes place within the psyche of the individual.

C. G. Jung describes individuation as "becoming an 'individual,' and, in so far as "individuality" embraces our innermost, last and incomparable uniqueness, it also implies becoming one's own self."[63] He explains that the goal of the individuation process is a more complete understanding of the persona's effects on the individual.[64] Through this process a person "becomes the definite, unique being he in fact is."[65] Jung also explains that although it is true that a child's parents are the most important relations, as the child grows older, the parents "become increasingly shut away from consciousness, and on account of the restrictive influence they sometimes continue to exert, they easily acquire a negative aspect."[66] This is the rejection factor mentioned earlier. Jung sees this denial as a necessary action, if the child is to develop in a psychologically healthy manner. It is imperative that the child free itself from portions of parental control while retaining other valuable elements.[67] As the individual becomes more aware of itself, "the layer of the personal unconscious that is superimposed on the collective unconscious will be diminished."[68] This action allows the consciousness to assert itself more freely.[69] This increased awareness of one's particularity results in the production of a socially more successful person. Jung maintains that "adequate consideration of the peculiarity of the individual is more conducive to a better social performance than when the peculiarity is neglected or suppressed."[70]

Throughout his writings, Jung describes individuation primarily as the process of the male seeking his appropriate anima.[71] It is possible, however, for the female to look for her animus, the male counterpart of the anima.[72] Thus it is appropriate to refer to the process the daughter undergoes as she rejects and moves away from her parents as part of individuation.

Other authors refer to the phenomenon of the daughter moving away from the father's control as a manifestation of her individuation. Greif comments that "experiences away from parents" are seen as necessary during maturation.[73] Davis views the process not simply as moving away from the parents, but as "*moving into* the social organization."[74] In this manner, the child's personality expands, his entire future lies before him. Conversely the parent's life focus shifts to the past. Indeed, the child represents the parent's future,[75] and the parent depends vicariously upon the child for continuation of a meaningful existence. The child on the other hand seeks greater exclusion of the parent as its independence increases. Thus conflicting interests may arise between parent and child - the parent depending more heavily on the child while the child continues to free itself from parental control.[76]

A principal cause for the child's movement away from the father is the repression of individuality occurring within the family unit. Such repressive socialization results from the father's inability or unwillingness to allow the child to develop in a manner that does not directly reflect the parent's expectations. For individuation to take place, the youth requires room to explore. As we saw above, a family's standards of behavior are often rigid; there is little, if any, opportunity for the individual to deviate from these norms as a part of maturation. This includes the inability of the youth to gather experiences outside the home situation. Mitterauer and Sieder report that under such circumstances there is little chance for children "to develop their own interests or to foster individual talents and ambitions."[77] When children are socialized solely by their parents, a danger exists because the parents and children are, "at any given moment, in different stages of development."[78] What the parents learned at the stage where the child currently finds itself, is different from the stage the child now internalizes. The danger lies in the parents' attempts to instill in the child the older, now inappropriate content.[79] The rule of thumb for this type of socialization is, "If it was good enough for me, it is good enough for her."

The reaction of the child to such repressive socialization is revolt. As the discussion of the plays will demonstrate, degrees of revolt can range from openly defying the parents to secretly doing what the individual wishes (and perhaps living in constant fear of being discovered, thus causing despair). Ruth Nanda Anshen explains that rebellion has taken place throughout history whenever "the realms of the mind - spirit, reason, language, all aspects of nature's manifoldness which have claims in universality" - have found themselves repressed.[80] Such revolt is an assertion of independence. Independence manifests itself by "revolting against what are felt to be the standards of the adult world."[81] This denial is accompanied by a compulsive desire to fit into the tightly-knit group of adolescent peers, thus rejecting the authority of adults.[82]

Although denial seems an inevitable manifestation of the repressive socialization performed by the family, revolt was not expected in a normal family, nor was it perceived as a natural expression of adolescent autonomy.[83]   Indeed, the possibility of avoiding rebellion exists, but this involves a change in parental treatment of individuals who are at a turning point in life. Such change centers on "a progressive readjustment . . . in the respective positions of parent and child."[84] Lucarini writes that the father must remember that the children live in a different dimension: they are ahead of the fathers - living in the future while the fathers live in the present.[85] If parents alter their own socialization techniques in a way allowing for the child's inherent necessity to differ from the parents as it develops its own personality, caustic revolt can be avoided.

Under the rubric of parent-child socialization, the father-daughter relationship holds a special place.   Gilbert and Webster see this relationship as "the laboratory for learning heterosexuality, in its sexual and social aspects; it prepares the daughter to enter the world with an accurate map of the sexual status quo."[86]   The father can provide a model of autonomy and individuality for imitation by the daughter, aspects of the self that the mother is either unwilling or unable to validate.[87] If, however, the daughter wants to continue to have a positive relationship with her father, she may not openly rebel against him and what he represents; she must remain submissive, particularly regarding the father's expectations for the daughter's (lack of) sexual activity.[88] The father's rules, especially in sexual matters, may certainly be designed to protect the daughter from teen-age pregnancy, but, as Gilbert and Webster maintain, the element of a "bad reputation" is also a part of this picture.[89] While the daughter may believe that her actions affect only her, the fact remains that the entire family is touched by what she does. Especially the father becomes associated with and made responsible for his daughter's behavior. Thus the daughter's reputation helps establish (or ruin) that of the family and of the father. Under such circumstances it is not surprising that the daughter "learns that real or feigned sexual abstinence will be necessary to maintain her father's respect, approval, and love."[90] Deviation from this practice would indicate denial of the moral standards the father tries to instill as society's representative in the family.

Having considered the father's role in child development and the daughter's status in the father-daughter relationship, let us now consider some additional factors of this relationship peculiar to the nineteenth century to provide a clearer socio-historic basis for the literary examination. Lamb points out that, during the eighteenth and early nineteenth centuries, the father's role in child development centered on "moral oversight and moral teaching."[91] The father's principal responsibility lay with ensuring that his children "grew up with an appropriate sense of values, acquired primarily from the study of religious materials like the Bible."[92] This notion corresponds to the assertion made by Coser about the significance of religious value systems for child development. Without a doubt, the nineteenth century was an era of patriarchy.[93] As Drewitz describes, women began about 1800 to become more aware of themselves socially and politically, but the "direct struggle for their rights is a phenomenon of the industrial society . . ."[94] This struggle did have some positive effects on the status of women, for example in Prussia where equality between women and men was legally mandatory. Nevertheless, with the rise of industrialization, such developments were "wiped out for more than 100 years."[95] The advance of industrialization changed the status of the man as well. It brought with it the removal of some business production from many private households. This resulted in the loss of a certain amount of the father's economic authority.[96] Nevertheless, in matters concerning the family, the father continued to reign supreme.[97] One reason for the continuation of this well-established practice is that the nineteenth century glorified the Middle Ages, complete with their authoritarian form of existence and emphasis on knighthood.[98] Another related factor is the concomitant rise of absolutism and patriarchy.

With its emphasis on patriarchy, the nineteenth century functions as a good example of how an individual, especially a daughter, had to deal with a socially repressive system while establishing an autonomous identity.

We have seen how the father's role in child development includes concern for the honor and reputation of his family, representation of social norms in the family and domination, objectification and possible rejection of the daughter. The daughter's place in the relationship with her father is characterized by her possible denial of parental ethos and isolation. These become important elements of the child's maturation and individuation process. They are also important topics in the dramas.

Chapter II

Precursors to the Nineteenth Century

In the eighteenth century, German dramas appear in which the interaction between fathers and daughters becomes an especially significant aspect of the works.[1] These *bürgerliche Trauerspiele* are relevant to a study of nineteenth-century dramas because they indicate a "dramatic heritage,"[2] and show the conflict arising between father and daughter when the daughter's natural desires to leave the family assert themselves. The conflict stems from the discrepancy between the daughter's desires and the father's expectations of socially accepted behavior.[3]

Two works by Lessing, *Miß Sara Sampson* and *Emilia Galotti*, Wagner's *Kindermörderin* and Schiller's *Kabale und Liebe* demonstrate many of the sociological and psychological elements of the father-daughter relationship described in the first chapter. Another important feature in each of these dramas is the difference in social class. Each work shows the author's critique of the abuse of the bourgeoisie by members of a higher class. Thus the aspect of social class consciousness, a topic of these plays that has been examined elsewhere,[4] must be considered for its significant, albeit indirect role in the father-daughter relationships of these dramas. Moreover, if we accept Jochen Hörisch's notion that the origin of psychology lies in the essence of these *bürgerliche Trauerspiele*,[5] their significance increases greatly. Although in his article on *Miß Sara Sampson* Denis Jonnes does not always examine each possible argument in his interpretation of that play (see below), he does point out that we can discover important psychological information about fathers and daughters through the dramas,[6] with special emphasis being placed on the daughter's virtue, specifically her sexual purity.[7]

The first line of *Miß Sara Sampson* develops that portion of the drama's plot centering on the father, Sir William, and the daughter, Sara. Sir William states: "Hier meine Tochter? Hier in diesem elenden Wirtshause?"[8] This is not to say that this play focuses solely on the father-daughter relationship. Indeed, as Bornkamm maintains, the plot centers on the situation of the man (Mellefont) between two women.[9] But the task here is to analyze the relationship between father and daughter, not to examine the entire play - this has often been done already.[10] In Sir William's opening statement quoted above, we experience a sense of the concern and forgiveness this father brings to his daughter. She is described by Waitwell, Sir William's manservant, as "Das beste, schönste, unschuldigste Kind, das unter der Sonne gelebt hat . . ."[11] Sir William has come to reconcile himself with his daughter after she left him to live with Mellefont. According to Waitwell, Mellefont has led Sara astray.[12] Sir William thinks only of being rejoined with his daughter and is prepared to overlook any and all of Sara's actions as long as she is reunited with him:

> Ich kann sie länger nicht entbehren; sie ist die Stütze meines Alters, und wenn sie nicht den traurigen Rest meines Lebens versüßen hilft, wer soll es denn tun? ... wenn diese Vergehungen auch wahre Verbrechen, wenn es auch vorsätzliche Laster wären: ach! ich würde ihr doch vergeben. Ich würde doch lieber von einer lasterhaften Tochter, als von keiner, geliebt sein wollen.[13]

In this instance, the father has overcome the harsh patriarchy attributed to this parent by most sociologists: he is remorseful and seeks to foster a positive relationship with his daughter.[14] Although this is superficially true, Sir William nevertheless puts himself in the position of feeling that he has something to forgive. While his arrival at the "elende Wirtshaus" is seen on the surface as a magnanimous act, his principal desire lies in ensuring the love of his daughter for himself - egocentric behavior. Therefore, we should not view his actions as totally altruistic.

Like her father, Sara is concerned with her "guilt," as demonstrated by her dream that she describes to Mellefont:

Es war der Ton meines Vaters - Ich Elende! kann ich denn nichts von ihm vergessen?   Ach! wo ihm sein Gedächtnis eben so grausame Dienste leistet; wo er auch mich nicht vergessen kann! - Doch er hat mich vergessen. Trost! grausamer Trost für seine Sara![15]

Sara realizes that she has broken with her father by leaving him to live with Mellefont. She cannot believe that her father desires to reconcile himself with her and is unwilling to enjoy herself at the expense of her father.[16]   She perceives her flight, an action Mauser interprets as an outward sign of Sara's self-realization, as an affront against the norms represented by Sir William.[17] Furthermore, Sara maintains that she has lost all her virtue and desires to hear that her father has given up on her: "Aber nun sage mir wenigstens, Waitwell, daß es ihm nicht hart fällt, ohne mich zu leben."[18] Waitwell asserts that Sir William does indeed still love his daughter, that he is the same tender father, "so wie sein Sarchen noch immer die zärtliche Tochter ist, die sie beide gewesen sind."[19] But Sara is not convinced by this statement and continues to play the martyr, demonstrated by her desire for self-punishment.

Although Sir William and Sara view her actions as morally incorrect, they do become reconciled with each other, but only as Sara lies dying after being poisoned by Marwood.[20] Suddenly Sir William comes to the realization that the actual problem lies in the fact that he should never have put Sara in a position that forced her to flee. He asks himself: "Warum vergab ich dir nicht gleich? Warum setzte ich dich in die Notwendigkeit, mich zu fliehen?"[21] These are hard questions for a father to ask, especially as his daughter lies on her death bed. But for this father and daughter, there is an apparent happy end in their reconciliation. Sir William is prepared to fulfill Sara's last wishes to accept Mellefont as a son and look after Mellefont's child as a granddaughter.

This happy end is only a superficial appearance. To be sure, Sir William and Sara are rejoined, but the questions Sir William asks himself at the conclusion point to the real conflict in this father-daughter relationship: "Soll ein Vater so eigennützig handeln? Sollen wir nur die lieben, die uns lieben?"[22] This father-daughter relationship has not been beneficial for Sara's psychological and sociological development, and her entire manner of behaving has centered on her concern for her father.[23] But this concern was not always present. Sara first felt the need to flee from her father - a consequence of her natural adult development that includes moving away from parental control. In Mellefont Sara found someone she believed would be her life's partner, but the family situation prevented her from fulfilling this need in a psychologically healthy and independent manner. Thus she had to leave. Nonetheless, she was so closely tied to her family, especially to her father, that she was unable to overcome her feeling of guilt for having left. The act of leaving itself brought Sara (and Mellefont as well) into conflict with social norms.[24] Sara herself believed that her virtue suffered as a result of her actions (see above). This notion of self-guilt, coupled with the fact that Sir William suspected his daughter of being less than virtuous,[25] placed Sara in a hopeless situation.[26]

As we have seen, reconciliation plays an important role in the drama. But the question must be asked, what kind of reconciliation does Sir William truly offer? Waitwell alludes to re-establishing the status quo - *Sarchen* (most likely the name used for Sara when she was a little girl) and her father would become the beings they always *had been*! No development, no self-realization, no individuation can take place in such a situation. Sir William's deep-reaching questions come much too late for him and his daughter. This is part of the tragedy of this drama: There is a light, an indication of change, but it simply does not appear soon enough. Father and daughter remain tied too tightly to the conception of virtue that prevents each from sharing thoughts and feelings with each other. Sara's entire situation could have been avoided if communication had occurred between father and daughter *before* she felt it necessary to leave.

The father-daughter relationship in *Emilia Galotti* is also significant, this time leading directly to the daughter's death. Indeed, the actions of Odoardo and Emilia at the end of the play have caused interpreters some consternation as they have struggled to explain why the drama concludes as it does.[27] But, as in *Miß Sara Sampson*, the father-daughter relationship plays an important role from the beginning of the work. At the outset, the Prince describes Odoardo as "Ein alter Degen, stolz und rauh, sonst bieder und gut."[28] Here a principal characteristic of Odoardo's personality is mentioned that forms the basis for this father's actions throughout the drama: virtue. He is primarily concerned with the moral development of his daughter[29] and is happy that she is about to marry a man of good standing in the community. Moreover, he does not view the marriage as the loss of his daughter, but rather is comforted by the fact that she will be secure "in den Armen der Liebe."[30] Whereas Sir William Sampson sought to regain his daughter's companionship, Odoardo appears prepared to relinquish his daughter so that she may lead a life with her husband. But such autonomy is not yet present as we see when Odoardo explains to his wife how important Emilia's existence is for his own. When he discovers that the Prince has spoken with Emilia in the past, Odoardo becomes incensed, demonstrating a second characteristic of his personality: rage. But, instead of considering the effect of a relationship with the Prince on Emilia, Odoardo merely sees how he might be affected: "Ha! wenn ich mir einbilde - Das gerade wäre der Ort, wo ich am tödlichsten zu verwunden bin! . . . der bloße Gedanke setzt mich in Wut."[31] Here manifestations of Odoardo's virtue and rage appear. Odoardo expresses his concern for his daughter's virtue, but couples this with anxiety about what an affront to her virtue would mean for him. Virtue becomes a fixation, as his life apart from the larger community in order to preserve his own virtue suggests.[32] As Poynter maintains, virtue is "Odoardo's sole sense of his *self* and his own personality."[33] Even Claudia, Emilia's mother, associates Odoardo with raw virtue.[34]

This patriarchal head of the family is interested in the preservation of his daughter's virtue. This desire places the rest of the family in a state of fear, leading the mother to explain to Emilia: "Ha, du kennest deinen Vater nicht! In seinem Zorne hätt' er den unschuldigen Gegenstand des Verbrechens mit dem Verbrecher verwechselt."[35] Here we see the second characteristic: rage.[36] In Odoardo's conversation with the Prince's former mistress, Orsina, causes Odoardo to recognize what will happen to his daughter if she is left in the Prince's hands: "Schlimmer? schlimmer als tot? - Aber doch zugleich auch tot? - Denn ich kenne nur *ein* Schlimmeres -."[37]   He thus sees rescuing Emilia from this situation as his purpose; he must protect his daughter. Finally it becomes apparent to Odoardo and to Emilia that only one method exists to preserve her virtue: she must die.

But what brings Emilia and her father to this decision? Emilia, like her father, is viewed as a paradigm of virtue.[38] She goes to church every day and will be a "pious bride," as Graf Appiani calls her. But another side of Emilia exists about which only she knows, a side she has difficulty admitting even to herself: she can be passionate. She alludes to this aspect of her character in Act II when she hurriedly comes home from church after the Prince has spoken with her. Emilia explains to her mother that she found it difficult to pray. The mother maintains: "Dem Himmel ist beten wollen auch beten." Emilia counters: "Und sündigen wollen auch sündigen."[39] Emilia clearly articulates her perception of her emotional capabilities. Another expression of this passion appears when she tells her father of her inner turmoil, something she may not be able to control:

> Ich habe Blut, mein Vater, so jugendliches, so warmes Blut als eine. Auch meine Sinne sind Sinne. Ich stehe für nichts. Ich bin für nichts gut. Ich kenne das Haus der Grimaldi. Es ist das Haus der Freude. Eine Stunde da, unter den Augen meiner Mutter; - und es erhob sich so mancher Tumult in meiner Seele, den die strengsten Übungen der Religion kaum in Wochen besänftigen konnten.[40]

When coupled with the statement "sündigen wollen auch sündigen," it becomes clear that Emilia possesses the ability to be passionate. She has been placed in a situation from which she sees no escape.[41] Since she is not allowed to flee, but will be held in the Grimaldi house, a place she associates with her passion already,[42] she sees death as the only remaining means of escaping from the present situation and of preserving her own virtue.[43] Emilia must choose between her natural urges and the bourgeois norms her father represents.[44] She begs her father to kill her because she sees no other way out.

Odoardo also believes that Emilia's death is necessary to preserve her virtue. Jonnes maintains that the concluding scenes of the play bring about a "transformation of Odoardo's character, which necessitates the confrontation" between father and daughter.[45] This transformation, Jonnes believes, causes Odoardo to kill his daughter. There is, however, no transformation in Odoardo's character: he remains steadfast in his belief that virtue is the most important feature of human existence. For the sake of its preservation, Emilia must die. Thus the characteristic Odoardo has instilled most predominantly in his daughter becomes the reason for her death. To this degree, Odoardo is guilty not only of killing his daughter, but, in combination with the expectations of society, of causing the situation that made her death necessary.[46] Odoardo reacts quickly and without thought to Emilia's chiding remarks that there once was a father who was willing to kill his daughter (referring to the Virginia story) by thrusting a dagger into her.[47]

Emilia and Odoardo are products of the same moral education. This father has fulfilled the sociological role of instilling in the child his mores and modes of social behavior. Unfortunately for Emilia it is impossible for her to continue to exist and at the same time remain true to her father's lessons. Thus, the tragedy of this play depends greatly on the father-daughter relationship since the moral conflict that rages within Emilia, causing her to desire death over life, is a manifestation of the contradiction between her inner passions and her moral development - something for which the father and his society are responsible.

A third eighteenth-century drama in which the father-daughter relationship plays a significant role is Heinrich Leopold Wagner's *Die Kindermörderin*. This work, like others written by Wagner, has been widely overlooked until recent years.[48] Otto Mann in *Geschichte des deutschen Dramas* mentions Wagner's play only in passing as an influential work for Hauptmann's *Rose Bernd*.[49] In another standard text, Fritz Martini's *Deutsche Literaturgeschichte*, only a three-line description of the work is given.[50] Perhaps one reason for the work having been widely forgotten is the fact, "Was Wagner zeigte, und wie er es zeigte, wurde bereits von den Zeitgenossen als unzulässig, weil anstößig, gebrandmarkt."[51] Wagner's topic was not a creation of his own mind, but rather a reflection of eighteenth-century reality.[52] Many could have found this reality too caustic, especially the first act's seduction scene - especially problematic in Wagner's day.[53] The presentation on stage of infanticide also contributes to the crass realism of the work.

Of primary concern for this brief analysis is why Evchen is driven to commit infanticide. The answer depends greatly on the father-daughter relationship. As pointed out in the first chapter, a father is responsible for a child's moral development and, more specifically, the reputation. Shame becomes a significant element in establishing reputation because it indicates awareness of improper behavior. Shame works on Evchen's mind throughout most of the drama. She becomes more and more aware of the fact that her actions are in opposition to social norms, represented by her father, and infanticide is her attempt to rid herself of the physical manifestation of her shame as an unwed mother. Paradoxically, however, infanticide serves only to increase the shame she brings upon herself and her family and, more importantly, sharpens the penalty imposed on her.[54] Almost immediately after having intercourse with von Gröningseck while attending a ball, Evchen is concerned about her shame and feels her honor has been disgraced. She calls her "lover" an "Ehrenschänder" and responds to his promise to return in five months to marry her, "Fünf Monat, sagten Sie? gut! so lang' will ich mich zwingen, mir Gewalt anthun, daß man meine Schande mir nicht auf der Stirne lesen soll."[55]

In the next scene, Evchen's father, Humbrecht, is incensed to learn that Evchen and her mother were at the ball the night before and explains that he feels attending a dance of this type is inappropriate behavior for "Bürgersleut'."[56] Thus Humbrecht displays his understanding of the difference in classes - the bourgeoisie ought not to associate with the aristocracy (as Evchen has with *von* Gröningseck). Moreover, Humbrecht concerns himself with Evchen's sexual purity and readily expresses his conception of what happens at such parties:

> Wenn denn vollends ein zuckersüßes Bürschchen in der Uniform, oder ein Barönchen, des sich Gott erbarm! ein Mädchen vom Mittelstand an solche Örter hinführt, so ist zehn gegen eins zu verwetten, daß er sie nicht wieder nach Haus bringt, wie er sie abgeholt hat.[57]

Humbrecht unknowingly describes just what has happened to his daughter. Evchen expresses the fear that her father has already discovered her secret: "sollt' er meinen Fehltritt schon entdeckt haben?"[58] Her fear is not unfounded or unreasonable since Humbrecht has no sympathy for "dishonorable" people. Furthermore, he is concerned with what other members of the community think about what happens in his home as well:

> . . . die schöne Jungfer dahinten hat sich von einem Sergeanten eins anmessen lassen, die Mutter weiß darum, und läßt alles so hingehen; die ganze Nachbarschaft hält sich drüber auf. - Jetzt marsch! und kündig' ihnen das Logis auf: du weißt jetzt, warum? - Wollt eher den ganzen Hinterbau zeitlebens leer stehen lassen, Ratten, Mäusen und Nachteulen preisgeben, eh' ich solch Lumpengesindel beherbergen wollt'. - Meine eigne Tochter litt ich keine Stund' mehr im Haus, wenn sie sich so weit verging.[59]

Humbrecht is a morally rigid individual. Evchen understands her father's words as her own judgment and feels all is lost as Act II concludes.[60] With the presence of an attitude such as her father's, Evchen becomes ever more aware of her shame, which was not simply part of a good reputation, but rather a manifestation of the repressions practiced within the family and the closely-knit social relationships present in Evchen's community.[61]

Not only does Evchen fear her father's anger, but also his love.[62] The father-daughter relationship has become problematic for Evchen because she sees personified in her father social norms with which she has collided as a result of her sexual activity with von Gröningseck.[63] Like her father, Evchen is concerned about the neighbors' opinions - even what they might think about something as insignificant as how late the lights burn at night.[64] Indeed, Evchen remains a captive of the bourgeois ethos personified by her father; she is unable to free herself from the fixation with shame and disgrace. Ultimately Evchen's concern for social morality results in her forced withdrawal from society as she attempts to rid herself of life's reality through isolation. Infanticide then becomes Evchen's final attempt to conquer her isolation by removing the physical manifestation of her dishonor. In the same moment, the murder of the child demonstrates Evchen's unceasing compliance with her father's Weltanschauung: It drives her into a hopeless situation from which she perceives only one escape.[65]

When the Magister comes and relates Evchen's behavior in church as the ordinance about infanticide was read aloud during the worship service, Humbrecht surprisingly demonstrates that he trusts his daughter. He refuses to equate Evchen's fainting with her guilt.[66] This marks the double nature of the relationship between Humbrecht and Evchen. The father seems almost schizophrenic as he vacillates between love and hate for his daughter. One moment he is understanding and the next he is in a rage.[67] The reunion scene between Evchen and her father at the end of the play demonstrates this tendency:[68]

> Humbrecht. Wo? wo ist sie, mein Evchen? - meine Tochter, meine einzige Tochter! *Erblickt sie auf dem Bett.* Ha! bist du da, Hure, bist da? . . . Hängst den Kopf wieder? hast's nicht Ursach, Evchen, 's ist dir alles verziehn, alles! - *Schüttelt sie.* Komm, sag ich, komm! wir wollen Nacht-ball halten - - ja, da möcht' man sich ja kreuzigen und segnen über so ein Aas; wenn der Vater zankt, so lauft's davon, giebt er gute Wort, so ist's taub - *Schüttelt sie noch heftiger.* Willst reden? oder ich schlage dir das Hirn ein![69]

Even after the dead child is discovered, Humbrecht continues to think of honor and, although he states that the world has become too small for him, is prepared to finance von Grön-ingseck's attempt to obtain a pardon for his daughter.[70] Thus we see at the end of this drama a positive act by the father as he struggles to save what is left of his daughter's existence. Although she has clearly acted in opposition to the social norms both by having sexual relations with von Gröningseck and then subsequently killing the product of this action,

Evchen's father does not turn his back on her. To be sure, he is angry; but, if his final words are believed at face value (and we have no reason not to believe them), then they indicate a continuation of parental support for the daughter in spite of her actions. Evchen's fear of her father does indeed drive her away from home, but in their reunion we witness Humbrecht's deeply felt concern for his daughter. Here the catastrophe is a result of the father-daughter relationship; Evchen's actions were necessitated by her realization of having rejected the social norms represented by her father, demonstrated through her awareness of shame, and then acting in order to remedy the situation.[71]

In Schiller's *Kabale und Liebe*, the catastrophe of the drama is *not* a result of the daughter's rejection of the father and all that he represents. On the contrary, Luise dies because she refuses to abandon the norms her father holds dear in her desire to save his life.[72] Miller's interests concerning his daughter are expressed in the first lines of the play: "Einmal für allemal. Der Handel wird ernsthaft. Meine Tochter kommt mit dem Baron ins Geschrei. Mein Haus wird verrufen."[73] Miller is anxious not only for his house and its reputation, but also for his daughter, as he soon expresses to his wife. He believes that if the situation goes unchanged, the girl will be "verschimpfiert auf ihr Leben lang."[74] Miller bears the responsibility for his family's image and the well-being of his daughter. Fritz Martini convincingly summarizes the father's position in this family when he explains that Miller is not only the tyrannical head of the family, but also its natural law giver; Miller "bedeutet . . . eine entscheidende moralische Bindung."[75] Indeed, Miller represents the opinion of the wider community in the family. He believes that Luise behaves improperly for a girl of her class, thus imposing the beliefs of society on his family: "Das Mädel setzt sich alles Teufelsgezeug in den Kopf; über all dem Herumschwänzen in der Schlaraffenwelt findets zuletzt seine Heimat nicht mehr, vergißt, schämt sich, daß sein Vater Miller der Geiger ist. . . ."[76]

Miller acts out of genuine concern for Luise. Although he is a stern individual, she is nevertheless emotionally attached to him, as Wurm's comment to the President indicates: "Sie liebt ihren Vater - bis zur Leidenschaft, möcht ich sagen. Die Gefahr seines Lebens - seiner Freiheit zum mindesten - Die Vorwürfe ihres Gewissens, den Anlaß dazu gegeben zu haben."[77]

In addition to her devotion to her father, Luise's perception that her relationship with Ferdinand is impossible further demonstrates her awareness of what is fitting for her. She maintains that their liaison would "die Fugen der Bürgerwelt auseinandertreiben, und die allgemeine ewige Ordnung zugrund stürzen."[78] In theory Luise believes what she has said, but when she must actually decide whether she will abandon her bourgeois attitudes and intentions for the sake of her love, Miller has to convince her to keep silent about the deception Wurm has instigated. Finally Miller forces Luise to choose between Ferdinand and himself.[79] He convinces Luise to adhere to his way of thinking. She destroys the letter to Ferdinand explaining what has truly happened, demonstrating her inability and unwillingness to deny her father's ethos.

For Luise freedom was not a possibility because it would have meant acting as she really wanted, loving Ferdinand and rejecting her father.[80] She considers the consequences of remaining true to her father and following his directive or fleeing with Ferdinand and thus abandoning her family and its bourgeois traditions. Because Luise decides for herself which avenue she will follow, she demonstrates that she has become "a responsible individual, a tragic subject capable of self-determination."[81] Luise does choose her mode of behavior, but this does not negate the fact that she is forcefully compelled to decide in favor of the behavior corresponding to her father's perceptions.

Finally, however, Luise's inability to free herself from her father's domination causes Ferdinand to poison himself and her. Although Ferdinand commits the actual murder, it can be asserted that Miller kills his own daughter indirectly since his domination causes her to remain silent until it is too late to save herself. Because she abides by her father's wishes, the daughter places herself in a situation that finally proves fatal.

Happiness may have come to Luise had she rejected the ideals her father represented. But such an action is impossible for her because she is so firmly entrenched in the bourgeois value system her father represents; she remains dominated by it. To this extent, the father-daughter relationship in *Kabale und Liebe* is like that in *Emilia Galotti*. Each daughter dies as a result of obeying the norms set up by society and represented by the fathers; both remain dominated by their fathers' world view. In contrary fashion, the father-daughter relationships in *Miß Sara Sampson* and *Kindermörderin* are comparable as the daughters die (or, in the case of the latter, will almost certainly be put to death) because they reject their fathers' beliefs. Thus it is impossible to reduce the father-daughter relationship of these four plays to a single common denominator. In each play, the daughter does come into conflict with the social norms represented by the father, but the plays differ as to the extent of the daughter's denial of these norms. Unfortunately for the daughters, no matter whether they accept or reject their fathers' ideals, life ends.

Chapter III

Grillparzer's *Das Goldene Vließ*

The action of Wagner's *Kindermörderin* moves progressively toward the murder of the child by its mother. In Grillparzer's trilogy *Das goldene Vlieβ*, a similar progression occurs. While this work and *Des Meeres und der Liebe Wellen* utilize topics from antiquity, demonstrating Grillparzer's desire to follow the tradition of Goethe's Classicism, the representation of familial interaction nonetheless resembles that of the bourgeois tragedies. Specifically, Medea's infanticide corresponds to Evchen's and, as we will subsequently see, to Klara's and Rose's as well. Thus, while Grillparzer sets his plays in the mythical past, the subjects he treats are indeed current for his time. Medea's killing of her children is not merely an act of revenge against her estranged husband Jason, but also a manifestation and consequence of her individuation process.[1] Although the murders happen toward the end of the last play, they do *not* indicate the final level of self-development achieved by Medea. Indeed, these murders, and subsequently that of Kreusa, must be addressed by any examination of this work. But it would be improper to focus on the importance of only these actions for Medea's psychological development. While the murders serve as the climax of the entire trilogy,[2] they are just a few pieces in the puzzle formulating Medea's self-understanding. It is necessary to study a number of aspects that contribute to the total picture of this character and her individuation.

In order to comprehend more fully the process of self-realization occurring in this work, it will be helpful to examine briefly a key aspect of Grillparzer's dramatic thought. Politzer and Schaum agree that Grillparzer was concerned with the inner development of humans.[3] This inner development is most simply characterized as the confrontation the individual experiences between a *vita contemplativa* and a *vita activa*,[4] that is, a life of seclusion - where one exists in harmony with nature and one's past - versus a life of attempted activity in the outer world. In the latter instance, an active life stands in opposition to one's former mode of existence; one departs from and even attempts to deny the past. Thus the *vita activa* seeks to conquer and exclude the *vita contemplativa* as the individual moves from one milieu of existence to another.

A principal component of Grillparzer's characters is the necessity for action because, "Es ist einmal Pflicht des Menschen, sich der Menschheit hinzugeben mit dem, was er vermag. . . . [D]er Mensch ist nun einmal nicht da, um rein zu sein, sondern zu nützen, zu wirken."[5] Obligatory action becomes an integral aspect of the departure from the past. Human existence is incomplete without motion from one sphere to another, making activity unavoidable. But through their actions Grillparzer's characters become tragic (consider, for example, Sappho and Libussa). Thus, while individuals cause their own tragic situations by virtue of their actions, they cannot behave differently. This necessary action was an expression of human development for Grillparzer: "Alle Bildung geht schrittweise. Jeder Sprung, wenn er ein wirkliches Vorwärtskommen sein soll, muß zurückgemacht und das Vorwärts schrittweise noch einmal durchgemacht werden."[6] Even more significant is the idea that this constant change forms the basis of human existence: "Immer-währender Wechsel auf den alten Grundlagen ist das Gesetz alles Daseins."[7] Change, brought about through action, is a necessary component of existence for Grillparzer's characters.[8]

Once the individual has moved into the sphere of active life, it is impossible to undo what has already been done; one cannot go back to the contemplative sphere.[9] In this manner, Grillparzer's characters are caught in a situation of inevitable tragedy. They must act, but by acting they become tragic. Grillparzer's dramas symbolically present this tragic process, specifically the juxtaposition of the *vita contemplativa* and *vita activa*.

Grillparzer dealt with a significant aspect of symbolic literary expression when he wrote in his diary in 1837:

> Zum poetischen Gehalt ist erforderlich, daß es Ideen, d.h. notwendig und ewig wahre Gedanken und Gefühle, die über das irdische Dasein hinausgehen, in sich abspiegle und bildlich zur *Anschauung bringe*.
>
> [. . .]
>
> Das Symbolische der Poesie besteht darin, daß sie nicht die Wahrheit an die Spitze ihres Beginnens stellt, sondern, bildlich in allem, ein *Bild* der Wahrheit, eine Inkarnation derselben, die Art und Weise, wie sich das Licht des Geistes in dem halbdunklen Medium des Gemütes färbt und bricht.[10]

The purpose of literature, according to this statement, is to demonstrate truths of life and human existence symbolically. The author shows us through his characters and their actions not an actual piece of life, but rather a description of eternal truths reflected through a symbolic situation. This concept provides a vital point of reference as we examine the father-daughter relationship. In *Das goldene Vließ* we learn about Medea. But beyond this, Grillparzer shows us something about human development in more general terms, at least human development as he comprehended and depicted it.

Critics have discovered a wide variety of topics in *Das goldene Vließ*, although no one has ever focused on the father-daughter relationship throughout the entire work.[11] Grillparzer himself described the first section, *Der Gastfreund*, as showing "Von wo der Mensch beginnt, womit er endet . . . ."[12] He quoted Rousseau's *Confessions* when he described the general theme of the entire work:

> L'on a remarqué que la plupart des hommes sont dans le cours de leur vie souvent dissemblables à eux mêmes, et semblent se transformer en des hommes tout différens.[13]

Treating the work in its entirety was also a concern for Grillparzer. In a letter to the director of the *Hoftheater* in Vienna at the time of the completion of the trilogy (November 8, 1820), Grillparzer wrote:

> Darf nicht etwa nur das eine oder das andere der beiden [d.h. drei] Stücke, sondern sie müssen *beide*, und zwar, bei der ersten Vorstellung

ohne Zwischenraum, in zwei unmittelbar aufeinanderfolgenden Tagen gegeben werden. Dieses ist durchaus notwendig, damit das Gedicht als ein Ganzes erfaßt werde, und weil die beiden Abteilungen sich wechselseitig bedingen und erklären.[14]

In keeping with Grillparzer's desire, we will analyze the father-daughter relationship throughout the entire work. This relationship in *Der Gastfreund* and *Die Argonauten* focuses principally on Medea's objectification by her father, Aietes. This objectification is active and intentional. Whenever Aietes finds himself in a threatening situation, he requests the assistance of his daughter and her magical capabilities. At the beginning of *Der Gastfreund*, Medea is shown in harmonious union with nature and the wilderness of Kolchis as she hunts game. Gora almost immediately identifies Medea as "Aietes Tochter, / Des Herrschers von Kolchis fürstliches Kind."[15] Medea speaks of herself in the same terms: "Ich bin Aietes königliches Kind."[16] No mention is made at this point of other members of the family and, at least initially, it is not surprising that Aietes comes to solicit his daughter's aid: "Du rufst Geister / Und besprichst den Mond, / Hilf mir, mein gutes Kind!"[17] Ironically, however, such an action on Aietes' part appears uncommon, as Medea explains:

> Bin ich dein gutes Kind!
> Sonst achtest du meiner wenig
> Wenn ich will, willst du *nicht*
> Und schiltst mich und schlägst nach mir;
> Aber wenn du mein bedarfst,
> Lockst du mich mit Schmeichelworten
> Und nennst mich Medea, dein liebes Kind.[18]

From Medea's own words, we discover that Aietes seeks her company only when he needs assistance. She serves as a mere helper for her father; he treats her as an "Instrument und nicht als verehrungswürdig in sich selbst."[19]

From the outset of the play Medea and her father are not of one mind; there is an underlying current of opposition between them. Phryxus alludes to this difference upon his arrival when he recognizes that Medea is not simply a barbaric figure (as Aietes proves to be). Phryxus states: "Halb Charis steht sie da und halb Mänade."[20] In this manner, Medea is described as a *Doppelwesen*: she is tied partially to her barbaric father, but she also possesses a characteristic that Phryxus finds appealing. This phenomenon further manifests itself in the scene depicting the murder of Phryxus by Aietes. Medea supports her father by obeying his command to request Phryxus' sword, the last form of defense Phryxus possesses. In this request, the objectification of Medea by Aietes is expressed. Here the father uses his daughter, whose beauty Phryxus has already praised, as a means to attain his goal - the murder of Phryxus in order to gain possession of the fleece. Phryxus gives Medea his sword readily as he believes himself under the protection of the *Gastrecht*, a law forbidding harming a guest in any fashion. Aietes fails to abide by this law and, moreover, denies the fact that Phryxus ever was his guest:

> Hab ich ihn geladen in mein Haus?
> Ihm beim Eintritt Brot und Salz gereicht
> Und geheißen sitzen auf meinem Stuhl?
> Ich hab ihm nicht Gastrecht geboten,
> Er *nahm* sichs, büß ers, der Tor![21]

In the critical scene where Aietes eventually kills his guest, Phryxus attributes at least a portion of the blame for this deed to Medea since she served as a means to his destruction:

> Du auch hier, Schlange?
> Warst du so schön und locktest du so lieblich,
> Mich zu verderben hier im Todesnetz?
> Mein Herz schlug dir vertrauensvoll entgegen,
> Mein Schwert, den letzten Schutz, gab ich in deine Hand,
> Und du verrätst mich?[22]

Medea denies the assertion that she betrayed Phryxus and even gives him the sword of one of the soldiers standing nearby, but to no avail, as Aietes mortally wounds him. Aietes himself has discerned that he has treated his guest improperly and has even stolen his property, the fleece. Aietes fears for himself. Phryxus refuses to take back the fleece and calls on the gods to take revenge on the man who has failed to abide by the *Gastrecht*. Aietes is unable to return the fleece and, in a fit of rage, strikes Phryxus. As Phryxus curses Aietes and his entire family with his dying words, Medea also curses her

father's action immediately after Phryxus dies: "Vater! Was
hast du getan! / Den Gastfreund erschlagen, / Weh dir! Weh
uns allen!"[23]

Medea perceives that her father's deed will subsequently
affect all members of the family. Although her cooperation
with Aietes was purely the act of an obedient child, she will
suffer along with her father for his wrongdoing. In her
abhorrence of Aietes's action, Medea expresses inner separation from her father. Aietes believes he represents the gods, as
his statement of revenge indicates: "Daß ich ihn [Phryxus]
strafe, daß ich räche / Des Gottes Schmach und meine?"[24] He
also sees therein justification for the murder. In this manner
Aietes stands as the representative of godly will and expectation in this small family unit. Medea comes into conflict with
the tradition her father represents when she condemns the
murder Aietes believes is justified by the gods.[25] Medea interprets this murder as an affront against the norms even of the
barbaric people of Kolchis since Aietes breaks the code of
ethics with regard to the guest.[26]

Aietes's action causes a break between Medea and her
father. In this break, we see the beginnings of Medea's
individuation, her coming to terms with the distinct person
she is and what she understands to be appropriate modes of
behavior. Furthermore, because of Aietes's action, Medea feels
guilty and, as a result of this guilt, she senses a certain separation from her former existence.[27] Subsequently this separation manifests itself between the first and second play when
Medea withdraws from her father's society and seeks seclusion
in her tower, a physical expression of the self-realization
Medea now begins to experience.

The relationship between Medea and Aietes centers on the
objectification that is expressed through Aietes's attempts to
use his daughter as a means to achieve his goals. Aietes fails to
recognize his daughter's intrinsic value as a human being.[28]
Indeed, he vacillates in his emotions for her - he loves her
when he needs her help; otherwise his treatment of her fails to
indicate parental affection. This aspect is reminiscent of the
relationship between father and daughter in Wagner's *Kindermörderin*. In that situation the father almost schizophrenically

shifted in his feelings for his daughter from love to hate (see chapter II). For Aietes, love and the desire for togetherness are felt only when he needs his daughter's assistance. Aietes depends on Medea for assured success in battles with his foes. But he fails to value her and seek her companionship for any other reason - for example, simply because she is his child. Furthermore, Aietes does not comprehend how he forces his daughter to act in a manner contrary to what she believes is proper - he is only interested in achieving a certain end. Indeed, Aietes appears in this fashion as a weak and isolated individual, incapable of expressing to his child a complex range of parental feelings, such as warmth, love, understanding and compassion.

These phenomena appear again in the second play of the trilogy, *Die Argonauten*. From the outset of this portion, we can discern the effects that the events of *Der Gastfreund* had on Medea's individuation. She now lives in seclusion from her family in a tower, thus indicating rejection and denial of her father's world.[29] Only in the seclusion Medea finds in withdrawal can she preserve her personal freedom.[30] But isolation does not remove the conflict between father and daughter because Medea has left home without permission, an improper act in this patriarchal society. When Aietes asks for an explanation of her absence, Medea replies: "Verhaßt ist mir dein Haus, / Mit Schauder erfüllt mich deine Nähe."[31] Medea explains that the reason for her feelings is based on Aietes's murder of Phryxus. At this point, one might believe that Aietes has come to seek reconciliation with his daughter. In one sense this is true; but the real reason Aietes has sought out his daughter is because he once again needs her assistance in combating a foreign force that has arrived on the island. Here a repetition of events from the first play appears at the beginning of the second: The experience with Phryxus has set the stage for the arrival of Jason. Through Phryxus, Medea encountered a new sphere of existence and new feelings that lay dormant in her being.[32] The formula in each play is the same: Aietes seeks out Medea because he needs her help in battle against strangers. He pleads: "Willst du mich verlassen, da ich dein bedarf? / Willst du sehen des Vaters Blut? / Medea, ich beschwöre dich, / Sprich! Rate! Rette! Hilf! / Gib mich nicht preis meinen Feinden!"[33] Medea's first reaction is: *"Ich soll helfen, hilf du selbst!"*[34] But, as in the first play, Medea finally agrees to obey her father: "Es sei! du gebeutst, ich gehorche!"[35] As Brauckmann and Everwien'note, Medea is by nature submissive.[36] That she has twice agreed to act against her will for the sake of her father demonstrates that she is essentially insecure about her true self. She needs acceptance, up to now acceptance by her father, even though she views life differently than he.

Aietes twice treats his daughter as a mere object,. a means to gain a certain end. In the second instance, however, Aietes fails in his attempt to kill the foreigner. Whereas in *Der Gastfreund* Medea served as an aid to Aietes, she repeatedly prevents a repetition of the same catastrophe in *Die Argonauten* (see below). This does not negate the fact that Aietes attempts to use Medea as a means to kill Jason. Indeed, Medea initially agrees to assist her father. But in the crucial moments when she can either allow or hinder Jason's murder, Medea saves the young man's life.

To understand more fully why Medea prevents Jason's murder, it is necessary to examine the early relationship between these two characters. They first meet when Jason gains entrance into Medea's tower. Within a few dozen lines, the mood of the encounter shifts from aggression to mutual attraction. Jason utters words reminiscent of Phryxus' understanding of Medea's character: "Scheinst du so schön und bist so arg, zugleich / So liebenswürdig und so hassenswert."[37] Shortly thereafter, Medea's brother, Absyrtus, unexpectedly enters the tower and tries to kill Jason. While Medea holds Absyrtus back physically, Jason quickly kisses her hand and disappears.[38] At the beginning of the next act we learn that Medea has thought much about Jason: "Ich habe lange darüber nachgedacht, / Nachgedacht und geträumt die lange Nacht."[39] Her thoughts are cut short by the appearance of Aietes and Absyrtus. Once again Aietes succeeds in convincing Medea to support him in his actions against Jason. Medea humbly obeys and prepares a poisoned drink for the stranger. But in the instant before he drinks, she warns him: "Du

trinkst Verderben!"[40] and saves his life a second time.
Furthermore, Medea shows through this action another step
toward her new self - a self separate from her father. What
was *physical* distance between Medea and Aietes at the outset of
Die Argonauten now becomes *metaphysical*, as Medea believes she
feels sensations previously unknown. Although Jason openly
declares his love for her, Medea refuses to accept this situation
and attempts to retreat into her former sphere of existence.
But even she must admit, "ich bin nicht mehr, die ich bin."[41]
For a third time in this play, Medea and her father reconcile
themselves to each other. Medea wants her father's protection
from Jason and the two part on very positive terms. While en
route to her new residence, she and Absyrtus encounter Jason.
As soon as she speaks his name, Jason is convinced of her love.
In a passage reminiscent of Gottfried's "Tristan, Isold, Isold,
Tristan," Jason states: "Medea, Jason; Jason und Medea, / O
schöner Einklang!"[42] From this point on, Jason and Medea
are inseparable; they become a single being, to which Jason
himself alludes when he discusses Plato's notion of two halves
coming together to form the whole in a love relationship (also
Jung's theory of the animus and anima seeking one another
and combining to form one being):

> Es ist ein schöner Glaub in meinem Land,
> Die Götter hätten doppelt einst geschaffen
> Ein jeglich Wesen und sodann geteilt;
> Da suche jede Hälfte nun die andre
> Durch Meer und Land, und wenn sie sich gefunden,
> Vereinen sie die Seelen, mischen sie
> Und sind nun eins![43]

When Jason and Medea subsequently meet Aietes, Medea
again seeks reconciliation with her father, but this time there
is a stipulation: Jason must be included in the "family."

> Heiß ihn dableiben, den Führer der Fremden,
> Nimm ihn auf, nimm ihn an!
> An deiner Seite herrsch er in Kolchis,
> Dir befreundet, dein Sohn![44]

This request marks a significant development in Medea's
individuation; she openly declares her union with this man

and thus departs still further from her former existence. Aietes counters with the exclamation that he intends to kill Jason, and Medea, too, if she chooses not to follow her father's wishes. He then curses his daughter as he banishes her from Kolchis forever:

> Du hast mich betrogen, verraten.
> Bleib! Nicht mehr betreten sollst du mein Haus.
> Ausgestoβen sollst du sein, wie das Tier der Wildnis,
> Sollst in der Fremde sterben, verlassen, allein.
> Folg ihm, dem Buhlen, nach in seine Heimat,
> Teile sein Bett, sein Irrsal, seine Schmach;
> Leb im fremden Land, eine Fremde,
> Verspottet, verachtet, verhöhnt, verlacht;
> Er selbst, für den du hingibst Vater und Vaterland,
> Wird dich verachten, wird dich verspotten,
> Wenn erloschen die Lust, wenn gestillt die Begier;
> Dann wirst du stehn und die Hände ringen,
> Sie hinüberbreiten nach dem Vaterland,
> Getrennt durch weite, brandende Meere,
> Deren Wellen dir murmelnd bringen des Vaters Fluch![45]

Aietes speaks just once more, and then only indirectly, with Medea in the entire play. By his own choice, he breaks off the father-daughter relationship. He refuses to accept Jason as his son-in-law and so forces Medea to choose between father and spouse, between loyalty to the past and the promise of love for the future. Medea had sought a reconciliation of the two opposing forces, but her father prevents it. Medea chooses to follow Jason.[46] When confronted with this decision, Medea stood on a dividing line between two forms of existence.[47] She tried to unite these into one special hybrid life situation, but her father prevented such a synthesis. In this manner, Aietes pushed Medea over the boundary and out of her former community. For this father, there can be no dual loyalty - either Medea remains fully obedient to him or she must leave.

Here we see an example of the rigid moral code described in chapter I. The father is unwilling to alter his outlook, to allow his daughter to develop beyond the being he has created. Medea's relationship with Jason clearly stands in conflict with Aietes's expectations. By stepping beyond this stage of development, Medea continues the individuation process she began when she first rejected her father's actions after the murder of Phryxus, manifested through seclusion in the tower. Now a second, more extreme withdrawal from the father's society is necessitated in order to intensify the process of self-realization Medea currently experiences. Medea's newly established persona of lover appears on one hand as "das Brechen von Loyalität, Verrat gegen die Landsleute . . . ,"[48] but it can also be construed as the natural development of the individual who has experienced and is still experiencing new perspectives of the self. Aietes, by remaining steadfast in his rigid attitude, rejects Medea and necessitates her physical withdrawal from her homeland. This behavior is reminiscent of Lessing's *Miß Sara Sampson* inasmuch as Sara felt the need to leave home in order to be with her lover. Neither Sara nor Medea found the parental support or openness of mind allowing a synthesis of both the childhood and adult spheres of existence. Sara's father eventually reconciled himself with his daughter, but, as we have seen, after Sara had begun to die. For Medea, no such reconciliation occurs. She begins a new life in which she commits herself totally to Jason.

The first manifestation of Medea's full commitment to Jason expresses itself through her assistance in regaining the fleece. Just as Aietes before him, Jason requires Medea's help, he needs her in order to attain his goal. She gives him a potion with which he successfully intoxicates the serpent guarding the fleece in a secret cave. Once again Medea has behaved submissively; even though she realizes that the fleece will only bring destruction to those who possess it, she nonetheless succumbs to Jason's wishes. Furthermore, the cave becomes not only the place where Medea submits to Jason's materialistic ambition, but to his sexual desire as well. Stiefel and Politzer write convincingly that the cave is a feminine symbol[49] and that Jason's entrance into it is symbolic of the sexual union between himself and Medea. Indeed, Grillparzer's text is quite explicit: "MEDEA. Geh hin, mein süßer Bräutigam, / Wie züngelt deine Braut!"[50]

Whether we agree with a sexually-oriented reading of this scene or not, the fact remains that Jason objectifies Medea, using her as a means to obtain his ambitious end. Without her, his success is impossible, but with her, he can attain his goal. As Stiefel points out, it is a basic perspective of Jason's character to view the world as "nichts als Stoff zu Taten."[51] Here it must be observed that Medea is in the same position with her husband as she was with her father. In each instance, Medea is asked to behave in a manner contradictory to her better judgment and to her own desire. She submits herself to the will of each man. As for Aietes and Jason, both fail to perceive Medea as a person, and instead instrumentalize her for the sake of their ambition. Thus Jason, like Aietes before him, fails to recognize Medea's intrinsic value as a human being.

Furthermore, Medea loses a part of her self through the act of objectification. Her total devotion to these men, albeit at different stages in her life, causes her to behave in a manner that contradicts the commitment to her inner being. Thus, when Medea agrees to help her father and Jason, she steps out of the realm of the *vita contemplativa* - unity with her true inner nature - and attempts to find a place in the sphere of the *vita activa* - acceptance by and involvement in a wider social system. Such action, which is unavoidable for Grillparzer's characters, ensures her tragedy. Medea's "fate" (a word used advisedly in this context) comes not from the curses either of Phryxus or Aietes, but rather from her own personal behavior in an attempt to fulfill the expectations of the two principal male figures around her and thus to live actively by assisting these men to realize their goals.

Medea's individuation does not stop once she has helped Jason gain the fleece. Indeed, this occurrence marks a significant step in the break with her former existence; but Medea's estrangement from her father and homeland increases continuously through the conclusion of *Die Argonauten* and into the final play of the trilogy, *Medea*. The final scene of *Die Argonauten* contains an especially crucial moment in Medea's self-realization process. She has a final opportunity to return to her father, who indicates that the break between them may not yet be total and complete. As Jason is about to board his ship with Medea and Absyrtus - whom Jason has just taken captive -, Aietes says: "Haltet ein! Meine Kinder! Mein

Sohn!"[52] Indeed, "Sohn" is the final word, but the preceding phrase, "Meine Kinder," includes Medea in the family once again, if only for a moment. Here Aietes's vacillation in his emotions for Medea manifests itself again. Whereas his earlier curse appeared to have indicated full rejection, his present statement contains a hint of acceptance. Aietes's words elicit a compassionate response from Medea: "Mein Bruder! - Vater!"[53] Medea still senses a bond to her former existence. But her father turns from his momentary concern for *both* children as he calls to his son only: "Komm, Sohn!"[54] Aietes repeats this phrase (or a slight variation thereof) four times before the curtain falls at the conclusion of this play. Jason has taken Absyrtus prisoner to ensure safe passage for the crew of the Argo, but Absyrtus commits suicide rather than remain hostage on board ship. Aietes's final words demonstrate that his full concern now lies with his son; there is no indication that his daughter ever existed: "Weh mir, weh, / Legt mich ins Grab zu meinem Sohn!"[55]

In the first scene of the final play, Medea tries to break the remaining ties with her former self by burying the chest of magical instruments (and the golden fleece) she has carried along since leaving Kolchis. Rismondo interprets this as an act of repression.[56] Indeed, in this action we see Medea's attempt to deny her past existence and, furthermore, to become an integrated component of the Greek society where she now finds herself with her husband and two sons.[57] Hoesch carries this notion even further when she writes: "Medea möchte Griechin werden, um so dem Zwiespalt in ihrem Leben zu entgehen. . . . Medea versucht, ganz im 'Es' aufzugehen und das 'Ich' zu unterdrücken."[58] Through the denial of the *Ich*, of her former self, Medea tries to become a part of this new world - a further step into the *vita activa*. Brauckmann and Everwien refer to the act of burying the chest as a "Widerspruch in der Entwicklung der Figur."[59] This assertion can only be credible if it is interpreted as focusing on Medea's failure to come to terms with her former existence and acknowledge it. Even this interpretation is problematic since Medea strives - at least initially - to please Jason in every way possible. By robbing herself of these vestiges of her past, including the veil and the staff, Medea seeks to ensure success in her future by gaining the acceptance of those now around her and thus becoming one with them.

For Grillparzer's figures, the act of changing clothes frequently indicates an inner - or at least attempted inner - change in the persona. Sappho, for example, appears initially "köstlich gekleidet"[60] when she is in the character of the victorious poetess. In Act II, when she tries to become the lover, she is "einfach gekleidet."[61]   Finally, after having discerned that she is incapable of the active life of love, she again appears "reich gekleidet, wie im ersten Aufzuge."[62]   Like Sappho, Medea marks her desire to become a different being by putting aside these physical manifestations of her previous self.   By burying the fleece with the tools of her former magical trade, she seeks to put an end to the hardship that befalls those who have contact with the fleece.

The golden fleece and the figures of Medea and Gora, Medea's nursemaid, are the three elements providing cohesion throughout all segments of the trilogy.   Indeed, the action of the entire work revolves around the fleece.[63]   It becomes the motivating force for the most significant events - the murder of Phryxus, Jason's voyage to Kolchis, Aietes's banishment of Medea, Jason's further difficulties in his homeland and Kreon's uncovering of Medea's buried chest.   The representation of Medea's life is shown in terms of how these actions affect her development.[64]

In addition to the fleece, there exists another object greatly significant for the depiction of Medea's inner development: the lyre.   Medea began her attempt to become an accepted member of Greek society by burying her chest of magical instruments.   This was a personal and private expression of her desire to begin a new existence.   When she tries to learn to play the lyre and sing a song Jason sang in his boyhood, she openly demonstrates to Jason, Kreusa and all of Greek society a longing to become what she perceives as Jason's ideal companion.   Furthermore, Medea even submits to the tutelage of Jason's former fiancée, thus humbling herself before her rival for Jason's affections.   Try as she might, Medea is unable to master the lyre and remember the song.   Jason suggests that

Kreusa take the lyre and sing the song after Medea's attempt
has failed. Medea grasps the instrúment, refuses to hand it to
Jason upon request and finally breaks it to pieces. Kreusa
exclaims: "Tot! / MEDEA *rash umblickend.* Wer? - *Ich* lebe!
lebe!"[65] This scene expresses important aspects of Medea's
individuation. Her inability to perform reflects the inner
truth of the situation - she is incapable because she attempts to
behave in a way contrary to her inner being. Medea has
changed externally by taking off and burying the outward
symbols and instruments of her witch-like existence. In the
lyre scene, she tries to impose this alteration on her inner self,
but her innermost being rejects such an unnatural element
and hence prevents her from succeeding in this latest attempt
to step out of the *vita contemplativa* into the *vita activa.*
Furthermore, as Hoesch explains, Medea redirects her goal
from becoming a member of Greek society after the failed
attempt: "die alte Medea, die Kolcherin wird nun wieder ganz
das Ziel ihres Strebens."[66] As we will subsequently ascertain,
this is not a lasting phenomenon.

The motivation for the lyre scene necessitates further
examination. Stiefel would have us believe that Jason *forces*
Medea to change. He writes: "Immer wieder verlangt er von
Medea die Verleugnung ihres Wesens. Die Amazone soll sich
in eine Griechin verwandeln, die, statt in der Wildnis zu
jagen, die Leier in der Hand hält und singt."[67] Indeed,
shortly before the lyre scene Jason makes it clear that Medea's
very presence truly disgusts him. After he has convinced her
to go and check on the children, a task she has just performed,
he says to Kreusa: "Ah! So, nun ist mir leicht, nun kann ich
atmen. / Ihr Anblick schnürt das Innre mir zusammen / Und
die verhehlte Qual erwürgt mich fast."[68] Medea is aware of
the difference between herself and, for example, Kreusa, as
she states at the beginning of the act: "Nur an den Wurfspieß
ist die Hand gewöhnt / Und an des Weidwerks ernstlich rauh
Geschäft."[69] Both Jason and Medea are aware of the difference between the Kolcherin and the Greeks. But Jason does
not *directly* articulate to Medea any desire or expectation on his
part for her to change, although his actions indicate this
indirectly. This indirect denial of Medea's being manifests itself

at the beginning of the lyre scene when Medea tries three
times to get Jason's attention so that he can listen to her song.
Only when Kreusa interjects: "Sie weiß ein Lied,"[70] does
Jason even notice that his wife has reappeared. The message
to Medea must be clear: As she is, she no longer fulfills his
wishes. But the fact remains, Jason does not encourage Medea
to play the lyre and sing the song. Indeed, he even suggests
that she lay the instrument aside and not sing at all:

> Willst du mit einem armen Jugendlied
> Mir meine Jugend geben und ihr Glück?
> Laß das. Wir wollen aneinander halten,
> Weils einmal denn so kam und wie sichs gibt.
> Doch nichts von Liedern und von derlei Dingen![71]

Thus we must proceed with caution and not speak of direct
demands that Jason places on Medea. To be sure, he clearly
expresses his feelings for Medea, but indirectly, making us
ponder Stiefel's statement quoted above.

After this important scene, where Medea begins to sense
confusion in her newly and falsely acquired active life, she
thinks more and more about her past, her father and the fate
that befell him and Absyrtus. Gora, Medea's nursemaid,
chides her: "Denn nicht Medea bist du mehr, / Des
Kolcherkönigs königlicher Sproß."[72] As Aietes had predicted,
Medea calls out for her homeland, knowing that she cannot
return: "O Kolchis! Kolchis! O Vaterland!"[73] In Act IV,
even more specific thoughts of the past occupy Medea: "Starb
mein Vater, hab *ich* ihn getötet? / Fiel mein Bruder, fiel er
durch *mich*?"[74] These questions could be answered both
positively and negatively. Indeed, Medea did not physically
strike down either father or brother; however, her departure
played a definite role in the deaths of both men. Medea does
sense some responsibility for the passing of her family. She
begins to comprehend that her departure did cause the demise
of father and brother. She directs the responsibility for this
series of events to Jason, whom she lovingly followed.[75]
Gradually one thought develops in Medea's mind:
"Vergeltung."[76] She focuses her revenge on Jason not only as
a result of the perception that he drew her away from her

family under false promises of love and since he has now rejected her as a partner, but also because her own children have rejected their mother in favor of Jason and Kreusa.

The subsequent murder of the children is also Medea's method of ironically saving her children from a fate similar to her own. Just as Gora intensifies Medea's thoughts about Aietes and Absyrtus, she also speaks of a woman who killed her own children and still lived.[77] Medea arrives at the conclusion that death for her children would be better than the life they would have among the Greeks:

> Bleiben sie hier beim Vater zurück,
> Beim treulosen, schändlichen Vater,
> Welches ist ihr Los?
> Stiefgeschwister kommen,
> Höhnen sie, spotten ihrer
> Und ihrer Mutter,
> Der Wilden aus Kolchis.
> Sie aber entweder dienen als Sklaven,
> Oder der Ingrimm, am Herzen nagend,
> Macht sie arg, sich selbst ein Greuel.[78]

This manner of thinking does not provide the complete motivation for the murders, as we can see from Grillparzer's own notes from January 1820:

> Medeens Gefühl gegen ihre Kinder muß gemischt sein aus *Haß* gegen den Vater, Jason, von dem sie weiß, daß er die Kinder liebt und ihr Tod ihm schmerzlich sein wird; aus *Grimm* gegen die Kinder, die sie flohen und ihren Feinden den schmerzlichsten Triumph über sie verschafften; aus *Liebe* gegen diese Kinder, die sie nicht mutterlos unter Fremden zurück lassen will; aus *Stolz*, ihre Kinder nicht in der Gewalt ihrer Feinde zu lassen.[79]

Medea's desire to save the children from an unpleasant future is coupled with feelings of revenge and betrayal. In Act III the children must choose which one wants to accompany its mother, but both decline. In this moment of total rejection, Medea mentions the similarity of one of her sons to Jason: "Ebenbild des Vaters! / Ihm ähnlich in den falschen Zügen / Und mir verhaßt, wie er!"[80] When neither child will follow Medea, Kreusa leads them away, causing Medea to feel betrayed.[81] Friedrich associates Medea's perception of the children's betrayal with the emotions she currently feels toward Jason. In this moment of choice by the children, the physical resemblance to Jason and the rejection by Medea's offspring and husband join together to cause her despair.[82] This despair, coupled with concern for her children's future finally motivates the murders. The concept of betrayal reflects feelings Medea perceives in herself about her own parents, as Stiefel suggests: "Medea tötet ihre Kinder, weil sie sich von ihnen verraten weiß, wie sie selbst Vater und Mutter verraten hat. In den Treulosen haßt sie ihr eigenes Selbst."[83] Here we see an interesting correlation between Medea's actions and the lingering relationship between father and daughter. Indeed, Aietes did not kill Medea; his punishment of her betrayal takes the form of banishment and curse. Medea grasps the ultimate means to punish her children's betrayal and, as we have seen, to prevent them from experiencing a fate similar to her own. Lastly, only through the murder of the children can Medea fully free herself from Jason,[84] a necessity for her self-realization. By murdering the children and Kreusa, Medea fully frees herself from all aspects of her former existence for her own inner self-development.

Kreusa's murder is closely associated with that of the children and results from Medea's desire for revenge. Ironically, Kreon indirectly facilitates his daughter's death because of his ambitious desire to recover the golden fleece. When he returns to Medea the chest she had buried in Act I and forces her to open it so he can gain possession of the fleece, he also returns to her the magical vestiges of her former existence. Medea puts on her veil and once more becomes the Kolcherin. This is not the final stage of Medea's inner development, but she does occupy it long enough to send Kreusa a deadly present; Medea also commits infanticide just after recovering her old instruments.

The significance of all three murders for Medea's individuation centers on the notion that this is really the first time in her life that she has not acted submissively; she has not tried to please anyone else and has been true to no one other than herself. Stiefel calls this "den Rückweg zu sich selbst."[85] The process Medea experiences here is not a returning to the self, in the sense of permanently going backward to her former ways; the return to the past is a momentary stage. Here Medea acts for the first time in accordance with her true self. She has reached a new level of individuation; she is no longer submissive. Medea makes her own decision and then acts accordingly.

The subsequent decision to go to Delphi and return the fleece to its place of origin, aside from rounding out the action of the entire trilogy, expresses the definitive level of self-realization reached by Medea. Here her commitment to justice is again expressed. The first manifestation of this commitment was demonstrated when she left her father's presence after he killed Phryxus. While she did comprehend her own partial guilt in this matter, her father's failure to abide by the *Gastrecht* - a great injustice - contributed significantly to Medea's decision to withdraw into the tower. At the end of the trilogy, Medea becomes judge and, we expect, executioner of herself. She understands that her previous existence no longer corresponds to her current view of life. Indeed, the final scene of the play depicts Medea in a fashion greatly divergent from all previous instances. While Jason bemoans his fate, Medea has reached a state of sublime understanding of life's complexities.[86] Her much-quoted "Was ist der Erde Glück? - Ein Schatten! / Was ist der Erde Ruhm? - Ein Traum!"[87] provides anything but a joyful picture of human existence and is reminiscent of the ancient memento mori theme. When this world view is coupled with the three imperatives: "Trage! . . . Dulde! . . . Büße!,"[88] which she utters as much for Jason's benefit as for her own, a clear image of Medea's new metaphysical state appears. Medea's thoughts reflect the Weltanschauung expressed in the final verse of Grillparzer's poem "Entsagung:"

Nur was du abweist, kann dir wieder kommen.
Was du verschmähst, naht ewig schmeichelnd sich.
Und in dem Abschied, vom Besitz genommen,
Erhältst du dir das einzig deine: Dich![89]

Medea has finally achieved herself. This acquisition has required the renunciation of father, brother, husband,

children and the fleece.   All of these have been necessary
facets in her individuation process and marked specific stages
of her self-understanding.   By finding herself, Medea gains
the final goal of the evolutionary process: "a new harmony."[90]
To this end, the father-daughter relationship and Medea's life
within the wider world reflect distinct stages in this daughter's
process of self-realization.

Indeed, we can see the necessity for Grillparzer's characters
to leave the sphere of the *vita contemplativa* for the *vita activa*.
Although this action becomes a catalyst for tragic occurrences,
without it there would be only stagnation in. existence.
Through Medea's actions, we see the expression of Grillparzer's general theme of the trilogy, which he found in
Rousseau's *Confessions*.   We perceive how she transforms
herself into a being "tout différens" just as all humans do
throughout their lives.   Unlike other human beings, however,
Medea becomes larger than life.   She reaches a state of total
self-reliance in active existence and assumes full responsibility
for her own behavior.   Medea is an ideal figure to the extent
that she achieves a level of individuation for which most
people merely strive and which they do not attain.   In this
manner Grillparzer has given us a symbolic image of what
human existence itself might become.

Chapter IV

Grillparzer's *Des Meeres Und Der Liebe Wellen*

In the last chapter, the issue of the symbolic nature of Grill-parzer's dramatic work was raised with the emphasis being placed on the function of literature as an example.[1]   From Medea's story we received a model of one person's psychological development. Grillparzer's tragedy *Des Meeres und der Liebe Wellen* also demonstrates the psychological nature of the main characters, Hero, Leander and the Priest.   Although the psychological aspect of this work has been observed in the past,[2] the work has never been examined on the basis of the father-daughter relationship as the background against which psychological development occurs.

We have already discussed the theme *vita contemplativa* and *vita activa* for Grillparzer's *Das goldene Vließ*. *Des Meeres und der Liebe Wellen* contains the same attempt, here by both Hero and Leander. Just as this movement from contemplative to active life was an expression of individuation for Medea, so it is for Hero and Leander. The sphere of *vita contemplativa* to which Hero belongs is governed by her uncle, the Priest, who becomes a surrogate father for the young woman. In Act I Hero explains that she left her parental house because she felt she was a burden to her parents:

> War ihnen ich doch immer eine Last,
> Und fort und fort ging Sturm in ihrem Hause.
> Mein Vater wollte, was kein andres wollte,
> Und drängte mich und zürnte ohne Grund.
> Die Mutter duldete und schwieg.
> Mein Bruder - von den Menschen all, die leben,
> bin ich nur einem gram, es ist mein Bruder.[3]

Hero's home life has been anything but pleasant, and her relationship with her natural father, as illustrated in the preceding passage, demonstrates hostile feelings of the father toward the daughter and other members of the family. As Hero leaves the home of her biological father, she disassociates herself from his sphere of existence - a first step into the *vita activa*. But, as will be discussed below, Hero's life as a priestess will in reality become an extension of the *vita contemplativa* she has previously experienced. Nevertheless, Hero does indeed actively reject her natural father. However, she moves into a situation in which she is under the control of a second father figure. Hero's family, headed by her father, relinquishes all control of her to the Priest, as Grillparzer mentions in his notes on the drama: "Heros Vater ganz der Meinung seines Bruders untergeordnet . . ."[4] The Priest functions as a father *de facto*, taking over the active parenting role Hero's real father gives up. Hero's natural father does continue to live, however, appears briefly in the play and then disappears into the background, leaving the Priest as the clear father figure.

It is interesting to note that the figure of the Priest proved difficult for Grillparzer both while writing and revising the play. He expresses, for example: "Ursprünglich war dem Priester beiläufig die Rolle des *Schicksals* zugedacht. Eben so verhüllt, kurz, kalt. Das muß wohl einige Modifikation leiden."[5] While reflecting on the failure of the play and its shortcomings, Grillparzer states in his diary: "Vor allem ist die Figur des Priesters dabei zu kurz gekommen."[6] Indeed, the Priest can be understood as a shallow character if seen only as the representative of fate, as Grillparzer originally intended.[7] In Act IV the Priest expresses the notion that he is the agent of the divine: "In meinem Innern reget sich ein Gott."[8] But he is certainly more than the deputy of the Gods and representative of fate: He becomes a father for Hero in his own right, that is, in addition to the fact that Hero's natural father has failed to make life at home bearable for his daughter.[9] In Act III, the Priest refers to himself as Hero's second father.[10] Through his statements of love and concern for Hero, he expresses his role of father:

Mein Innerstes bewegt sich, schau ich sie.
So still, so klug, so Ebenmaß in jedem;
Und immer däucht es mir, ich müßt ihr sagen:
Blick auf! Das Unheil gähnt, ein Abgrund neben dir![11]

Even after Leander's body is discovered and the truth of the situation between Hero and Leander is exposed, the Priest still calls her "Mein starkes, wackres Mädchen. / So wieder du mein Kind!"[12]

By serving as her guardian and mentor, the Priest becomes a replacement father figure for Hero. Furthermore, in his role as representative and guardian of the social and religious norms for himself, Hero and the inhabitants of Sestos, the Priest takes on the typical father position outlined in chapter I. In Act I, he briefly describes local practices:

Nicht ehrt man hier die irdsche Aphrodite,
Die Mensch an Menschen knüpft wie Tier an Tier,
Die Himmlische, dem Meeresschaum entstiegen,
Einend den Sinn, allein die Sinne nicht,
Der Eintracht alles Wesens hohe Mutter,
Geschlechtlos, weil sie selber das Geschlecht,
Und himmlisch, weil sie stammt vom Himmel oben.[13]

The Priest's adherence to the law is expressed in the scene with the dove. He demands that the bird be removed because it is an animal that mates, a forbidden activity within the vicinity of the temple. When asked to explain why this is so, he remarks simply: "So wills des Tempels Übung;"[14] he unquestioningly accepts the ethos of his society. A speech in Act III demonstrates how the Priest embodies the attributes of the *vita contemplativa*, which he believes is the proper mode of existence since it enables completeness and perfection:

Doch wessen Streben auf das Innre führt,
Wo Ganzheit nur des Wirkens Fülle fördert,
Der halte fern vom Streite seinen Sinn,
Denn ohne Wunde kehrt man nicht zurück,
Die noch als Narbe mahnt in trüben Tagen.[15]

Here the Priest also expresses the advantages of a contemplative life of *Innerlichkeit*; it functions as a necessary escape from a more dangerous outer, active existence. Furthermore, the

Priest remains true to the rules of the temple that require him to allow Leander's body to be taken into the temple. The *Tempelhüter* explains: "So wills der Brauch! / PRIESTER. Wills so der Brauch, wohlan! / Die Bräuche muß man halten, sie sind gut."[16]   The Priest adheres rigidly to the laws, which ultimately require that he move to stop the liaison between Hero and Leander. This fact might indicate that the code itself is negative. Such is not the case, however.[17] Indeed, for the Priest the code is positive. But, as we shall subsequently see, the positive aspect does not apply to Hero. While the Priest's actions are motivated by a desire to adhere steadfastly to the moral code he represents, he is forced into conflict with Hero as a result of her divergence from this ethos. Since he is its representative, her divergence necessitates his actions and subsequently involves him in the ensuing tragedy.   Thus, while the Priest behaves with the highest of intentions, he also becomes guilty because of his actions. Through his culpability he becomes tragic. However, the Priest is a human being and must therefore be allowed failings and imperfections.[18]

By adhering to his code of ethics, the Priest comes into conflict with Hero when he perceives that she no longer abides by it. Hero's part in this conflict will be analyzed below. Here it is of interest to examine the conflict from the Priest's perspective. On one level the difficulty between Hero and the Priest may be understood as the failure of a priestess to abide by the laws of her order. This is the reading possible when merely considering the external plot of the play.[19]   On another level, the conflict may be seen as the daughter's denial of her father's ethos. The daughter rejects the father, his world and all it represents as she develops into an autonomous being, an aspect of Hero's individuation considered below. Finally, a third interpretation of this conflict centers on the movement from the *vita contemplativa* to the *vita activa*. As we have seen, the Priest represents the contemplative sphere of life. As we will see in the discussion of Hero, the relationship between her and Leander is a manifestation of the *vita activa*; through love both enter an active sphere of existence and come into conflict with the contemplative. As the representatives of the *vita activa*, Hero and Leander thus stand in conflict with the personification of the *vita contemplativa*, the Priest. By striving to save Hero for a life as a priestess, the Priest tries to overcome the conflict between himself and Hero on each of these levels. It must be understood that the Priest does not seek to punish Hero for her actions; his goal is to gain her return to her former sphere of existence.[20]

Not only is the Priest the representative of the law and the *vita contemplativa*, but he also becomes the "guardian of the self which Hero has consecrated to the temple."[21] Therefore he must try to prevent a repetition of the indiscretion that occurred when Hero and Leander spent the night together. This perception can be discerned in two passages. The Priest believes his actions are divinely guided and maintains that prevention is now necessary: "In meinem Innern regt sich ein Gott / Und warnt mich, zu verhüten, ehs zu spät!"[22] In the following scene, when Hero and the Priest meet for the second time in Act IV, the Priest warns Hero:

> Man sah
> In deinem Turme Licht die ganze Nacht.
> Tu das nicht mehr.
> HERO.   Wir haben Öl genug.
> PRIESTER. Doch siehts das Volk und deutets, wie es mag.
> HERO. Mags denn!
> PRIESTER. Auch riet ich dir, den Schein zu meiden,
> Den Schein sogar; viel mehr noch wahren Anlaß.[23]

In addition to demonstrating the Priest's attempt to prevent any recurrence of previous events and thereby save Hero for an existence as a priestess, these lines also express the Priest's concerns about what other people will think should they see the light shining in Hero's window. This points to a concern for Hero's reputation, typical of a father figure. Through the word play on "Schein," the Priest's anxiety becomes apparent. Concern about a light burning late into the night is reminiscent of a scene in Wagner's *Kindermörderin* where the same apprehension is expressed. In Wagner's play it is indeed the daughter who is anxious about what the neighbors might think, but this misgiving is simply a manifestation of the father's way of thinking, here deeply instilled in the daughter. Thus the concern, "Was denken da die Leute?" plays a significant role in the Priest's attempt to achieve Hero's return to her life as a priestess and preserve her reputation. By trying to force Hero's reversion to the priesthood, the Priest actively objectifies his niece. He uses her to fulfill the family tradition and fails to see that she has intrinsic worth and an existence apart from the office she has entered. By seeing the young woman *only* as a priestess, this father figure demonstrates his inability and unwillingness to understand her for who she actually is.

As we will see in the following discussion of Hero's character, the Priest fails to recognize the young woman's true nature and, moreover, tries to force a set of values and a mode of behavior on her that do not fit Hero's true persona. This is not to say that the Priest's values are intrinsically false for all people. Indeed, Papst is convincing when he criticizes those who see the Priest solely as "the embodiment of an unnatural moral law."[24] The moral code he represents is not *unnatural* at all for *him,* but it becomes so for Hero. The Priest's failure lies in his continuing attempt to impose this behavior on Hero, an expression of the rigid adherence to a moral code typical of fathers (see chapter I). Thompson writes that the Priest believes "wrongly that he can still save her from the ultimate indiscretion and preserve her for the priesthood."[25] What is "wrong" here is not the moral code itself, but rather the Priest's unwavering application of it. His intentions are sound but in this instance, unrealistic. His understanding of Hero's true nature is defective. Indeed, the Priest acts "in what he believes to be Hero's own interest."[26] But the fact that the moral code is of ultimate importance for the Priest, even at the expense of individual existence, signifies his inhumane and exaggerated application of it. In his attempt to return Hero to the *vita contemplativa,* the Priest fails to perceive fully Hero's true inner being and thereby causes in part the ensuing tragedy of human existence.

Let us now turn to an analysis of Hero's role in the conflict and trace her individuation process as Grillparzer demonstrates it in the drama. Besides leaving home because of the animosity she feels toward her father and brother, Hero believes she is destined to a high calling, namely the priesthood. Indeed, as Janthe states, this is part of Hero's family tradition:

> JANTHE. Verzeih, wir sind gemeines, niedres Volk.
> Du freilich, aus der Priester Stamm entsprossen -
> HERO. Du sagst es.
> JANTHE.   Und zu Höherem bestimmt.
> HERO. Mit Stolz entgegn ich: Ja.[27]

This passage directly reflects Grillparzer's plan. At the beginning of 1826 he wrote in his notes: "Hero auf ihre Geburt stolz. Alle ihre Vorfahren Priester und Priesterinnen desselben Tempels."[28]   Hero's choice to become a priestess is an active behavior; but because of its required isolation, this existence is passive and contemplative. The Priest describes this isolation: "Ein einsam Leben harrt der Priesterin, / Zu zweien trägt und wirkt sichs noch so leicht."[29] He not only describes the isolation but also alludes to the difficulty contained in such an existence: it is more difficult than sharing life with another individual. Hero fails to comprehend the Priest's warning fully. Because there have always been many people in the temple, Hero perceives the priesthood as requiring almost constant communication with others.

As we have seen, Hero regards the priesthood as secure and uses it as an escape from her parental home with all of its mistreatment. Because she withdraws from active life into the guarded world of the priesthood, we can interpret it as Hero's *vita contemplativa*.[30]   This notion is strengthened when we further consider that the priesthood Hero now enters requires isolation and withdrawal from the outer world, as reflected in the Priest's remarks quoted above. Hero's failure to comprehend fully the consequences and requirements of her new office point from the very outset of the play to the inevitability of her ensuing conflict.[31] This fact is also recognized by other characters in the work.[32] Hero's mother provides the most penetrating and foreboding observation: "Was soll ich dirs verhehlen? / Das Weib ist glücklich nur an Gattenhand."[33] The Priest expresses his reservations about Hero's devotion to the priesthood at the beginning of the play as well: "Doch kommt die Zeit und ändert Wunsch und Neigung."[34]

Hero's own actions at the end of Act I and in Act II demonstrate that she has not truly internalized her desire to become a priestess. The first example appears during the ordination scene. Here Hero merely goes through the ritualistic motions and becomes confused in the middle of her incantations. When she pours an overabundance of incense into the fire, "[zuckt] [e]ine lebhaftere Flamme . . . empor."[35] Thompson and Papst agree that this flame "reflects the flaring passion in her heart."[36] As she leaves, she looks "als nach etwas Fehlendem an ihrem Schuh, über die rechte Schulter zurück. Ihr Blick trifft dabei auf die beiden Jünglinge [Leander und Naukleros]."[37] Thus, without words, Grillparzer gives us a picture of Hero's inner confusion.

The second manifestation of Hero's confused state comes in the first face-to-face meeting between Hero and Leander when she sings the song of Leda and the swan. She catches herself and remembers: "Mein Oheim meint, ich soll das Lied nicht singen / Von Leda und dem Schwan. / *Weitergehend.* Was schadets nur?"[38] She not only initially forgets to follow her uncle's directive concerning the song, but, more significantly, consciously decides that singing it will not do any harm; she purposely disobeys the Priest's order.[39] When speaking with Naukleros and Leander, Hero boldly explains that she has sworn to remain celibate: "Ich aber bin der Göttin Priesterin, / Und ehelos zu sein heißt mein Gelübd."[40] She even repeats this statement, but follows the repetition with a further explanation exposing her real thoughts:

> Niemand, der lebt, begehr um mich zu werben,
> Denn gattenlos zu sein heißt mich mein Dienst.
> Noch gestern, wenn ihr kamt, da war ich frei,
> Doch heut versprach ichs, und ich halt es auch.[41]

Yesterday the situation was different; that is, Hero would have been available, and - we infer - willing. Had the priesthood been an internalized facet of her being, it should have made no difference when Leander came; Hero would have always been beyond his reach. Indeed, since she indicates otherwise, we must discern that the priesthood for her is merely an outer covering - *eine Hülle.*

Hero's psychological perspective begins to shift away from the priesthood; this life is no longer an internalized characteristic of her personality.[42]   Instead she begins to focus on Leander. In Act II this metaphysical realignment is still part of Hero's unconscious; it has not yet appeared outwardly. But the kernel of inner change has been planted. Grillparzer has prepared the audience for this change by demonstrating that Hero was never truly committed to the priesthood. Now Hero herself begins to become aware of this fact. She naively entered the priesthood without fully understanding what else life had to offer. Through the love now beginning to grow between Hero and Leander, both develop to a fuller understanding of themselves and life. Love has a further consequence: it brings both into the sphere of the *vita activa,* which is in direct opposition to the *vita contemplativa* still represented by the Priest.[43]

Leander undergoes a process identical to Hero's inner change. Before meeting her, Leander had been an isolated and quiet individual.[44] Once they encounter each other, he transforms into a talkative, active human being. Activity had been characteristic of Naukleros' life, but in Act IV Naukleros comprehends the change that has occurred: "Nun ja, ich seh es wohl, wir haben, / Die Plätze haben wir getauscht. Ich furchtsam, / Du kühn; Leander frohen Muts . . . ."[45] Love becomes the source of change for both Hero and Leander.[46]

Grillparzer himself alludes to the importance of love and its effects when he notes in his diary: "Vierter Akt. Hero mit dem Gefühle als *Weib.*"[47] From this observation, we see that Hero's inner change, which has transformed her into a woman, occurred in Act III, thus motivating her new mindset in Act IV. Hero begins the third act by removing her priestly cloak, saying: "Ein Leben hüllst du ein in deine Falten. / Bewahre, was du weißt, ich leg es ab mit dir."[48] The symbolic content of this action has been widely analyzed.[49] It is of greater interest to compare this action with Medea's removal and burying of her chest in the first act of *Medea.* In chapter III, this action was compared to Sappho's change of clothing as a reflection of her inner state. No matter to what we compare Hero's action, it is clear that by taking off the cloak she has removed the vestiges of her priestly office and no longer feels bound by them. This notion further manifests itself when she again sings the song of Leda and the swan. As demonstrated earlier, this song reflects Hero's psychological state. After singing two lines of the song she says to herself:

> Das ewge Lied! Wie kommts mir nur in Sinn?
> Nicht Götter steigen mehr zu wüsten Türmen,
> Kein Schwan, kein Adler bringt Verlaßnen Trost.
> Die Einsamkeit bleibt einsam und sie selbst.[50]

Here she thinks *indirectly* of Leander; a few lines later she begins to speak of him *directly*:

> Ich will dir wohl, erfreut doch, daß du fern
> Und reichte meine Stimme bis zu dir,
> Ich riefe grüßend: Gute Nacht!
> LEANDER *im Hintergrunde von außen am Fenster erscheinend.*
>   Gut Nacht![51]

Indeed, as Papst cleverly points out, this meeting between Hero and Leander marks the metaphysical turning point when the two young people are finally brought together without the presence of others and the physical center of the drama.[52] From this point to the conclusion of Act III, Hero becomes increasingly receptive to Leander and even begins to worry on his account after Janthe and the *Tempelhüter* inspect Hero's chamber. Hero herself finally recognizes this fact: "Ich zitterte - doch nicht um mich! - Verkehrtheit! / Ich zitterte für ihn!"[53] A microcosm of the inner change Hero experiences is demonstrated when she and Leander discuss when they will next meet. At first Hero suggests he send her a messenger, then tells him to come on the next festival day, then in ten days, and finally - after Leander's persistent chatter - commands him to come the next day![54] After their kiss, Hero begins to depart, expecting Leander to leave. But she returns and they consummate their love after the curtain falls on Act III.

Love alters the way Hero and Leander perceive themselves and the world; it brings them happiness and self-awareness. This love also causes conflict with the Priest and the existing sphere of *vita contemplativa* to which Hero had belonged and to whose code of ethics she is expected·to adhere. The conflict appears in Act IV. Much comment has been made by critics about Hero's new emotional state in this act.[55] Indeed, Hero has developed beyond the level of self-establishment the priesthood can offer. Through her new commitment to Leander she rejects the world represented by her father figure, the Priest, and thereby experiences individuation. But by denying the lifestyle the priesthood represents and to which the daughter's obedience is expected, the conflict between Hero and the Priest develops;[56]   Hero's denial of her "father" steadily increases.

The conflict readily makes itself apparent in Act IV when Hero does not passively accept the word of the Priest, but rather asserts her own will and speaks impudently:

PRIESTER. Doch ich will Klarheit, und Janthe scheide.
HERO. Verzeih! Du weißt, das kann nicht ohne mich,
Die Mädchen sind der Priesterin befohlen,
Und meine Rechte kenn ich so wie meine -
Ich kenne, Herr, mein Recht.
PRIESTER.   Wie meine Pflichten:
Du wolltest sagen so.
HERO.   Ich wollte, Herr,
Und sag es jetzt: auch meine Pflichten kenn ich,
Wenn Pflicht das alles, was ein ruhig Herz,
Im Einklang mit sich selbst und mit der Welt,
Dem Recht genüber sellt der andern Menschen.[57]

This passage represents Hero's unwillingness to comply blindly with the expectations and commands of the priesthood and expresses her newly found self-understanding. She no longer sees her duty to her former office; rather, the relationship of the individual with the wider world becomes most important. Here the disparity between Hero and the Priest, representing the *vita activa* and the *vita contemplativa*, is expressed. As we saw in the discussion of the Priest's character, an attempt is made to re-establish Hero's adherence to the priesthood's code of ethics. This is impossible because Hero has changed internally to such an extent that she no longer desires to live according to this set of rules. The conflict arises when the irreconcilable nature of the opposing world views becomes apparent.[58]   Through love Hero comes into opposition with the institution of the priesthood and its stern representative.

Love leads to Hero's realization of her inner self, thus bringing her into conflict with her former *vita contemplativa* and eventually causing the death of both Leander and herself. Thus, in this context, love might be considered a destructive force.   Indeed, this interpretation appears in the literature. Politzer and Naumann, for example, describe Hero as the victim of love and passion.[59]   Politzer explains Hero's passion "war nichts als Schein, Bild und Zeichen."[60]   If this is true, that is, if love and passion were really just an outer veil as Politzer suggests, why does the removal of the source of love for Hero through Leander's death cause her own demise? Indeed, Hero behaves differently as a consequence of love. As Yates points out, she must often resort to lies to hide the true situation from her uncle, as in the first garden scene with Naukleros and Leander in Act II and later while Leander is present in the tower.[61]   Through love Hero rejects her old form of existence and thus incurs guilt.   By her actions she becomes a tragic figure in terms of Grillparzer's juxtaposition of *vita contemplativa* and *vita activa*.   She acknowledges her partial guilt in Leander's death when explaining the situation to Naukleros in Act V: "Und fragst du, wers getan?   Sieh! Dieser [Priester] hier / Und ich, die Priesterin, die Jungfrau - So? - / Menanders Hero, ich, wir beide tatens."[62]

Love partially causes the tragic situation, but it is also a positive force in this drama even though its consequences are less than desirable. As Papst writes, love produces "a state of irreducible wholeness of being and recollected composure in which the self at once possesses, fulfils and transcends itself."[63] Love enables the individual to overcome self-limitation and broaden the life perspective to include another human being. Beyond simple inclusion, love produces, at least in the case of Hero and Leander, a complete union between the *Ich* and the *Du*.   That is, Hero and Leander become one being in a metaphysical sense, in addition to their physical joining at the end of Act III. This metaphysical unification of each *Ich* with the other's *Du* opens a new type of life for them. All of Hero's existence, her entire *Ich*, has become focused on Leander and his *Du*.[64]

The significance of this unity further manifests itself apart from the conflict between Hero, Leander and the Priest. While Leander's death is necessitated by the Priest's attempt to redirect Hero's metaphysical obedience, the exact reason for Hero's demise may remain mysterious if one fails to consider the unity of *Ich* and *Du*. In the final words she directs to her dead lover, Hero says: "Als Zeichen nur, als Pfand beim letzten Scheiden, / Nimm diesen Kranz, den Gürtel lös ich ab / Und leg ihn dir ins Grab."[65] In this action she gives Leander her entire self, symbolically captured in the *Kranz* and the *Gürtel*. Papst interprets the *Kranz* as Hero's priesthood and the *Gürtel* as her virginity.[66] In any instance, these are the only objects Hero still possesses, and as such they embody her entire being, pars pro toto, which she now places with Leander forever. Through this expression of the total and irreversible unity between Hero and Leander, the motivation for her own death becomes apparent. Since Leander has ceased to exist and because the two are physically and metaphysically insepa-rable, Hero must necessarily die. Her death reflects the eternal unification of the *Ich* and *Du*. Death does not destroy the love between Hero and Leander, but rather serves as a "Durchgang zu einer endgültigen Vereinigung."[67] As Politzer writes, in death Hero realizes her true self.[68] This true self has become Leander.

By causing the deaths, the Priest fails to act humanely; he does not allow Hero and Leander to develop autonomously and determine their own behavior. Indeed, Grillparzer described the Priest as "keine moderne Humanität."[69] Through his unrelenting adherence to the law, the Priest forces the conflict between himself and Hero and refuses to accept her as she is. Humane behavior would have required and included acceptance of Hero's *vita activa* and openness to this change. The Priest does not possess these capabilities; the rift between his *vita contemplativa* and Hero's new life remains beyond reconciliation. But, as we saw above, the Priest, as a human being, has faults and imperfections and, therefore, should not be blamed totally for the catastrophe that occurs in the drama.[70]

To be sure, the Priest fails as a father and as a human being to comprehend Hero's true inner self and to allow the process of her individuation. Herein lies the kernel of the tragic occurrences in this play. Thus the father-daughter relationship is a significant aspect of the work and affects all principal characters. The Priest, as a father, tries to prevent Hero from partaking of the individuation she has just begun to experience. As stated above, he remains unbending in the application of moral and social ethics and grasps the ultimate means to prevent his daughter from stepping irrevocably beyond the bounds of his world order. The father thus causes the catastrophe.

Hero also plays a significant part in the catastrophe, to which her admissions of guilt testify (see above). Her individuation process has forced her father figure to act. Had she better understood her defective use of the priesthood from the outset, the catastrophe could have been avoided. But we must recognize that to expect such an understanding by a young, developing individual is unrealistic. This misunderstanding is precisely the center of the individuation process. Plainly stated, Hero tries first one mode of existence, finds that it fails to correspond to her inner being and then develops to another. This process reflects her movement from the contemplative to the active sphere of life. What is interesting to note about Hero is that, unlike Sappho and Medea, Hero never tries to go back to the first stage of the *vita contemplativa*. Naumann misunderstands Hero's individuation process when he maintains that Hero's tragedy stems from her inability to return to "Sammlung."[71]   Such an attempt to return would have indicated Hero's incomplete commitment to the new life she sought with Leander, and her death would not have been unavoidable. But she is fully entrenched in the *vita activa* of love for Leander, and the total unity of her *Ich* with Leander's *Du* does not necessitate an attempt to seek readmission to the *vita contemplativa*. Hero dies in a state of physical and metaphysical satisfaction.

In chapter III we saw that Medea reached the state of renunciation expressed in the last lines of the poem "Entsagung:" "Und in dem Abschied, vom Besitz genommen, / Erhältst du dir das einzig deine: Dich!"[72] Through the unity with Leander, that is, by becoming one with his *Du*, Hero in essence reaches a stage of renunciation through death similar to Medea's. It is impossible to separate Hero and Leander from each other; they must be perceived as one entity when they cease to live, so strong and complete is their unification. By dying, Hero perfects this unity between her *Ich* and Leander's *Du*. By renouncing life, i.e., "Besitz," Hero fully achieves her new self, that is, *Dich*. While Medea must rely only on herself as *Dich*, Hero has the further perspective of Leander's contribution to the *Du*. Thus death becomes at the same time renunciation and fulfillment of the self for Hero. We do not see this final expression of individuation on the stage. It manifests itself as a "jenseitiges Verhältnis."[73]

We see a progression in Grillparzer's thought from *Das goldene Vließ* to *Des Meeres und der Liebe Wellen*. In each work, there is a movement towards self-establishment, manifested through the evolution from the *vita contemplativa* to the *vita activa*. In *Das goldene Vließ*, the author depicts the summit of the individuation process as the necessary isolation of the individual. Medea indeed realizes her true inner self and achieves individuation, but only through total withdrawal from all other people. In *Des Meeres und der Liebe Wellen*, this picture shifts slightly to include another person at the height of individuation. In both works, the individuation process manifests itself as a result of the father-daughter relationship and concludes with the renunciation of all possessions besides the self. The difference between the two plays lies in how the final self is defined. For Medea the self is based on the isolated individual while Hero's life includes Leander.

The possibility of union with another is a change from the conclusions of the four dramas analyzed in chapter II. Like the women in those plays, Hero's death is caused in part by the father-daughter relationship. Unlike them, however, Hero's individuation does not result in total isolation, but, as we have seen, includes another human being. While this play is yet a tragedy, there is this glimmer of hope for human existence[74] since Grillparzer now allows the inclusion of another individual into the individuation of the self.   But Hero's individuation is tainted by her continued dependence on another human being. She left the control of her natural father because her family situation was unpleasant. In the next stage of her maturation she came under the control of the Priest. Finally, Hero met Leander and became dependent on him to such a great extent that she ceased to exist when his life ended. This progression demonstrates that Hero never truly came to rely *only* on herself; she merely moved from one source of domination to another. While her love for Leander was indeed a new, active existence for Hero, her continued dependence indicates that complete individuation did not occur.

Chapter V

Hebbel's *Maria Magdalene*

More extensively than *Das goldene Vlieβ* or *Des Meeres und der Liebe Wellen*, Hebbel's *Maria Magdalene* emphasizes the lethal effects the father-daughter relationship has on the child. The conflict in this work results from the father's unyielding bourgeois morality, to which the daughter tries to remain committed. While analyses of this play are often combined with an explanation of Hebbel's dramatic theory, this discussion foregoes a detailed examination since it has been amply treated elsewhere.[1] Instead, the concentration lies on the father-daughter relationship and its brutal consequences for the child. Although elements of this relationship in *Maria Magdalene* have been the subjects of several critical examinations, lacking is a close textual analysis that effectively elucidates how the words spoken by Hebbel's characters demonstrate such concepts as honor, objectification of the woman and the inevitability of death.

The first scene establishes two significant elements in Klara's progression toward suicide. Klara's mother wears her wedding dress, to which she now refers as her "Leichenkleid."[2] This points to the proximity of death. Indeed, words directly or indirectly indicating death, such as *Tod, Sarg, Grab, Mord*, and *sterben* commonly occur throughout the entire work - especially, but not exclusively, in connection with the figure of the mother.[3] To be sure, death is ever-present in this work in which four of six principal characters die.

The second important factor expressed in the first scene is the mother's explanation of Meister Anton's personality. While describing her life's duties she mentions: "ich habe dich [Klara] und deinen Bruder in der Furcht des Herrn aufgezogen und den sauren Schweiß eures Vaters zusammengehalten . . . ."[4] In her comment about Anton are the key words *sauer* and *Schweiß,* indicating his strong work ethic, which, as we find out subsequently from Anton, corresponds to that of the Meister's own father.[5] In Therese's words also lies the strong commitment to religion, another concept permeating the work and establishing its moral tone.

In the second scene, Karl repeats the notion of hard work, this time with regard to himself, and modifies his mother's statement regarding Anton. Karl refers to his father as a "Brummbär,"[6] a grouch or grumbler. This is indeed a characteristic of Anton's stern nature. This aspect of Anton can be seen in scene three when Klara describes her father's behavior during Therese's recent illness. Klara noticed that he was crying; when she approached and touched him on the cheek, he said: "Versuch doch, ob du mir den verfluchten Span nicht aus dem Auge herausbringen kannst, man hat so viel zu tun und kommt nicht vom Fleck!"[7] Naturally it would have been out of place for a man of the mid-nineteenth century to express emotion, especially in front of his daughter; but this incident does help indicate Anton's inner nature.

In the third scene, three other significant occurrences take place. In her long explanation of the revered position of *Schreiber,* Therese indicates her inclination toward Leonhard as a possible mate for Klara.[8] This instills in Klara the idea that Leonhard is the right man as far as her mother is concerned and, therefore, ought to be right for her as well. This fact encourages Klara to attempt to bond herself to Leonhard, even though she does not love him. Secondly, an obvious foreshadowing of Therese's death occurs in this scene. Klara speaks of a dream she had three times showing her mother lying in a coffin. The motif of a dream foretelling future action is Kleistian: precisely the event Klara dreams about comes to pass.[9] Finally, Klara's search for a spiritual foundation manifests itself when she says: "Ich wollt, ich hätt einen Glauben, wie die Katholischen, daß ich Dir [Gott] etwas schenken dürfte!"[10] Klara wants an emotional support she can physically grasp. Her Protestant faith apparently does not provide sufficient spiritual sustenance. From her attempt to find a metaphysical foothold, we perceive that Klara is already emotionally unstable.

The fourth scene establishes the basis of Klara's search for spiritual sustenance as her relationship with Leonhard becomes illuminated. Klara's pregnancy resulted when Leonhard forced himself on her when he became jealous of Friedrich. Leonhard's words reveal his jealousy as well as another characteristic of his personality that turns out to be especially abhorrent:

> KLARA. O Leonhard, es war nicht recht von dir!
> LEONHARD. Nicht recht, daß ich mein höchstes Gut, denn das bist du, auch durch das letzte Band an mich fest zu knüpfen suchte? Und in dem Augenblick, wo ich in Gefahr stand, es zu verlieren? Meinst du, ich sah die stillen Blicke nicht, die du mit dem Sekretär wechseltest? Das war ein schöner Freudentag für mich! Ich führe dich zum Tanz, und [11]

Leonhard calls Klara his "höchstes Gut," his greatest property. In this fashion he objectifies her by making her into a thing to be won when he fears he might lose her to someone else. In Act III, Leonhard contemplates again why he had sexual relations with Klara and concludes: "Es war in mir wirklich mehr die Eifersucht als die Liebe, die mich zum Rasen brachte, und sie ergab sich gewiß nur darein, um meine Vorwürfe zu widerlegen, denn sie war kalt gegen mich, wie der Tod."[12]

This idea is made even more tragic when coupled with the fact that Klara gave herself to Leonhard in order to dispel the critical talk of her acquaintances, as she explains in Act II. Furthermore, as we have seen, the mother believes Leonhard is the proper man for Klara and encourages her to set her sights on him and forget Friedrich.[13] When Leonhard announces that he has come to ask Anton's permission to marry her, Klara speaks words more meaningful than she momentarily comprehends. After Leonhard asks, "Ist dirs nicht recht?" she responds: "Nicht recht? Mein Tod wärs, wenn ich nicht bald dein Weib würde, aber du kennst meinen Vater nicht!"[14] Klara unknowingly associates separation from Leonhard with death. In the same breath, she alludes to her father's stern nature; she worries about what his reaction to

the engagement will be.   Furthermore, Klara immediately
fears that he might discover the secret of her pregnancy.   Her
concern lies not with any consequence for herself or what
having to postpone the marriage for a year would would mean
for her, but rather her anxiety centers on her father.   To be
sure, Klara does not mention keeping the secret from *both*
parents, but only from her father.   Leonhard is also well aware
of Anton's personality, especially his sense of honesty.   Leonhard explains that Anton would rise from the grave, if necessary, to rub out an excess letter on his headstone: "denn er
würde es für unredlich halten, sich mehr vom Alphabet
anzueignen, als ihm zukäme!"[15]

Thus all three members of the family, Therese, Karl and
Klara, as well as Leonhard, have spoken of Anton's stern
moral character and exacting nature.   Finally Meister Anton
describes how he seeks to remain above social reproach when
he explains to Leonhard: "Ich stecke in meinem Hause keine
Kerzen an, als die mir selbst gehören.   Dann weiß ich, daß
niemand kommen kann, der sie wieder ausbläst, wenn wir
eben unsre Lust daran haben!"[16]   Anton takes care of his own
house and keeps to himself to prevent others from attacking
him and his family.   Here Anton's fixation with reputation and
honor begins to become clear.   As discussed in chapter I, this is
a common phenomenon for the father figure, especially in
nineteenth-century Europe, because of the father's responsibility for his family's reputation.

All principal characters have established Anton as the representative of social morality in the family.   Each has described
some facet of his stern, honest and honorable nature.   Indeed,
this aspect of Anton's figure is frequently mentioned in analyses of *Maria Magdalene*.[17]   As Benno von Wiese explains, the
picture   Hebbel   paints   is   an   accurate   account   of   mid-
nineteenth-century existence and reflects "die geschichtlich
entstandene kleinbürgerliche Moralität, die noch in einer
pietistischen Weltabkehr verwurzelt ist, dabei aber stark genug
bleibt, in dem durch die Familie gebundenen Umkreis eine
absolute Tyrannei auszuüben."[18]   Here the forceful nature
and possible negative consequences of this moral code appear.
Indeed, while Anton represents this ethos, he also, like the

other characters in the play, becomes its victim.[19]   The bourgeois morality victimizes Anton as he cannot free himself from it; instead he remains in steadfast accordance with this tradition.   Anton's rigid adherence to the moral code is demonstrated through his refusal to deviate from it even when it would require him to defend his enemy Adam.   Once Karl has returned home from jail he vows to even the score between himself and Adam, who brought shame upon Karl and his family by parading Karl through the entire town instead of taking him directly to prison. Anton warns his son: "Das tadle ich nicht, aber ich verbiet es dir! . . . Ich werde dich nicht aus den Augen lassen, und ich selbst, ich würde dem Kerl beispringen, wenn du dich an ihm vergreifen wolltest!"[20] From this example, we see how strongly Anton is possessed by the moral code and how it victimizes him as well as those about him.

References in the text to Anton's upright nature and adherence to his society's code of ethics are numerous.   Upon returning from church, Therese comments: "Hab ich nicht einen aufrichtigen Mann?"[21]   When the merchant comes to explain that his wife actually stole the jewels and that Karl was unjustly arrested, he comments that his suspicion naturally fell on Karl although he greatly respects Anton.[22]

Anton's ethics are based on his concept of religion.   Indeed, religious references appear frequently in the text.   Perhaps the most significant one is Anton's perversion of the Lord's Prayer, which he envisions Karl using while drinking in a bar instead of going to church:

> "Vater unser, der du bist im Himmel!" - Guten Tag, Peter, sieht man dich beim Abendtanz? - "Geheiliget werde dein Name!" - Ja, lach nur, Kathrine, es findet sich! - "Dein Wille geschehe!" - Hol mich der Teufel, ich bin noch nicht rasiert![23]

In this statement, Anton combines religion with proper social behavior.   He feels Karl contradicts proper social tradition by going to a bar rather than attending church. Through her perversion of this prayer at the end of the drama, Klara shows her direct and unshaken attempt to adhere to the same moral concept.   By having each speak this prayer, Hebbel most certainly wanted to associate father and daughter and establish the common basis of their world view.

The basis of this world view lies in a fixation with honor and an abhorrence of dishonor, *Schande*. As expressed in chapter I, the reputation of the family was a primary concern of the father. Preservation of the reputation necessitated prevention of dishonor within the family with regard to the wider social community. Anton concerns himself with shame and the threat of social censure throughout the entire play and makes his reputation contingent on Klara's honor. At the end of Act I, just after Therese has died of either a stroke or heart attack at the news of Karl's arrest, Anton explains to Klara the significance and necessity of her honor, good reputation and purity: "Der Vater blieb am Leben! Komm ihm zu Hülfe, du kannst nicht verlangen, daß er alles allein tun soll, gib du mir den Rest, der alte Stamm sieht noch so knorrig aus, nicht wahr, aber er wackelt schon, es wird dir nicht zu viel Mühe kosten, ihn zu fällen!"[24] In the first scene of Act II, we receive a clearer definition of Anton's notion of honor. He explains that it is up to Klara to prove to the world that her parents were honorable people: If she turns out properly, everyone will know it was not the parents' fault that Karl became a thief. But Anton does not stop here. He adds:

> In dem Augenblick, wo ich bemerke, daß man auch auf dich mit Fingern zeigt, werd ich - *Mit einer Bewegung an den Hals.* mich rasieren, und dann, das schwör ich dir zu, rasier ich den ganzen Kerl weg . . . . Ich kanns in einer Welt nicht aushalten, wo die Leute mitleidig sein müßten, wenn sie nicht vor mir ausspucken sollen.[25]

Anton's oath to commit suicide if Klara's honor were ever questioned centers around the word *rasieren*. Hebbel has cleverly prepared the listener for the use of this word in this context by introducing it earlier in Anton's version of the Lord's Prayer. There *rasieren* appeared in its normal context and had no connection with suicide. Furthermore, Anton did not use it in reference to himself. This personal reference appears in scene six of Act I. Upon greeting his wife he says: "So gibst du mir einen Kuß! Ich bin rasiert, und besser, wie gewöhnlich!"[26] Again, as in the word's first application, there is no implication of death. However, the notion of *rasieren* is now directly related to Anton, and the listener has been prepared for its use in Anton's oath to commit suicide.

In a similar fashion, Hebbel prepares the listener for Anton's threat of suicide when Leonhard relates to Klara the meeting between himself and the other candidate for the position of cashier, which Leonhard obtained by employing his friends to get his opponent intoxicated. Leonhard met him on a bridge and, as he was peering into the water, asked whether something had dropped in. The other responded: "'Jawohl . . . und es ist vielleicht gut, wenn ich selbst nachspringe.'"[27] Thus the listener has the concept of suicide in mind before Anton states his oath. Furthermore, the defeated man's statement begins to prepare us for Klara's suicide at the end of the work by establishing drowning as the means for taking one's life.

It is interesting to note that water in this work is associated with death. This is ironic because most commonly water is associated with life; water itself nourishes the earth in the form of rain and is comparable to the *semen virile*.[28] Furthermore, in a biblical context, wells were considered a source of life, the *aqua viva*, as these produced life-giving water.[29] In addition to its life-producing and life-sustaining aspects, water functions as a means of purification, as in baptism.[30] Lurker comments: "Im Traum kann das Wasser sowohl als schöpferische, lebensspendende, dem Weiblich-Mütterlichen verbundene Kraft erscheinen, aber auch in seiner bedrohlichen, zerstörenden Wirkung erfahren werden."[31] The notion that water destroys corresponds directly to its effect on Klara's mortal existence.[32] Indeed, Hebbel's use of *Wasser* and *Brunnen*, like *rasieren*, prepares the listener for approaching action.

As with the word *rasieren*, Hebbel has intensified the concept of Anton's stern moral nature. His oath is an extreme manifestation of his honor fixation. As we have seen, each character comments on this phenomenon. The development of this aspect of Anton's personality culminates in the passages in which Anton himself expresses the importance of social appearance and preservation of honor.[33] His fixation demands the continuation of honor for himself and his family. To ensure that dishonor is avoided, he forces an oath from Klara, who promises: "Ich - schwöre - dir - daß - ich - dir - nie - Schande - machen - will!"[34]

Anton and Klara have both taken oaths focusing on the concept of disgrace. In each, Klara's honor and its effects on Anton occupy the principal thrust of the oath. Neither Klara nor Anton considers what shame and disgrace would mean for *Klara*. Anton in his egotism and Klara in her devotion both fail to perceive that Klara's honor applies primarily to her person. When he forces Klara to take her oath, Anton uses her as a mere object to gain and preserve *his* standing in the community. In this manner, Anton resembles Medea's father, Aietes, who used his daughter to achieve selfish goals.[35] By objectifying their daughters, both fathers fail to recognize each woman's intrinsic value as a human being. While both fathers indeed objectify their daughters, Anton's objectification is passive in comparison to Aietes's. As we saw in chapter III, Aietes seeks to use Medea and her magical powers against the intruders, an active form of instrumentalization; Aietes uses Medea to preserve his *physical* existence. Anton does not use his daughter in such an overt manner; rather, he indirectly objectifies her by making his honor contingent on her reputation, thus remaining in the more *metaphysical* sphere of public opinion (metaphysical because opinion does not directly affect his mortal existence).

Like Anton, Leonhard makes Klara into an object, as mentioned above. Leonhard's objectification of Klara results first from his use of her as a sexual object. His objectification of her further manifests itself in connection with the thousand *Taler* Anton loaned to a pharmacist. Leonhard expects this money will become Klara's dowry. He first asks Klara whether she is aware of the money's status. In typical fashion, the daughter has been left totally in the dark on this aspect of her marriage.[36] In his conversation with Anton, Leonhard quickly turns to the subject of the dowry. At first it does not appear to concern him greatly whether Klara will bring some modicum of financial security to the marriage:

Ich hätte es gern gesehen, wenn seine Tochter mir ein paar hundert Taler zugebracht hätte, und das war natürlich, denn um so besser würde sie selbst es bei mir gehabt haben. . . . Es ist nicht der Fall - was tuts? Wir machen aus der Fasten-Speise unser Sonntags-Essen und aus dem Sonntags-Braten unsern Weihnachts-Schmaus! So gehts auch![37]

Since Leonhard has already named the exact sum of 1,000, his mention of a "paar hundert Taler" indicates that he is testing the waters with Anton to see what the carpenter's reaction will be to the notion of a dowry. Anton remarks that the thousand *Taler* have indeed been lost. To this Leonhard responds *"beiseite*. Also doch weg! Nun, so brauch ich mir von dem alten Werwolf auch nichts gefallen zu lassen, wenn er mein Schwiegervater ist!"[38]   Leonhard reveals that he thinks primarily of the money Klara will bring into the relationship. His materialistic inclinations have placed him in a situation from which he can no longer extricate himself.[39]   In Act III Leonhard further demonstrates that he is "ein Mitgiftjäger und Karrierist."[40]   Even though the obstacle of detriment to Leonhard's honor has been removed through Karl's release from prison, Leonhard explains to Klara in Act III that he cannot marry her for two reasons. First he has impregnated another woman.   If this were not sufficient, he continues: "Wer die Aussteuer seiner Tochter wegschenkt, der muß sich nicht wundern, daß sie sitzenbleibt."[41]   Thus, the lack of a dowry finally proves to have been the actual reason for Leonhard's rejection of Klara. Leonhard used Karl's situation as an excuse to break the engagement, as his words suggest in Act I after the arrest is reported: "Schrecklich!   Aber gut für mich!"[42] Once the dowry disappeared, Leonhard's interest in Klara vanished as well.

Leonhard is the supreme egotist.   His world view centers not on love for Klara or even humane treatment of her, but rather on how she may increase his sexual self image and material possessions.   His inhumane abuse of other people further reveals itself in his relationship with the mayor's niece, whom Leonhard courts so that she will put in a good word with her uncle on his behalf to help win him the job of cashier.[43]   Leonhard rejects Klara because she lacks the necessary dowry that will enhance his material wealth.   To this extent, he uses her as an object, just as he did when he insisted on their physical union during the dance in order to assure himself of her bond to him in the moment of Friedrich's return and Klara's rekindled interest in her former beau.

Another aspect of Klara's relationship with Leonhard focuses on an oath. Klara's oath to Anton that she does not want to dishonor him and Anton's promise to commit suicide force her into a hopeless situation. Klara believes that if she continues to live without Leonhard as her mate, she will cause her father's death.[44] Whether Anton would actually kill himself is doubtful, but the threat suffices for Klara. At the conclusion of Act II, Klara vows: "Ja, Vater, ich gehe, ich gehe! Deine Tochter wird dich nicht zum Selbstmord treiben! Ich bin bald das Weib des Menschen, oder - Gott, nein! Ich bettle ja nicht um ein Glück, ich bettle um mein Elend, um mein tiefstes Elend - mein Elend wirst du mir geben!"[45] Although life with Leonhard would be Klara's greatest misery, she tries to convince him to marry her. She does not succeed. In this failure, another oath, one Klara *refuses* to swear, plays an essential part. In her final conversation with Leonhard, he demands from Klara: "Kannst du schwören, daß du mich liebst? Daß du mich so liebst, wie ein Mädchen den Mann lieben muß, der sich auf ewig mit ihr verbinden soll?"[46] Klara refuses to swear this oath and thus suspends any possibility of a union between herself and Leonhard. Reinhardt points to the significance of Leonhard's requested oath, remarking that Klara is naturally unable to swear it, "und Leonhard fragt auch nur so, weil er weiß, daß sie es nicht kann, und weil er ferner weiß, was ein Schwur für sie bedeutet."[47] Garland sees Klara's refusal as establishing "unambiguously that not even under the shadow of death will she betray her individuality."[48] Unfortunately, Garland does not clarify completely what she means by "her individuality." What Klara refuses to betray by failing to swear the oath is her bourgeois attitude and her adherence to middle-class ethics. Like Luise in Schiller's *Kabale und Liebe*, Klara has internalized the significance of the oath.[49] By adhering to the oath, Luise remained a part of her class and thus placed herself in a deadly situation. Klara also remains steadfastly bound to the bourgeois world view preventing her from falsely swearing an oath. We can only speculate whether Leonhard would have married Klara had she sworn the requested pledge. Hebbel does not encourage this speculation. We must focus merely on the fact that Klara cannot free herself from the bond of bourgeois society; she remains dominated by it,[50] a situation reflecting historical phenomena of pre-1848 Germany.[51]

Klara's adherence to the bourgeois Weltanschauung, in addition to preventing her from swearing Leonhard's oath, places her in a situation making her death inevitable. The hopeless nature of her existence hinges on Anton's oath in combination with the one he forces her to make. She feels obligated to remain true to the oath she swore to her father. Furthermore, the social pressures to which she freely submits herself force her to act to save her father's life.[52] Through his oath, Anton prevents Klara from freely choosing her own mode of behavior; he gives her no choice.[53] Since she cannot break with the bourgeois code, she must bear the burden of Anton's death threat with her. Once she realizes that all possibilities of escape remain closed to her, Klara has no other choice than to commit suicide. As Garland observes: "Anton places his burdens upon Klara, who carries them for him into the water."[54]

One possibility of escape lay with Leonhard. Klara hoped he would accept her as his bride. As we have seen, this does not occur. Another opportunity for Klara's rescue from the necessity of death comes in Act II when Friedrich appears. In the fourth scene, Klara begins to realize her hopeless situation: "Nun sollt ich mich freuen! Gott, Gott! Und ich kann nichts denken, als: Nun bist dus allein! Und doch ist mir zumut, als müsse mir gleich etwas einfallen, das alles wieder gutmacht!"[55] At this very moment Friedrich enters the room, bringing hope for Klara. He repeats the message the merchant has reported, namely that Karl will soon be released from prison: "Du wirst deinen Bruder noch heut abend wieder sehen, und nicht auf ihn, sondern auf die Leute, die ihn ins Gefängnis geworfen haben, wird man mit Fingern zeigen."[56] Friedrich hopes this news will warrant a kiss and, after discovering that Klara is no longer promised to Leonhard, suggests marriage. Klara listens only partially to what Friedrich has to say, for at this moment she still entertains hopes of a life with Leonhard, the father of her unborn child. When Friedrich finally comprehends that Klara is indeed pregnant, he says the often quoted words: "Darüber kann kein Mann weg! Vor dem Kerl, dem man ins Gesicht spucken mögte, die Augen niederschlagen müssen?"[57] In these statements, Friedrich articulates his own unconquerable commitment to bourgeois tradition.[58] This commitment is demonstrated by his use of the same vocabulary as Meister Anton to express a world view: *mit Fingern zeigen* and *spucken*.[59] Like Anton, Friedrich implies with *spucken* dishonor and contempt for another individual; *mit Fingern zeigen* also points to dishonor, disgrace and a loss of reputation. Unlike Anton, however, Friedrich does not remain unbending in his adherence to the social code that momentarily prevents him from sacrificing his self-concept to save Klara's honor. But, he is prepared to marry Klara only *after* Leonhard is dead and the necessity "die Augen niederschlagen [zu] müssen" has been removed. To this extent, Friedrich acts egotistically; he must wait until he no longer needs to fear an affront against his honor by Leonhard. In his readiness to marry Klara there is a trace of humanity, but this humanity is *conditional*; it rests on the assurance of the continuation of his moral impeccability. Once this is established, through Leonhard's death, Friedrich is prepared to marry Klara. Like the others - Karl, Anton and Leonhard[60] - he fails to perceive the serious nature and complexity of Klara's crisis. Indeed, he finally comprehends, but only after she is dead.

Coupled with Friedrich's immediate rejection of Klara at the discovery that she carries Leonhard's child is Klara's new perception of the hopelessness of her own situation, which she clarifies at the conclusion of Act II:

> Nein, darüber kann kein Mann weg! Und wenn - Könntest du selbst darüber hinweg? Hättest du den Mut, eine Hand zu fassen, die - Nein, nein, diesen schlechten Mut hättest du nicht! Du müßtest dich selbst einriegeln in deine Hölle, wenn man dir von außen die Tore öffnen wollte . . . .[61]

Here Klara articulates her perception of the hopeless nature of her situation, caused in part by her inability to free herself from the confines of her middle-class mindset. As in her refusal to swear a false oath to Leonhard, in her decision not to accept Friedrich's sacrifice, even if he had made it, Klara's adherence to the bourgeois ethos further manifests itself. She refuses to consider the possibility of salvation through a life with Friedrich. Her only hope lies with Leonhard. As we have already seen, this is also an impossibility. Klara feels she must commit suicide or, as she unfailingly believes, cause her father to kill himself.[62] In her last scene with Leonhard, Klara verbalizes her conclusion that suicide is necessary:

> LEONHARD. Du kannst Gott Lob nicht Selbst-Mörderin werden, ohne zugleich Kindes-Mörderin zu werden!
> KLARA. Beides lieber, als Vater-Mörderin! O ich weiß, daß man Sünde mit Sünde nicht büßt! Aber was ich jetzt tu, das kommt über mich *allein!* Geb ich meinem Vater das Messer in die Hand, so triffts ihn, wie mich! Mich triffts immer! Dies gibt mir Mut und Kraft in all meiner Angst![63]

Anton's continuing patriarchal control of his daughter appears when Klara does not equate her suicide with the murder of her unborn child. Her concern centers exclusively on her father. Furthermore, Karl's appraisal of what Anton's reaction would be if Klara were ever the cause of dishonor, helps establish the inevitability of her death.[64] Klara firmly believes that the continuation of her life will cause her father's death. Moreover, she will have to bear the guilt for his death. In her statement to Leonhard, Klara's comprehension of her guilt should she commit suicide is also expressed. Thus, guilt is inescapable for Klara; she fully understands this fact. In her own suicide, she believes she can spare her father the guilt he would incur through taking his own life. To this extent, Klara is fully selfless;[65] her concern focuses solely on her father.[66] Kraft maintains that it is not so much for her father that she dies, but for the bourgeois order he represents.[67] But Klara has no lofty notions of dying for a way of life; rather, she views the consequences of the continuation of her life for her father.[68] In the plot of the drama, this is the motivating force behind Klara's suicide. Through this action, she hopes to save Anton from shame and ultimate guilt.

Guilt is an important and complex issue for Hebbel's dramatic theory and the dramas themselves and necessitates a brief analysis. In "Mein Wort über das Drama," Hebbel writes about guilt:

> [Es] . . . ist nicht zu übersehen, daß die dramatische Schuld nicht, wie die christliche Erbsünde, erst aus der Richtung des menschlichen Willens entspringt, sondern unmittelbar aus dem Willen selbst, aus der starren eigenmächtigen Ausdehnung des Ichs, hervorgeht, und daß es daher dramatisch völlig gleichgültig ist, ob der Held an einer vortrefflichen oder einer verwerflichen Bestrebung scheitert.[69]

From this statement it can be discerned that for Hebbel, guilt is incurred merely through existence.[70] This phenomenon results from the fact that by virtue of existence, each individual (Hebbel's "das Werdende") comes into conflict with the universal whole ("das Seiende").[71] Hebbel notes in a diary entry from 13 June 1844:

> . . . der Begriff der tragischen *Schuld* [darf] nur aus dem Leben selbst, aus der ursprünglichen Inkongruenz zwischen Idee und Erscheinung, die sich in der letzteren eben als Maßlosig-keit, der natürlichen Folge des Selbst-Erhaltungs- und Behauptungstriebes, des ersten und berechtigsten von allen, äußert, entwickelt werden . . . , nicht aber erst aus einer von den vielen Konsequenzen dieser ursprünglichen Inkongruenz.[72]

Ross explains this somewhat complicated statement by noting that the conflict between the individual and the universal is a manifestation of the individual's assertion of his independence, thus causing the struggle with "the necessity of the whole."[73] The guilt incurred by the individual through the conflict with the universal does not result from "any act which is morally wrong;"[74] rather, it is "eine Art Erbsünde, die dem Menschen a priori anhaftet."[75]

The other essential feature of the guilt issue in Hebbel's work focuses on the death of the individual as the means of atonement: Only through death can the conflict between the individual and the whole be overcome.[76] Hebbel refers to overcoming the conflict between the individual and the universe as "Versöhnung:"

. . . der Begriff der tragischen Versöhnung [ist] nur aus der Maßlosigkeit, die, da sie sich in der Erscheinung nicht aufheben kann, diese selbst aufhebt, indem sie sie zerstört und so die Idee wieder von ihrer mangelhaften Form befreit, zu entwickeln.[77]

(It is essential to realize that the term "Erscheinung" is Hebbel's description of the individual in juxtaposition to the existing universal whole, representing the Idea.)

Thus, the destruction of the individual is necessary in order to overcome guilt and to establish reconciliation with the universe. This concept is a fact in terms of Hebbel's dramatic world, and provides a release for Klara from the guilt of her personal existence. Hebbel considered taking one's own life a sin if the deed were motivated by one single element of life and not by all of life itself: "Selbstmord ist immer Sünde, wenn ihn eine Einzelheit, nicht das Ganze des Lebens veranlaßt."[78] As previously indicated, Klara's *entire* existence has become hopeless, and, therefore, she does not sin when she kills herself. Most importantly, Klara sees in suicide her single possibility to prevent Anton from incurring guilt.

Anton's final statement, "Ich verstehe die Welt nicht mehr!"[79] bitterly expresses his incomprehension not only of the world, but also of Klara's attempt to prevent his guilt. In a diary entry made just after completion of the work, Hebbel explains the motivation of Anton's final words: ". . . er darf nicht weiter kommen, als zu einer *Ahnung* seines Mißverhältnisses zur Welt, zum Nachdenken über sich selbst."[80] Indeed, throughout the entire play, Anton remains in rigid compliance with the bourgeois tradition he represents in the family. As stated above, Anton's willingness to defend Adam from an attack by Karl - although Adam falsely accused Karl and, thereby, caused the death of Anton's wife - demonstrates how strongly the Meister holds to his societal beliefs. But the question arises, as in chapter IV with reference to the Priest, whether the societal beliefs themselves or rather the rigid adherence to them ultimately causes the inhumane behavior present in *Maria Magdalene*.

As expressed in chapter I, unrelenting parental observance of methods of socialization, which demand from children the reproduction of the exact same social content as the parents have instilled in themselves, becomes repressive. Such repressive socialization leads to revolt. Medea demonstrated revolt by openly defying her father and physically distancing herself from him. Hero, on the other hand, tried to hide the fact that she stood at odds with the expectations and ethical demands of the Priest; she neither attempted to flee with Leander nor did she speak openly to her uncle about the new type of existence she had found. In these two plays, the daughters moved beyond the confines of the father's world. In *Maria Magdalene* a different situation exists. Klara commits suicide because she is unable to free herself from the confines of the social milieu personified by her father. To this extent, Klara resembles Schiller's Luise Miller, who dies because she is unwilling to reject bourgeois standards and break the oath in order to tell Ferdinand the truth. This adherence to social norms ultimately leads to her death. Anton also remains fixed to the social expectations that finally bring about his daughter's death. The depth of Anton's commitment to these social expectations manifests itself when the Meister is prepared to kill himself for the sake of earthly honor.

Anton's culpability is not a consequence of the social tradition itself; it results from his perverse and unceasing application of it. Here a correlation with Lessing's *Emilia Galotti* can be drawn. Emilia's father, Odoardo, remains steadfast in his belief that virtue is the most important feature of human existence. This is his fixation. For the sake of the preservation of virtue, Emilia must die. The concept of virtue is not at issue in that play, but rather the unquestioning adherence to a Weltanschauung that demands the death of a human being in order to achieve that concept's preservation.

Thus we may perceive that the source of inhumanity in *Maria Magdalene* lies in Anton's rigid adherence to the social milieu and its ethical traditions. But it is an oversimplification to place the entire burden of inhumanity on Anton. Leonhard clearly behaves in an inhumane fashion and thus incurs guilt in terms of Hebbel's own correlation of objectification with sin[81] when he reduces Klara to an object of his materialistic and sexual desires. To this extent, Anton also sins when he uses Klara as an object for the preservation of his honor. In his long speech at the conclusion of the play, Friedrich includes himself in the culpability of all principal male characters in Klara's inhumane demise: "Er [Anton] hat sie auf den Weg des Todes hinausgewiesen, ich, ich bin schuld, daß sie nicht wieder umgekehrt ist."[82]

Indeed, all are guilty. But, as Hebbel expresses in a diary entry, all are also correct:

> Jetzt sind alle Mauslöcher ausgestopft und ich bin zufrieden, besonders damit, daß sie eigentlich alle recht haben, sogar Leonhard, wenn man nur nicht aus den Augen läßt, daß er von Haus aus eine gemeine Natur ist, die sich in höhere nicht finden und an sie nicht glauben kann, und daß also die Gebundenheit des Lebens in der Einseitigkeit, aus der von vornherein alles Unheil der Welt entspringt, so recht schneidend hervortritt . . . .[83]

A key concept in the passage is "Einseitigkeit," which may be interpreted in this context as egotism. Leonhard fails to contemplate how his treatment of Klara will affect her; he is concerned only with his own sexual gratification, monetary well-being and social standing. As we have seen, the other male figures think only of themselves and fail to consider the consequences Klara's situation may have on her life. Indeed, Friedrich finally considers Klara, but only after his social position has been assured through Leonhard's death. Although Anton is unaware of her pregnancy, which he does appear to sense at the end of Act I, he clearly centers his thinking on the effects Klara's dishonor would have on his own existence and fails to contemplate what the consequences might be for her. This failure stems from a "Defizit an Humanität und Aufklärung."[84] In the final analysis, this deficit of humanity is a product of the society Hebbel depicts. He criticizes Anton, Leonhard and Friedrich along with the social order whose ethos exacerbates Klara's situation.[85] From this unrelenting adherence to bourgeois ideals stems the inhumanity Klara experiences.

In contrast to the inhumanity inflicted on her, Klara demonstrates monumental compassion. The magnitude of Klara's humanity clearly manifests itself with regard to Friedrich, Leonhard and Anton. Klara comes to the realization that she could not accept the sacrifice Friedrich would have to make to marry her. Unlike Ibsen's Nora, Klara does not expect this man to stand up and accept full responsibility for the situation and, as a consequence of this action, overcome his conception of honor. In this instance, Klara takes the responsibility upon herself, thus releasing Friedrich from all duty to her in her own mind. She does not expect "the wonderful thing" to happen.

Klara also demonstrates humanity towards Leonhard as she forgives him just before leaving for the well. Klara's great inner confusion appears when she tries to pray the Lord's Prayer, which she momentarily cannot remember properly:

> Vater unser, der du bist im Himmel - Geheiliget werde dein Reich - Gott, Gott, mein armer Kopf - ich kann nicht einmal beten - Bruder! Bruder! - hilf mir -
> KARL. Was hast du?
> KLARA. Das Vaterunser! . . . Vergib uns unsere Schuld, wie wir vergeben unsern Schuldigern! Da ists! Ja! Ja! ich vergeb ihm gewiß, ich denke ja nicht mehr an ihn! Gute Nacht![86]

In her final moments of life, Klara forgives the man who forcefully planted the seed of her demise.

Finally, the situation surrounding Anton does not require Klara's forgiveness or understanding; she never questions the inevitability or necessity of her death to save her father's life. She makes the ultimate sacrifice to save Anton and preserve his honor. She has even prepared his *Abendtrank* before leaving the house. If her sacrifice of life were not enough to establish Klara's selfless humanity, Anton's unbelievable and totally incomprehensible lack of compassion and his harshness at the end of the work heighten the selfless character of Klara's act: Anton, by virtue of his past and present actions toward his daughter, is in no way worthy of such a sacrifice. After Karl has reported that someone saw Klara throw herself into the well and Friedrich has explained why she felt compelled to commit suicide, Anton remarks:

> MEISTER ANTON. Sie hat mir nichts erspart - man hats gesehen!
> SEKRETÄR. Sie hat getan, was sie konnte - *Er wars nicht wert, daß ihre Tat gelang!*
> MEISTER ANTON. Oder *sie* nicht![87]

In his continued contemplation of what other people will say, even in the moment of his daughter's tragic death, not to mention the comment that Klara herself was not worthy enough to have succeeded, Anton fails miserably as a father and, more importantly, as a human being to comprehend the magnitude of the daughter's sacrifice.[88] As von Wiese notes, Klara rises above the metaphysical state of her father, his world and the inhumanity present there.[89] Her life's development - her individuation - has ended in humane forgiveness and self-sacrifice.

The question remains whether Klara occupies a metaphysical state at the end of the drama different from her psychological level at the outset of the work. To be sure, during the course of the play, Klara does not experience individuation in Jungian terms, i.e. the meeting of anima and animus as happens to both Medea and Hero. However, because Jung perceived water to be the "commonest symbol of the unconscious,"[90] it may be maintained that Klara's return to the water via suicide is, in essence, a return to the unconscious itself, indicating that lasting individuation has not occurred. Nevertheless, Klara has been exposed to the individuation process. Given the analytic nature of Hebbel's drama,[91] reminiscent of Kleist's *Der zerbrochene Krug*,[92] it can be perceived that the union of animus and anima occurred before the play commences; the important occurrences have taken place prior to the first scene. Moreover, the action of the play itself is an unfolding of the consequences of these previous events. What can be said for Klara's attempt at individuation in her union with Leonhard is that the very focal point of her self-establishment is flawed from its inception. As the play unfolds and the true nature of Leonhard is revealed, Klara maintains that the episode in the park, during which her child was conceived, will result in her father's death if she does not legitimize the pregnancy. We have seen that such legitimization becomes impossible, forcing Klara to the only alternative: suicide. Ultimately Klara's inability to free herself from her social milieu and its devastating ethical demands necessitates her own death as she attempts to remove the physical manifestation of her future shame.

Hebbel depicts only the last half of Klara's individuation process, which ends in the prevention of her continued existence. This process and, more importantly, its failure, manifests itself as a consequence of the father-daughter relationship. Through his rigid and unrelenting insistence on the ethical principles of his patriarchal society, Anton necessitates his daughter's search for a way out of her precarious position. The first attempt centers on trying to join herself to a man whom she does not love and who does not love her. When this avenue of hope ends and the momentary notion of a life with Friedrich vanishes as well, Klara finds no alternative other than death. This is the tragic, but unavoidable consequence of this father-daughter relationship. Because of his unyielding adherence to the bourgeois ethos, Anton ultimately causes the death of four people. As a parent, his chief duty is protector of his daughter; but ironically he forces her into death. Through suicide she kills her unborn child in order to prevent her father's demise. Moreover, the deaths of Friedrich and Leonhard directly result from the father's rigid observance of social norms. Thus the father-daughter relationship becomes a central element of this work's tragic nature.

Chapter VI

Hauptmann's *Rose Bernd*

The daughters analyzed in the previous chapters have struggled with emotions and commitments, leading to one catastrophe or another. Each woman has experienced suffering and has reacted to overcome it. Such is the case in Gerhart Hauptmann's *Rose Bernd*, which, like Wagner's *Kindermörderin* and Grillparzer's *Das goldene Vlieβ*, depicts an inexorable process climaxing in infanticide.

In his dramas Hauptmann depicts suffering as the basis for human existence. Ernst Alker, writing in general about Hauptmann's dramatic works, remarks, "Hauptmanns Dichten ist ein Spiegel eines zerrissenen Ich . . . ,"[1] thus indicating the aspect of inner struggle and suffering present in the plays.[2] Hans Joachim Schrimpf, whose thorough analysis of *Rose Bernd* greatly adds to a full understanding of this work in particular and Hauptmann's entire production in general, notes that Hauptmann understood the "Weltgrund selbst . . . als endlosen Kampf, Qual und Leiden."[3] Through these observations, the motifs conflict and suffering appear as essential elements in Hauptmann's plays. Indeed, suffering is the very basis of *Rose Bernd*.[4]

In this tragedy, other themes basic to Hauptmann's entire dramatic production readily appear. The most fundamental of these elements is the family.[5] Although the family relationships in *Rose Bernd* do not correspond to those in *Vor Sonnenaufgang* or *Vor Sonnenuntergang*, for example, the family nevertheless plays a central role in the drama. Another characteristic element is the use of dialect, or as Schulz defines it, sociolect.[6] Hauptmann uses language variation to establish the characters in their strata and to indicate the geographical location of the play's events.[7] In *Rose Bernd* a difference in language reflects a difference in class: Bernd, Rose, August and Streckmann speak dialect while the language of Flamm and his wife approximates a regional standard, thus demonstrating different levels of society. As indicated by the function of language, the social milieu also becomes significant as the backdrop against which the concepts of the play are expressed.[8]

Although realistic, *Rose Bernd* lacks crass naturalism, which openly demonstrates all actions important to the play, no matter how upsetting they might be to the audience. To this extent, Hauptmann's work forms a contrast to Wagner's *Kindermörderin*. While Wagner allows the rape scene to be experienced by the audience, albeit only by means of the audience hearing the sounds, Hauptmann sets the corresponding scene between Rose and Streckmann between acts. The audience learns of it later through dialogue:

> Rose. Was sag'n Sie? Wer sein Sie den ieberhaupt?
> Streckmann. Wer ich bin? Verflucht ja: das werscht du schonn wiss'n.
> Rose. Wer sein Sie? Wo hätt ich Ihn denn schonn gesehn?
> Streckmann. Du?? Miich? Wo du mich gesahn hätt'st, Madel? Fer an'n Aff'n such du d'r an'n andern aus.
> . . .
> Streckmann. Denk an a Kerschbaum! Denk du ans Kruzifix![9]

By stressing the rape's effects on Rose rather than depicting this abrasive act on stage, Hauptmann's emphasis of the psychological aspect of the work becomes apparent.

In addition to the tempered naturalism of *Rose Bernd* is the auto-biographical perspective of the work.[10] In April 1903, Hauptmann served as a juror in an infanticide trial against Hedwig Otto, in which the accused was acquitted.[11] Maurer points out additional autobiographical aspects, especially that Hauptmann fathered an illegitimate son while married to another woman. While Hauptmann may thus be compared to Flamm, he eventually left his wife for the other woman, something Flamm refuses to consider.[12]

Another interesting facet of this work is the correlation of the succession of the acts with the progression of the seasons: spring through late autumn. Act I occurs in the morning and Act V ends in the gloom of twilight. The movement through the stages of the day from morning to night and the progression of the seasons from spring to late autumn symbolically underscore the aura of human destruction present at the conclusion of the drama inasmuch as the coming of winter and the approach of night may be equated with death.[13]

In this drama, Rose's murder of her child becomes her attempt to preserve her social honor, which has become questionable through the abuse she has experienced at the hands of Streckmann and, to a certain extent, Flamm. Her struggle is an inner phenomenon and results from the treatment she receives from the four men surrounding her. This treatment places her in conflict with society as represented by her father's concept of honor, which is deeply embedded in her persona as well. Rose's situation becomes so greatly exaggerated that the humanity offered by Frau Flamm remains unaccepted, and that of Keil is too late to prevent the catastrophe of infanticide.

Like the fathers analyzed in the previous chapters, Rose's father represents honor and the social norms with which Rose comes into conflict. Bernd is the typical father figure of the *bürgerliche Trauerspiele* for whom honor becomes a fixation[14] and who thinks of order and proper behavior as the guiding principles of human existence.[15] Rose expresses these aspects of her father at the beginning of the play: "Und dann is das halt o sei Lieblingsgedanke, daß endlich amal nu ane Ordnung wird."[16] Bernd and Rose have been evicted from their dwelling; for Bernd, Rose's marriage to Keil will establish the order and stability now lacking in life. For a man of Bernd's middle-class mindset, it is proper for the daughter to be married, especially to a respected individual such as Keil. To this extent, Bernd demonstrates concern for his daughter's reputation, which ultimately reflects the way others see the entire family. Bernd's fixation with honor is often alluded to in the secondary literature,[17] but attempts at textual verification of this phenomenon are generally incomplete. Because Bernd's concept of honor expresses a significant aspect not only of his character, but also of Rose's world view, it is necessary to examine the text more closely to discover all perspectives of honor for this father figure.

Bernd's notion of honor and proper behavior includes abstaining from drink, something reminiscent of Alfred Loth in *Vor Sonnenaufgang*: "Aber gerne hab ich keen Schnaps ni gebrannt, und ei der Zeit hab ich erscht recht ni getrunken."[18] This attitude befits a "Waisenrat und Kirchenvorsteher,"[19] as Frau Flamm describes him in Act II. Again, as in his desire that Rose marry an honorable citizen, Bernd's contemplation of what society considers appropriate behavior is exemplified itself through his abstention from alcohol. Indeed, his concern for his position in society molds his manner of thinking. When Streckmann makes remarks questioning Rose's honor and purity of character, Bernd reacts severely: "Den Streckmann, den wär ich noch miss'n anzeigen."[20] He rejects out of hand any notion that his daughter is something other than he believes; no daughter of his could ever be dishonorable: "Herr Leutnant, Sie kenn die Geschichte nich! Will a Mädel an'n Ehrenmann so hinzerren und rumreißen, da kann se nich meine Tochter sein."[21] Although Bernd's comment demonstrates trust for his daughter, it also shows the extreme importance of reputation for this father. Furthermore, Hauptmann suggests here that Bernd is prepared to reject her. To be sure, the words currently express his faith in Rose's character, but they also indicate the severity of his reaction should his beliefs ever be proven incorrect. This reaction would result in total rejection and denial of his child. Keil recognizes this fact when he comments to Frau Flamm:

> Nu, Frau Flamm, was a alten Bernd anbetrifft, aso himmelweit is der von solchen Gedanken, daß da irgend was kennte nich richtig sein, also felsenfest in der Sache dahier: der ließ sich d'rfier beede Hände abhacken. A is aso strenge, das gloobt eener nich.[22]

Keil's description is an excellent summary of Bernd's understanding of Rose. The father totally accepts his daughter because it never enters his mind to think otherwise. This is a very positive aspect of the father-daughter relationship in this work. Taken by itself, it indicates *unconditional* love. However, the descriptions of Bernd's apparent trust are always tempered by the notion that he would reject his daughter if it were demonstrated that his trust were unfounded. To this extent, Bernd's love for Rose is merely *conditional*; he would readily reject his child if she failed to live up to his expectations. Furthermore, through the repetition of possible denial, Hauptmann prepares the listener for Bernd's rejection of Rose at the conclusion of the drama.

Bernd's initial support of Rose manifests itself most significantly through the suit he brings against Streckmann for the remarks made about the girl's virtue, further demonstrating Bernd's rigid fixation with honor and reputation. When he and Keil discuss the possibility that Bernd should drop the suit, it becomes clear that the father is concerned not only with his daughter's honor, but, more significantly, with his honor and that of the entire family: "Das beansprucht mei Weib, das im Grabe liegt! O meine Ehre beansprucht das! Meine Hausehre und meines Mädels Ehre! Und o deine Ehre zu guter Letzt."[23] Bernd refuses to budge from his moralistic stance, even when Keil pleads with him to drop the suit. To this extent, Bernd makes his reputation and that of his family contingent on Rose. By refusing to soften his moral stance, he ceases to function as a vital psychological support for his daughter.[24] Bernd has appointed himself the guardian of everyone's honor, typical behavior of the father-figure. He is indeed responsible for the honor of his home, but his daughter is singled out because of her ability to disgrace all through socially unacceptable behavior. Like Hebbel's Meister Anton, Bernd is concerned with the opinion of the wider social network and feels that the honor of his entire family was called into question by Streckmann's remarks against Rose.

Another facet of this father's character with regard to Rose is his objectification of her. Through her marriage to Keil Bernd intends to provide himself with a stable life. In this fashion, Bernd uses Rose to secure his personal situation and thus objectifies her; she must serve as the means for his security in life. Instead of viewing Rose as an end in herself, he reduces her to an object. Through this objectification, Bernd resembles Aietes and Meister Anton, who both use their daughters for selfish purposes. What matters most to Bernd is how the community perceives Rose and himself; for this father, honor must be maintained. In addition to providing stability, the marriage between Rose and Keil would be an honorable arrangement. When Rose refuses to follow her father's wishes to the letter by not agreeing to marry Keil at the moment demanded, Bernd immediately distances himself from her without attempting to discover why his daughter has reacted in this fashion: "Nu hat a genug! Wer will's 'n verdenken! All's hat ane Grenze! Recht hat a dermit! Aber nu sieh du, wo du bleibst, was du willst; ich mag mit dir o keen'n Staat nich mehr mach'n."[25] Bernd rejects Rose in the moment she fails to adhere to his guidance. Like Aietes, Bernd demands total and unquestioning obedience from his daughter; when this fails to appear, the father counters by rejecting his child. In this fashion, Bernd continues to think of Rose as an unintelligent little girl who is unable to make her own decisions and determine her own life process. Indeed, he perceives that Rose needs to be taught; moreover, he believes Keil is the man for this task: "Se is gutt! Sie braucht ock ane richtige Leitung, und du hast ane gude und sanfte Hand."[26]

Through his conditional acceptance and love, and by making Rose responsible for his own honor, Bernd objectifies his daughter. Furthermore, the element of false piety plays a significant role in Bernd's character. Bernd is an openly pious individual, as his position as *Kirchenvorsteher* reflects. His piety is expressed in Act I when he comments with disdain on the fact that Rose fails to attend church.[27] To this extent Hauptmann combines an important aspect of the relationship between Hebbel's Karl and Meister Anton, namely that it is inappropriate and even disgraceful not to attend church. For Bernd, religion and outward expression of worship are integral components of an honorable person. When he enters his home in the last act, he instructs his other daughter, Marthel: "leg m'r de Heilige Schrift zurechte! Hauptsache is: in Bereitschaft sein."[28] Shortly thereafter, he refers to himself as a Christian.[29] Indeed, piety is part and parcel of Bernd's notion of honor and proper public behavior. But Bernd uses his religion as a means of escape from the reality of Rose's situation. After he discovers that Streckmann's remarks were true and that Rose had a physical relationship with Flamm as well, he states: "Gott verzeih mir de Sinde! Ich mag se ni sehn!"[30] The following stage directions are indicative of Bernd's misuse of religion: "Er setzt sich . . . an den Tisch, hält mit den Daumen die Ohren zu und senkt den Kopf tief in die Bibel."[31] Bernd calls himself a Christian, but fails to demonstrate two basic principles of Christianity: forgiveness and compassion. In the moment he discovers that Rose's life does not correspond to his expectations, he rejects his daughter and withdraws from her, physically immersing himself in his religion, rather than offering her support in a truly Christian manner. Hauptmann thus criticizes the bourgeois mentality Bernd represents.[32]

Aside from providing an escape for this father from the reality of this situation, Bernd's piety and his entire lifestyle have kept him from understanding Rose's situation before the moment of catastrophe; they have shielded him from reality. He has failed throughout the play even to entertain the idea that Rose's honor might be in question. While this is laudable, it also demonstrates Bernd's failure to perceive reality. By the time he can no longer avoid it, the weight of the situation has increased to an unbearable extent.[33] Bernd can think only of himself, and he uses religion and his concept of honor to preserve his own psychological status. This egocentricity, a feature of Bernd's honor fixation, contributes to the final catastrophe of infanticide because it prevents him from altering *his* behavior and impeding an exacerbation of Rose's situation. Had Bernd not rigidly forced his ethos upon his daughter, she would have been able to deal with her difficult situation more readily and positively. But Rose has internalized the same concept of shame and disgrace as her father (see below). In this manner Bernd's behavior intensifies the tragic situation, a common phenomenon of Hauptmann's works.[34]

Although Bernd clearly plays an important role in the motivation of the final catastrophe, total culpability cannot be attributed to him alone. The treatment of Rose by Flamm and Streckmann worsens the girl's situation and contributes significantly to her suffering and despair. Both Flamm and Streckmann use Rose as an object, another typical characteris-

tic of Hauptmann's works.[35]   The treatment of Rose by both
Flamm and Streckmann reflects images of men after wild
game.   Indeed, the notion of the hunt is often associated with
the relationship between men and women in Hauptmann's
works.[36]   This applies directly to Flamm, whose prowess as a
hunter is demonstrated by the many trophies adorning his
Jagdkammer.[37]
  Flamm claims to love Rose, and their actions at the beginning of the play seem to indicate this.   Both come out of the
bushes obviously joyful over what has just occurred, and
Flamm sings of his happiness as a hunter(!):

> Im Wald und auf der Heide
> da such' ich meine Freude!
> Ich bin ein Jägersmann!
> Ich bin ein Jägersmann![38]

Shortly after proclaiming that he wishes Rose were his wife, he
explains that he is nonetheless still attached to his wife
emotionally.[39]   We discover that his wife is an invalid and has
been confined to a wheelchair for nine years.   His conclusion,
"Na zum Donnerwetter, was soll denn das mir nützen?!"[40]
reveals that he has turned to Rose to enjoy the physical
relationship such a "schönes und kräftiges Bauernmädchen"[41]
as Rose can offer.   Thus, because of the emphasis on the physical aspect of this relationship, which clearly can never become
permanent, Flamm's love for Rose reveals itself as conditional;
he says he would like to marry her, but stops short of leaving
his wife for this young, healthy girl - something greatly at odds
with the social customs of that time.[42]   Furthermore, Flamm's
continued adherence to his marriage vows, if only for the sake
of custom, prepares his later rejection of Rose after he discovers that she has also had sex with Streckmann.
  Flamm continues to pursue Rose and attempts to arrange a
time when they can meet because he "muß alles bereden" with
her.[43]   The fact that he wants to meet behind the barn
indicates that he has more in mind than talking.   Rose refuses,
appearing to understand how she has been used by Flamm:
"Immer schlagt uff mir rum, ich verdien das nich besser!
Immer putzt euch an mir eure Stiefeln ab, aber . . ."[44]   Later,

Flamm manages to seize Rose and embrace her, but she begs him to release her. Flamm counters: "Du meenst also, ich sollte dich loslassen? Jetzt, wo ich dich endlich jetz hab' amal?! Nee, Mädel, so leichte geht das nich!"[45] Flamm continues to pursue Rose even against her will, thus objectifying her as a means of his sexual gratification. As we have seen, Flamm is interested in Rose primarily for physical purposes. Like Streckmann, he treats Rose as a second-class citizen who, he believes, has no choice other than to succumb to men's sexual demands. Neither Flamm nor Streckmann considers what sexual activity would mean for Rose, that she might become pregnant and dishonored.

When Frau Flamm discovers that her husband is the father of Rose's child, she points out that Flamm treated Rose as an object since he misused his position of authority:

> Grade so a'm Mädel die Zukunft zersteeren, wo mir hier . . . wo ma alle Verantwortung hat! Wo ma se hat ins Haus gezogen! Wo se haben a blindes Vertrauen gehabt! O nee, 's is zum ei de Erde sink'n! Als hätt' man's reen heimlich druff angelegt.[46]

According to Frau Flamm, her husband is guilty of more than adultery. Because Rose entrusted herself to them, his abuse of her becomes even more abhorrent. Besides the emotional abuse Rose suffers in her relationship with Flamm, their sexual activity becomes the catalyst for the ensuing tragic situation.[47]

Indeed, Flamm does not force Rose to do anything against her will, but his continued advances reflect the true reason for his desires: He wants to possess her. The moment it becomes apparent to Flamm that Streckmann has had the same privilege, he rejects Rose totally. At the beginning of the play, Flamm's egotism and concern for his own honor are expressed when he quickly disappears as other people approach. He does not want anyone to suspect that he and Rose are having an affair, a natural desire for a married man. But his disappearance serves as further preparation for his subsequent abandonment of Rose after he learns of Streckmann's liaison with her:

Nu, Mutter, da nimm mir nur alles nich übel, verzeih mir nur, was du verzeihen kannst! Von der Sache weiß ich nu klipp und klar, daß sie mich nu auch ganz und gar nichts mehr angeht! Ich lache drieber! Ich niese drauf.[48]

When Flamm discovers that he is not the only man in her sexual life, he feels jealous and immediately rejects her without any moment of contemplation or question about why the other relationship came about. To this extent, Flamm shows himself to be egocentric and lacking of true feelings of love and devotion for Rose. The rejection Rose experiences here augments the problematic relationship she has with her father.

The relationship between Rose and Streckmann adds to Rose's despair that results from the lack of parental support. As with Flamm, jealousy also becomes the driving force behind the liaison between Rose and Streckmann. The important role jealousy plays here is reminiscent of Hebbel's *Maria Magdalene*. In that work, Leonhard slept with Klara because he was jealous of her former beau, Friedrich. Furthermore, just as Leonhard used other women, such as the mayor's niece, Streckmann objectifies members of the opposite sex. We discover, for example, that he beats his wife.[49] Streckmann, like Büchner's Tambourmajor,[50] is a handsome man and readily gets his way with women: "Was ich will bei am Weibe, das setz' ich o durch."[51] In this manner, Streckmann is in the habit of using women as objects. It is ironic and tragic that such a man should see the actions between Rose and Flamm at the beginning of the play.[52] He uses this information to force Rose into a liaison. But Streckmann is not interested in Rose only for his sexual pleasure. He rapes her in order to prove that he is of the same caliber as Flamm and can possess the same woman: "Wo Flamm-Schulz hiereicht, komm' ich o no mit."[53]

If Streckmann's physical abuse of Rose were not enough to make the girl despair of her existence, he further torments her during Act III by insinuating that she physically pursued him when she came to his room. Rose counters:

Schubiack! Schuft! Was hust du jetzt noch um mich rumzuschnup-
pern? Wer bist du? Wer sein Sie? Was hätt ich gemacht? Du hast dich
an meine Fersen gehängt! Du hast mich gehetzt . . . ei de Heechsen
gebissa. Schuft! Schlimmer als wie a Fleescherhund![54]

Rose then describes how Streckmann raped her. Streckmann
becomes enraged at these comments and, after Bernd and
other workers appear on the scene, insults Rose openly:
"Wegen dem Frovolke da, die mit all'r Welt a Gestecke hat
. . ."[55]

Rose gave herself to Streckmann in order to gain his silence
and hide the fact that she has a relationship with Flamm,
"thereby injuring her social honor in the attempt to shield
it."[56] This situation is ironic and intensifies the importance of
Rose's relationship with Flamm. This liaison becomes the
impetus for all ensuing disaster; it provides Streckmann the
necessary leverage to force Rose to fulfill his sexual wishes.
Thus the physical bond between Rose and Streckmann is the
direct consequence of that between Rose and Flamm and leads
to Streckmann's insult of her honor. This insult causes
Bernd's legal suit, which is further necessitated by his strict
adherence to a harsh moral code. Thus Rose's suffering
increases and propels her ever closer to despair. Her relationships with Flamm and Streckmann ultimately lead to the
conflict between father and daughter. Bernd's refusal to drop
his suit, as expressed above, adds to Rose's suffering, despair
and confusion, which increase to the point where she swears
the false oath in court.

All the seeds of Rose's suffering were planted in Act I
through her relationship with Flamm and Streckmann's
discovery of it. The actions in the following scenes help
increase the girl's despair, and she is transformed from "dem
übermütig lachenden Mädel der Anfangsszene" into "die
Geängstigte,   verzweifelt   Flehende,   Gehetzte   des
Aktschlusses."[57] Indeed, Rose's situation of increasing suffering and despair results from several factors. As expressed
above, she is physically and emotionally surrounded by
Flamm, Streckmann, and her father. In addition, Keil - whose
character will be analyzed below - also figures in this constella-

tion. Critics often maintain that Rose is encircled by three male figures: Keil, Flamm, and Streckmann. In these analyses, Bernd is merely included as a variant to Keil.[58] But, as we will see below, the primary function of Keil differs from that of Bernd, thus placing Rose in juxtaposition to four men. This phenomenon intensifies the dramatic complexity present in *Maria Magdalene*. Klara was surrounded by three men, all of whom contributed to her hopeless situation. Hauptmann separates the role of Hebbel's Leonhard into two characters, Flamm and Streckmann, thus heightening Rose's difficulties considerably.

Rose's suffering and despair are indeed motivated in part by the four men around her. However, a portion of the young woman's own inner being contributes to the despair she experiences. Because Rose remains a captive of her society, like Schiller's Luise and Hebbel's Klara, the ever-present expectations of her milieu increasingly determine her behavior and cause her psychological despair. Just after she and Flamm emerge from the bushes at the beginning of the play, Rose twice expresses her concern that someone might see them together: "Die Kirchleute kommen ja gleich, Herr Flamm."[59] Aside from preparing for the ensuing action with Streckmann, this anxiety demonstrates how Rose, like her father, is concerned with what other people think. Honor remains an important and determining factor of life for Rose; she is unable to free herself from its domination. This phenomenon also becomes apparent when Streckmann begins to threaten Rose with publicizing her liaison with Flamm. Rose responds: "Wenn doas e Mensch im Dorfe derfährt. . . ."[60] In a slightly different context, Rose further demonstrates her dependence on honor when she explains to Flamm that the presence of her father and Keil prevent her from acting according to her desires: "Ohne August und Vater, wer weeß, was ich machte!"[61] Moreover, after Streckmann has insulted her publicly, Rose no longer gladly leaves the house. As Keil explains to Frau Flamm: "Se is ebens reen scheu in a letzten Zeit'n."[62] Finally, like Hebbel's Klara, Rose is concerned that her father's supper stands prepared for his arrival at home, and this after she has suffered through murdering her child![63] These anxieties join together to form a montage depicting Rose's adherence to social customs and concern for her position in society. This concern contributes to her isolation, dependence and captivity; she feels caught not only by the men in her life, but is also held by notions of social expectations that prevent autonomous activity and self-determination. As Karl Holl maintains, we see in this play how "an individual character, this time a woman, is indissolubly connected with its social milieu and its whole structure predestined by it to its own doom."[64]

Rose's dependence on her society reflects one aspect of her persona. Her shyness is a manifestation of this bondage to society. Furthermore, Rose's shyness indicates the isolation motif present in this drama. Her isolation begins to appear when Flamm rejects her in Act IV. She finally expresses her perception of alienation to her sister in Act V: "Das gloob ich ni! Kumm, Marthla, greif a wing, stitz mich a wing! Ma is halt zu sehr ei d'r Welt verlass'n!"[65] Rose senses that she has been abandoned, that she has nowhere to turn. She has been rejected not only by Flamm, but also by her father when she refused to marry Keil in Act II. Although this situation reverses itself, the possibility of paternal rejection is ever present. Indeed, Bernd makes statements throughout the play indicating that he could reject his daughter, as described above, and ends by totally separating himself from her. Rose's isolation becomes a consequence of both external and internal motivations. The external factors center on Flamm, Streckmann and Bernd, the internal on Rose's own knowledge of the truth of her situation. As we will see, Frau Flamm offers a possible escape for Rose from the isolation brought on by her pregnancy, but Rose's steadfast adherence to her society prevents her acceptance of Frau Flamm's generosity.[66] Rose's isolation develops inexorably to its culmination in infanticide: "Unaufhaltsam vollzieht sich die Tragödie grenzenloser Vereinsamung in einer inhumanen Welt."[67]

The metaphysical encirclement by the four male characters, her own captivity in society and finally her isolation combine to cause Rose's suffering and despair. These feelings become apparent in Rose's own words in Act IV:

's verfolgt een'n vorher o Tag und Nacht, was der Mann [Keil] fer
Schmerzen hat missen leiden . . . suster mißt a mich ja oaspein dahier.
Nu hält ma immer a Arm ei de Hieh, ma will immer was aus'm Feuer
rett'n, da brechen se een alle Knoch'n entzwee.[68]

This statement is mild in comparison to the outburst of
passion when Rose explains why she perjured herself: "Ich
hoa mich geschaamt! Ich hoa mich geschaamt!"[69] Rose's
shame is the climax of her despair vis-à-vis her inner and
outer worlds. While at one point she tried to repress the fact
that the liaison with Streckmann had ever taken place (in Act
III), or that she is even pregnant, her acknowledgment of
shame reflects the young woman's cognizance of behavior she
herself considers improper. In an attempt to overcome the
despair, and thus free herself from the psychological suffering
she has increasingly felt, she perjures herself. The expression
of shame is Rose's explanation for swearing the false oath in
court. Completely without her intention or control, Rose is
placed in a situation giving her two choices: bringing shame
on herself by admitting that Streckmann has spoken the truth,
or committing perjury. To this extent, Rose is the victim of
both internal and external forces; she finds herself in a
situation in which she must choose between two actions that
will both cause suffering.[70]

In her admission of guilt and shame, we perceive the
change that has occurred within Rose in the course of the
play. At the beginning, Rose was happy and self-assured; at
the end she despairs and has no sense of foundation.[71] All
actions in the drama collide and push Rose beyond rational
comprehension of her deed's consequences.[72]

Rose attempts to free herself from this net of despair
through perjury. Gradually it becomes apparent that this
behavior is also defective. She feels attacked from every side
and perceives nothing that can serve as a psychological
support, not even her religion. In Act V Rose asserts that in
her greatest moment of suffering, need and despair, "Da hoa
ich wull ernt in de Sterne gesehn! Da hoa ich wull ernt
geschrien und geruffa! Kee himmlischer Vater hat sich
geriehrt."[73] Rose senses that her scream of despair fell on
deaf ears, that her isolation is complete both in terms of

heaven and earth. Like Hebbel's Klara, Rose seeks a spiritual foothold, but fails to find one in her faith. This stands in sharp contrast to Bernd, whose creed is expressed in words just preceding Rose's statement of condemnation quoted above: "Herr Gott, meine Zuflucht fier und fier."[74] Thus, a basic contrast between Rose and her father appears in their views of God and religion. Bernd continues to believe unquestioningly and remains steadfast in his faith. Rose seeks and does not find an affirmation of God's support, not to mention human assistance, in her time of crisis. As Hilscher comments, "Sie zweifelt an der Gerechtigkeit der bestehenden Ordnung, der angeblich göttlichen und der irdischen, denn ihr Verlangen nach Liebe blieb ohne Erfüllung, ihr Menschenrecht auf Liebe wurde mit Füßen getreten."[75] Rose feels betrayed by both heaven and earth. When she realizes that her perjury cannot possibly resolve her fateful situation, after Flamm totally damns and rejects her, and finally when she perceives no assistance from her last possible source of support, God, Rose does the only thing she can to try to free herself from the utter suffering and despair she experiences: She kills her new-born baby.

The motif of infanticide is frequent in the *bürgerliche Trauerspiel*, beginning with Wagner's *Kindermörderin*, continuing in the *Urfaust* and reappearing in Hebbel's *Maria Magdalene*. In Hebbel's play, the fact that Klara kills her unborn baby by committing suicide demonstrates a slight variation on the infanticide theme.[76] But even more significant than merely fitting into this tradition, Rose's murder of her child shows an important characteristic for Hauptmann's entire dramatic production. For Hauptmann's women characters force became a means of self-protection and a method for acquiring freedom while under the control of non-relenting males. Schurz explains: "Gewalt als weibliche Schutz- und Befreiungsreaktion findet sich bei Hauptmann in den verschiedensten Formen. Dazu gehört das Töten des eigenen Kindes bei Rose Bernd . . ."[77] Indeed, infanticide is Rose's attempt to free herself from the apparently hopeless situation. Through this murder, Rose seeks to rid herself of the physical manifestation of her disgrace. Aside from the aspect of freeing the self, the murder of the child is the first real demonstration of Rose's autonomy. At no time in her life has Rose actually done what she wanted; she has consistently reacted to a series of events motivated by behaviors of the men around her, either to please them or, in the case of Streckmann, to gain his silence. To be sure, Rose's refusal to marry Keil in Act II expresses a momentary break with this pattern of obedience, but Rose soon alters her decision to comply with her father's wishes. Infanticide becomes the first event Rose performs for herself and as a result of her own decision.

But even in this action of attempted freedom and self-determination, Rose comprehends that she and the entire group of men encircling her have acted. To be sure, Rose kills the child alone, but as the words preceding her confession illustrate, she believes that all have had a hand in this heinous deed: "Ihr hott mei Kind derwergt. . . Streckmann? Der hat mei Kind derwergt! . . . Ich ha mei Kind mit a Hända derwergt!!"[78] Rose then explains where the murder occurred and, in her explanation, more directly addresses the fact that no one has understood the suffering she has experienced, not to mention the men's inability to perceive life in general: "Ihr wißt ebens nischt! Ihr seht ebens nischt! Ihr habt nischt gesehn mit offnen Augen. A kann hinger de große Weide sehn . . . bei a Erlen . . . hinten am Parrfelde draußen . . . am Teiche . . . da kann a das Dingelchen sehn."[79]

Indeed, the murder results from the "geistige Verwirrung"[80] to which Rose has been driven by the unperceiving men around her. To this extent, infanticide was a source of freedom and expression of self-determination for Rose. But another reason exists for the murder, as Rose herself explains: "'s [das Kind] sullde ni laba! Ich wullte 's ni!! 's sullde ni meine Martern derleida!"[81] Like Medea, Rose killed her child in order to preserve it from the same sorrowful existence she has experienced. Indeed, Medea had other reasons for murdering her children, as discussed in chapter III, but the notion of rescuing them from a fate similar to their mother's significantly motivates her action just as it plays an important role for Rose. Infanticide may be perceived as an ironic expression of motherly love and devotion[82] because it demonstrates the mother's desire for a better life for the child. Ironically, the only way of achieving this superior existence is through death, a variation on the memento mori theme, focusing on the despair of earthly existence.

An interesting aspect of infanticide in *Rose Bernd* is the fact that it occurs next to a pond, and is thus directly linked to water. As expressed in chapter IV, water has many symbolic meanings, both positive and negative. The association of the water of the pond with the water inside a mother's womb during pregnancy, which breaks during childbirth, establishes an ironic juxtaposition in this drama. On the one hand, water is the provider of nourishment and sustainer of life for the unborn child. The irony of the situation becomes clear when we discern that water is ultimately the location of death for Rose's baby. Instead of providing sustenance or cleansing, as in baptism, water becomes associated with destruction.

The mistreatment Roses experiences culminates in infanticide and is a result of the inhumanity of Bernd, Flamm and Streckmann. In contrast, Keil and Frau Flamm should be lauded for their unceasing devotion to Rose.[83] Indeed, Keil and Frau Flamm do demonstrate humanity, a topic requiring greater analysis.

At the outset of the play, Flamm describes his wife as "so gut wie 'n Schaf," and explains to Rose, even if Frau Flamm knew of the liaison between them, "'n Kopf würde die uns noch lange nich abreißen."[84] Indeed, Frau Flamm appears as the essence of goodness, mercy and compassion, qualities frequently expressed in her dealings with Rose. Frau Flamm functions to a certain extent as a mother for Rose, whose natural mother died. Frau Flamm's goodness toward Rose results from the kindness Rose showed Kurt, the Flamms' son, who died as a small child. Frau Flamm remarks to Rose: "du denkst doch nich, daß ich's mit dir ni gut meene? . . . Das wär' woll ooch etwan! Na, abgemacht. Du hast noch mit mein Kurtel gespielt."[85] Frau Flamm and Rose are kindred spirits because they experienced the loss of a vital family member at approximately the same time. But beyond this fact, Frau Flamm remains unwavering in her support of Rose, even when it is revealed that Rose is carrying an illegitimate child:

"Ich will nischt wissen! Verlaß dich uff mich! Mir sein ieber-
haupt de Väter ganz gleichgiltig."[86] Even after she discovers
that her own husband has fathered Rose's baby, Frau Flamm
continues to swear her support - both emotional and financial
- to Rose: "Es bleibt dabei, Rose, was ich gesagt habe: es wird
immer gesorgt sein für euch zwei."[87] By virtue of her suffering, both through the loss of her child and because of her
illness, Frau Flamm is more keenly aware of the sufferings
other people experience.[88]   Furthermore, she becomes the
spokesperson for the misused, single mother.[89]

Another aspect of humanity, demonstrated by both Frau
Flamm and Keil, is total understanding of Rose's situation.[90]
Frau Flamm is the first person to comprehend Rose's difficulty
and subsequently acts to relieve Rose of her suffering and
despair. But Rose does not accept this generosity. Instead she
withdraws, due to Flamm's rejection and damnation, and seeks
to deal with the circumstances herself.

While Frau Flamm's humanity manifests itself during the
entire play, Keil's compassion and understanding emerge
primarily in Act IV, after he has had the opportunity to
experience suffering through the loss of an eye. It is interesting to note that it is the partially blind Keil who is able to see
the truth, recalling images of the blind man who tells Oedipus
of his coming fate and of the blind grandfather in Kleist's
Familie Schroffenstein who is the first to perceive the catastrophe
that has occurred in the darkness of the cave.[91] In his attempt
to convince Bernd to drop the suit against Streckmann, Keil's
truly humane, Christian nature appears:

> August. . . . Vater, Ihr mißt Eure Klage zuricknehm!
> Bernd. Alles, August! Das kann ich nich.
> August. Es is nich christlich. Ihr mißt se zuricknehm.
> . . .
> August. Vater Bernd, Vater Bernd, wie soll ich da anfang, wenn Ihr gar
> so unversehnlich seid! Ihr habt von so vieler Ehre gered't. Ma soll
> aber seine Ehre ni suchen, sondern Gottes Ehre und sonst keene
> nich![92]

Indeed, this is Keil's notion; his devotion to God does not
waver and he accepts his fate without question as he feels his
suffering on earth will simply increase his reward in heaven.[93]

Like Frau Flamm, Keil refuses to abandon Rose after he discovers her true state. He is even willing to sell his house and move away to start a new life with her. To this extent, Keil could be contrasted with Hebbel's Friedrich, who is concerned with his own public stature. Indeed, Keil even uses the word "Pharisee" when referring to those who refuse to help someone in need.[94] Keil's hope to start a new life crumbles at the conclusion of the work as Rose is led away by the constable. His often-quoted concluding line, "Das Mädel . . . was muß die gelitten han!,"[95] further demonstrates his understanding, compassion and humanity.[96]

An important element of Keil's progression toward humanity is his gradual movement away from the stern morality of Bernd.[97] While Bernd remains unswerving in his adherence to the code of ethics, Keil's understanding of morality undergoes a change allowing forgiveness and acceptance. To this extent, Keil is purer than Hebbel's Friedrich in terms of humanity because Keil's compassion is not contingent on the elimination of those who could call Rose's character into question. Friedrich would marry Klara only after Leonhard was dead, thus making his humanity conditional. Keil's commitment to Rose, on the other hand, is unconditional; he accepts and supports her without question. But, like Friedrich's, Keil's well-meaning humanity comes too late to alter Rose's situation.[98] This does not diminish the importance of Keil's compassion; on the contrary, it heightens the tragedy of the situation because the audience now knows there was an escape for Rose: she had an option other than infanticide. The tragic element lies in the reality that Rose remained unaware of this solution to her hopeless situation. Her inability to free herself from the world view her father represents, especially the concept of honor, prevented her from sharing her despair with Keil and discovering the true depth of his love and devotion for her.

The humanity exhibited by Frau Flamm and Keil exemplifies the type of change Hauptmann felt necessary in human society. At the conclusion of his discussion of Hauptmann's dramatic works, Gerhard Schulz states: "Als Dramatiker stellt Hauptmann Konflikte, also Kollisionen von Menschen dar, und er tut es in der Überzeugung von der Notwendigkeit des 'Anderschwerdens.'"[99] Frau Flamm and August Keil demonstrate change that has already taken place. It is the logical conclusion that this change, i.e., the humane treatment of others in the spirit of caritas, would spread to all people and form the basis for all human relationships.

In terms of humane behavior, the father-daughter relationship in *Rose Bernd* fares as poorly as the one in *Maria Magdalene*. Rose's father, by remaining sternly couched in his piety and rigid moral ideals, renders himself incapable of fully comprehending his daughter, her suffering and despair. Like the other fathers examined in the preceding chapters, Bernd fails to love his daughter unconditionally, that is, no matter what happens. He is absorbed in himself to such a severe extent that he simply cannot release his traditions and give of himself to his daughter even in the moment of her greatest need. Furthermore, Rose's inability to free herself from her father's ethos heightens the despair that finally engulfs her. Although Bernd's failures in this play are augmented by the shortcomings of Flamm and Streckmann, he is nonetheless guilty of pushing his daughter into a hopeless situation. Thus we can see once more how the father-daughter relationship contributes to the daughter's psychological demise as she attempts to hide the denial of her father's ideals. To be sure, Bernd does not promise to commit suicide, as Meister Anton does; rather, the notion of the family's dishonor, resulting from the daughter's actions, moves into the position of paramount importance. Bernd and Rose must both "anderschwerden" if humane treatment is to flourish and if Hauptmann's goal, which he articulated most clearly years later during a speech commemorating the centennial of Goethe's death, is to be met:

> ... die Welt wird weder mit Gold noch durch Gewalttat erlöst, sondern allein durch Menschlichkeit, durch Menschenachtung, durch Humanität. Immer waren es Einzelne, die uns die frohe Botschaft gebracht und zur Humanität ermutigt haben, die als reiner Gedanke die größte, ja fast einzige Legitimation des Menschen als Menschen ist. Nicht Revolutionen bringen die Fortschritte, aber eine immerwährende, wie das Leben selber gegenwärtige, stille Reformation.[100]

Chapter VII

Domination, Dependence, Denial and Despair

In the preceding analyses of the father-daughter relationships themes common to the presentation of this relationship have become apparent, such as objectification, domination and possible rejection of the daughter by the father, concern with honor, attempts to deny societal norms by the daughter and her individuation. Each daughter's suffering, struggle and despair have also appeared. Indeed, the terms domination, dependence, denial and despair reflect the most essential elements of the father-daughter relationships discussed here.

Domination clearly reflects the role of the father in the relationships illustrated in the plays. Important perspectives of the fathers' domination is their constant fixation with honor and the objectification of their daughters. Beyond objectification is the sexual factor: In all eight dramas, sexual objectification plays some type of role and is demonstrated through the relationships of the women with their lovers. The Prince in *Emilia*, Mellefont, Jason, Leonhard, Flamm and Streckmann seem interested in the women only for sexual gratification, in addition to material enrichment in the cases of Jason and Leonhard. This treatment of women as sexual objects indicates their second-class status: The men indeed misuse these women, but the men are not considered dishonorable. The women must act to try to salvage their reputation; they are clearly victims of a double standard that condones active sexual behavior among males but condemns it among women. Such treatment is, however, not characteristic of all the men in these works. Leander and Keil appear as men who sincerely and unconditionally love the women with whom they are associated. Wagner's von Grönungseck could be included in this group, especially since he undertakes efforts at the end of the play to save Evchen's life.

In *Miß Sara Sampson, Emilia Galotti, Kindermörderin, Das goldene Vlieβ, Maria Magdalene* and *Rose Bernd* the sexual abuse of the women, while not a feature of the father-daughter relationships, nevertheless contributes significantly to the difficulties arising between father and daughter, often leading to the fathers' domination over the daughters and to the women's despair. This phenomenon reflects a critical element of the father's general socialization of the daughter inasmuch as daughters were closely guarded and not readily allowed out into the wider community. One result of this protection was the objectification of the daughter; another was often the daughter's inability to deal with problems when they arose. This phenomenon becomes most apparent in *Maria Magdalene* and *Rose Bernd*.

Another aspect of the father's role in the father-daughter relationship is his rigid adherence to a code of ethics. Here the father's normal action to restrict his children's behavior becomes perverted through its overemphasis, often leading to rejection of the daughter and resulting in the fathers' inhumanity.

A subtopic of the rigid observance of a certain ethos and the rejection of the daughter is the fathers' egocentricity. The fathers often base their honor on their daughters and, in so doing, think not primarily of their children but of themselves. The overriding factor for these men is what other people say or think about them and their families. Rather than considering how society views the daughters, the fathers are primarily concerned with themselves.

The daughters' sexual activity becomes a motivating factor in the fathers' rejection as it demonstrates their denial of the fathers' ethos and domination. A significant issue for the figure of the daughter is the degree of denial or obedience she demonstrates toward her father and the effect this has on her existence.

Denial and its consequence, paternal rejection, join together with objectification to cause each daughter's despair. Such a feeling manifests itself in the perception of hopelessness. Each daughter believes she has been placed in a situation from which escape can come only in the form of death - either her own or her child's.

In addition to causing despair, denial becomes an indication of the level of individuation attained by the daughters. Evchen, Emilia, Luise, Klara, and Rose lack the rejection factor Jung sees as essential in individuation, thus making their self-realization incomplete. The degree of self-realization reached by Sara, Medea, and Hero is much more extensive than that of the other five daughters. All three openly reject their fathers, although Hero initially tries to hide this denial. Based on the dramas analyzed, successful self-establishment appears to depend on the ability of the individual to rely on the self. When the daughter is unable to deny the father's world view, as in the case of continued concern for honor and reputation at the expense of physical existence or emotional well-being, she fails to rely on her self and become free from her father's domination. This self-development depends on escaping from the bonds of family and society that force the daughter into isolation and despair. Such self-realization can be augmented through a relationship with another human being, but dependence must be avoided. The exclusion of domination and dependence are therefore part and parcel of successful individuation. The third component is denial, through which independence expresses itself. Absence of sufficient denial results in despair. In the dramas examined, the daughters' despair leads either to the catastrophe, i.e., infanticide - followed by the expected death of the daughter - or her demise within the work itself. Despair and the subsequent catastrophe stem from the daughters' inability to free themselves from dependency on their fathers and the world view these men represent. Because the women do not distance themselves from these conditions that determine and restrict their behavior, they fail to create a self which can cope adequately with the despair life produces. A low degree of individuation causes the daughters' inability to realize their true persona. The failure to establish a clear self-image becomes a consequence of several factors: lack of denial, obedience to the father's standards, continued dependence on a male, and domination.   While Medea achieves the highest degree of individuation of all the daughters, the catastrophe of infanticide results from her continued domination by a male. Only after, and in essence as a result of, the murder of her children does Medea free herself from this final domination. Thus we perceive that the failure to establish individuation appears as a principal feature in these tragedies, complementing the notion that the denial of the fathers' Weltanschauung causes the disasters present in the works.

The fathers' world view finds a common base in the inhumane treatment of the daughters. One result of this inhumanity is the destruction of the father-daughter relationship, stemming from the refusal of the fathers to alter their ideology. In juxtaposition to such unbending behavior, rejection by the daughter to one degree or another is a normal expression, as indicated in chapter I. Furthermore, the refusal to change leads to despair and catastrophe. The conclusion to be drawn from these facts centers on the notion of change. In the quotation cited at the conclusion of chapter VI, Hauptmann pointed not to revolution, but to reformation in inter-human relationships as the basis for improving the world. The ultimate goal of such improvement was to further humanity. Indeed, the fathers' inhumane treatment of their daughters leads to the women's despair, culminating in the disasters of each work.   To be sure, Humbrecht and Sir William alter their behavior and begin to treat their daughters in a more humane and accepting manner, but only after the destruction caused by their former mode of action has irreparably damaged the existence of the daughters. In these two men an example of change is indicated; reform has occurred.   Hauptmann's notion of transformation reflects Hebbel's goal of improving the existing social institutions rather than replacing them completely.   Indeed, *Maria Magdalene* does not indicate that any reform has taken place in Anton's mind: His final line demonstrates that he does not understand what Klara's actions mean; he simply contemplates the meaning of life.   However, Friedrich's statements at the end do point to the reform Hebbel had in mind. From Grillparzer's *Das goldene Vlieβ* and *Des Meeres und der Liebe Wellen* can be extrapolated a further example of transformation inasmuch as the reader may perceive that the author indicates an example of the need for change. While the latter work ultimately demonstrates the destructive consequence of a lack of reform, the character of Medea rises above the confines of the non-accepting world and enters a realm of existence where inhumanity no longer affects her.

But Medea's example is not a positive manifestation; it results in the total isolation of the individual. In such a situation of withdrawal, the actions of other humans certainly cannot affect the one who separates herself from the wider community. Such separation as Medea finally experiences is mirrored by Karl's decision to leave his home and become a sailor. This flight is not a solution to the problem of inhumanity, but rather a means of escape. The difficulty with such escapist behavior centers on the fact that it changes the life circumstances only for that individual and in no way reforms the social network causing the inhumane treatment. The plea for reform in *Rose Bernd* is clearly expressed in the examples of humanity found in Frau Flamm and Keil. Whether stated directly or indirectly, we see in each play the need for change and reform vis-à-vis the humane treatment of other people.

In the first sentence of chapter I, it was remarked how literature tells about human behavior in the past in order to help us learn something for our present. We can apply this concept to the notion of transforming present life in such a manner as to increase humanity and humane treatment of all forms of life, thus permitting positive self-determination. The dramas serve as examples from the past that show us the negative and inhumane consequences of certain behaviors, especially centering around the father-daughter relationship. Each drama depicts a critical turning point in human existence, something all people experience. By examining these works and contemplating their examples, we receive an indication of how we might act when confronted with our own moments of change or those of others. By applying the dramas' message of reform - with the goal residing in the seemingly simple, but yet infrequently achieved ideal of caritas -, we can better understand and accept ourselves and others not only in the present but also in the future.

Notes

Chapter I

1 Michael Mitterauer and Reinhard Sieder, *The European Family* (Chicago: University of Chicago Press, 1982) 20. The authors also write: "When we compare the present-day situation of the young in the family with that of earlier times, we find that relationships and influences from outside the family (that is, those of school, work and peer groups) have become much more important" (112).

2 Ingeborg Weber-Kellermann, *Die deutsche Familie. Versuch einer Sozialgeschichte* (Frankfurt am Main: Suhrkamp, 1974) 19.

3 Talcott Parsons, "The Social Structure of the Family," *The Family: Its Function and Destiny*, ed. Ruth Nanda Anshen (New York: Harper, 1959) 263.

4 Rose Laub Coser, "Authority and Structural Ambivalence in the Middle-Class Family," *The Family. Its Structures and Functions*, ed. Rose Laub Coser (New York: St. Martin, 1974) 367.

5 Coser 365.

6 Coser 371.

7 Wade C. Mackey, *Fathering Behaviors. The Dynamics of the Man-Child Bond* (New York: Plenum, 1985) 4.

8 See: Bronislaw Malinowski, "Parenthood, the Basis of Social Structure," *The Family. Its Structures and Functions*, ed. Rose Laub Coser (New York: St. Martin, 1974) 59.

9 Malinowski 59.

10 Michael Lewis and Marsh Weinraub, "The Father's Role in the Child's Social Network," *The Role of the Father in Child Development*, ed. Michael Lamb (New York: Wiley, 1976) 179.

11 Mitterauer and Sieder 4. See also Weber-Kellermann 12. Here she writes: "Vom Patriarchalismus war die Familie der Vergangenheit geführt und gehemmt."

12 Reay Tannahill, *Sex in History* (New York: Stein and Day, 1980) 353.

13 See: Max Horkheimer, "Authoritarianism and the Family," *The Family: Its Function and Destiny*, ed. Ruth Nanda Anshen (New York: Harper, 1959) 382.

14 D. B. Lynn, *The Father: His Role in Child Development* (Monterey, California: Brooks/Cole, 1974) 39. Drewitz alludes to the fact of patriarchy when she explains that the "emancipation documents handed down to us are individual testaments to rebellion against a patriarchal society which allots to women the position of work-horse or status figure alone or chooses as its model those whose silence is not only kept in church" (quoted in Ingeborg Drewitz, ed. *The German Women's Movement* (Bonn: Hohnwacht, 1983) 18.

15 Lynn 39.

16 Emile Benveniste, *Indo-European Language and Society*, trans. Elizabeth Palmer (London: Faber and Faber, 1973) 165. He describes the linguistic basis of patriarchy and states that "the structure of the family implicit in the [Indo-European] vocabulary is that of a patriarchal society, resting on descent in the paternal line and representing the type of 'Grossfamilie' (still observed in Serbia in the nineteenth century) with an ancestor, around whom are grouped the male descendents and their immediate families ..." (165).

   Jean Haudty, *Les Indo-Européens* (Paris: Presses Universitaires de France, 1981) 74 notes the same relationship between "father" and "God" as Benveniste: "Les dieux indo-européens se nomment **deywós* 'ceux du ciel-diurne', désignation qui remonte à une époque où le Ciel-diurne *dyéw-pHtér-* [Jupiter] était le premier de tous les dieux."

17 See: John Nash, "Historical and Social Changes in the Perception of the Role of the Father," *The Role of the Father in Child Development*, ed. Michael Lamb (New York: Wiley, 1976) 70.

   Weber-Kellermann 80 writes: "Gerade in der protestantischen Familie erfolgte durch den Fortfall der priesterlichen Vermittlerrolle eine Stärkung der väterlichen Autorität in der Familie-und von daher eine Übertragung auf die weltliche Autorität überhaupt." See also 82 and Lynn 32.

18 Bryan E. Robinson and Robert L. Barret, *The Developing Father. Emerging Roles in Contemporary Society* (New York: Guilford, 1986) 6.

19 Malinowski 54.

20 Lucy Gilbert and Paula Webster, *Bound by Love: The Sweet Trap of Daughterhood* (Boston: Beacon, 1982) 52.

21 Gilbert and Webster 41.

22 Lynn 39. Inge Stephan, "'So ist die Tugend ein Gespenst': Frauenbild und Tugendbegriff im bürgerlichen Trauerspiel bei Lessing und Schiller," *Lessing Yearbook* 17 (1985): 7, writes of the father's paradoxical,

yet all-powerful role during the eighteenth century: "Ökonomisch und gesellschaftlich gesehen wurde der Bürger zusehends ein kleines Rädchen in einer großen Maschinerie, die er weder befehligte noch kontrollierte. Als Oberhaupt in der Familie erhielt er eine Entschädigung für die reale Einbuße an Bedeutung. Als Herrscher über Frau, Kinder und Gesinde könnte er sich mächtig fühlen."

23 Marsha Weinraub, "Fatherhood: The Myth of the Second-Class Parent," *Mother/Child, Father/Child Relationships*, eds. Joseph H. Stevens, Jr., Marilyn Mathews (Washington D.C.: National Association for the Education of Young Children, 1978) 127.

24 Michael E. Lamb, *The Role of the Father in Child Development* (New York: Wiley, 1976) 22-23. (Subsequent reference made to *Role*.)

25 Robinson and Barret 43.

26 Lamb, *Role* 25.

27 Lamb, *Role* 29.

28 Esther Blank Greif, "Fathers, Children, and Moral Development," *The Role of the Father in Child Development*, ed. Michael Lamb (New York: Wiley, 1976) 219.

29 See Malinowski 59 and Gilbert and Webster 51.

30 Lamb, *Role* 11. See also 17.

31 Lynn 194 writes: "Father-working in the community, knowledgeable of its rules and principles, aware of the price of their violation, and eager that his children take their responsible place as citizens-might be expected to urge his children to internalize the culture's basic rules and values."

32 Weber-Kellermann 94 writes: "In der Gemeindeordnung und -verwaltung vertrat er [der Hausvater] sein 'Haus' mit allen seinen Bewohnern auch rechtlich als eine Wirtschaftseinheit, und die Gemeinde funktionierte gewissermaßen als eine Gemeinschaft der Hausväter."

33 Paul Schrecker, "The Family: Conveyance of Tradition," *The Family: Its Function and Destiny*, ed. Ruth Nanda Anshen (New York: Harper, 1959) 493 remarks that "the family operates as the most appropriate conveyance, at any time and place, of the traditions and conventions to be impressed upon the offspring whose future life and work are to be determined by the norms thus transmitted." See also 506. In the same vein Mitterauer and Sieder state: "Traditional European society passed on norms, attitudes, manners and skills in a familial or domestic framework" (106).

34 See Mitterauer and Sieder 94-95.

35 Lamb, *Role* 12.

36 Lynn 217.

37 Coser 363.

38 See Werner Pols, *Deutsche Sozialgeschichte 1815-70* (Munich: Beck, 1979)
    8.

39 Mitterauer and Sieder 115.

40 Robinson and Barret 71.

41 Coser 366.

42 Sabean 2.

43 Weber-Kellermann 47 writes: "Gehorsam und demütige Unterwer-
    fung, geduldiges Ertragen auch von Züchtigungen seitens des Mannes
    predigte man als Teil der göttlichen Weltordnung . . ."

44 See Weber-Kellermann 118.

45 Gilbert and Webster 3.

46 Gilbert and Webster 16.

47 Mitterauer and Sieder 101.

48 Gilbert and Webster 19.

49 See Gilbert and Webster 16.

50 Gilbert and Webster vii (Preface) write: "The forced march to feminin-
    ity begins when we are daughters in the family. Daughterhood creates
    a common past for all women since it is the only shared structural
    feature of our lives. It is our first social identity and psychologically our
    most enduring."

51 Gilbert and Webster viii (Preface).

52 Tannahill 349.

53 Drewitz 48 writes: "The social supression of women stems from their
    economic dependence. Their domestic activity is only apparently of
    equal value with the money-earning work of the man, because he pays
    for the maintenance of the family. This makes the woman his
    property." See also 56, where more specific information concerning
    the nineteenth century is given. Of particular interest is the statement:
    "Women were under male guardianship, not allowed to practice any
    profession or sign any contract without their husband's permission; on
    marriage their property passed into their husband's hands for adminis-

tration and whatever they earned while married also passed into the possession of the husband 'according to the law.'"

54 See Weber-Kellermann 26 and 30. Indeed, Fichte supported the notion that women were merely property when he wrote: "Die Frau gehört nicht sich selbst an, sondern dem Manne. . . . Der Mann wird ihre Garantie bei dem Staate; er wird ihr rechtlicher Vormund; er lebt in allem ihr öffentliches Leben; und sie behält lediglich ein häusliches Leben übrig." (Quoted in: Susan L. Cocalis, "Der Vormund will Vormund sein: Zur Problematik der weiblichen Unmündigkeit im 18. Jahrhundert," *Amsterdamer Beiträge zur neueren Germanistik* vol. 10 1980, *Gestaltet und Gestaltend. Frauen in der deutschen Literatur*, ed. Marrianne Burkhard (Amsterdam: Rodopi, 1980) 54.

55 Friedrich Kluge and Alfred Götze, *Etymologisches Wörterbuch der deutschen Sprache* (Berlin: de Gruyter, 1948) 121. See also Benveniste 193.

56 See Weber-Kellermann 28. Inge Stephan writes at some length about the phenomenon of the daughter as property as it applies specifically to eighteenth-century Germany: "Die Konzeption der Tochter als Eigentum des Vaters und als Ware in den Beziehungen zwischen Männern läßt sich . . . nur verstehen als Ausdruck eines patriarchalischen Machtanspruchs, der im Rahmen des bürgerlichen Emanzipationskampfes neu formuliert und bekräftigt wurde" (15). See also Stephan 12, 13.

57 Tannahill 351.

58 See Weber-Kellermann 27. Indeed, as Stephan points out, marriage did not bring about a significant change in the woman's status: "Als Frau eines anderen Mannes und als zukünftige Mutter in einer neuen Familie wechselte die Tochter von einem Familienbund in einen anderen und entglitt damit erst einmal dem Herrschaftsanpruch ihres Vaters. Von daher ist es verständlich, daß die Väter versuchten, die Sexualität ihrer Töchter zu kontrollieren und den Übergang auf den zukünftigen Schwiegersohn in ihrem eigenen Sinne zu regeln" (15).

59 See Weber-Kellermann 27. See also Cocalis 40.

60 See Weber-Kellermann 27. Especially in the Middle Ages there was no choice on the part of the daughter in marriage settings. Daughters were often married at 14, a fact which precludes any notion of free choice (see Weber-Kellermann 41-42).

61 Mitterauer and Sieder 101.

62 Drewitz notes that the educational system did not promote the development of such self-understanding during the nineteenth century: "The girls were fed on half-knowledge and fixed prejudices. They were not guided towards independent thoughts and were therefore unable to develop any sense of self-valuation" 58.

63 C. G. Jung, *The Collected Works of C. G. Jung* vol. 7 *Two Essays on Analytical Psychology*, 2nd edition, trans. R. F. C. Hull, Bollingen Series 20 (New York: Bollingen Foundation, 1966) 173.

64 Jung, *Essays* 174.

65 Jung, *Essays* 174.

66 Jung, *Essays* 188.

67 C. G. Jung *The Collected Works of C. G. Jung* vol. 2 *Experimental Researches*, trans. Leopold Stein, Bollingen Series 20 (Princeton: Princeton University Press, 1973) 478, maintains: "It should be one of the most important aims of education to free the growing child from his unconscious attachment to the influences of his early environment, in such a way that he may keep what is valuable in it and reject whatever is not."

68 Jung, *Essays* 178.

69 See Jung, *Essays* 178.

70 Jung *Essays* 173-4.

71 See, for example, "Anima and Animus," *Essays* 188-211.

72 See Jung, *Essays* and C. G. Jung, *The Basic Writings of C. G. Jung*, ed. Violet Staub De Laszlo (New York: The Modern Library, 1959) 274.

73 Greif 223.

74 Kingsley Davis, "The Sociology of Parent-Youth Conflict," *The Family. Its Structures and Functions* ed. Rose Laub Coser (New York: St. Martin, 1974) 454.

75 Davis 454.

76 Davis 454. See also Parsons 268 for a discussion of adolescent behavior patterns.

77 Mitterauer and Sieder 98.

78 Davis 448.

79 Davis 448. In a similar vein Mitterauer and Sieder write: "There are also causes of conflict that may be explained by the retention of traditional parental control. For example, the sex life of the young person is still frequently restricted (or perhaps we should say they attempt to restrict it)" (114).

80 Ruth Nanda Anshen, "The Conservation of Family Values," *The Family: Its Function and Destiny*, ed. Ruth Nanda Anshen (New York: Harper, 1959) 519.

81 Parsons 269.

82 Parsons 269.

83 Lynn 40.

84 Davis 454.

85 Spartaco Lucarini, *The Difficult Role of a Father*, trans. Hugh Moran (New York: New York City Press, 1979) 42.

86 Gilbert and Webster 57.

87 Gilbert and Webster 44.

88 See Gilbert and Webster 47 and 51.

89 Gilbert and Webster 54.

90 Gilbert and Webster 54.

91 Michael E. Lamb, "The Changing Roles of Fathers," *The Father's Role: Applied Perspectives*, ed. Michael E. Lamb (New York: Wiley, 1986) 5.

92 Lamb, *Perspectives* 5.

93 See Weber-Kellermann 10.

94 Drewitz 7.

95 Drewitz 46.

96 See Weber-Kellermann 16.

97 See Weber-Kellermann 159.

98 See Weber-Kellermann 105.

Chapter II

1 See Hans Helmut Hiebel, "Mißverstehen und Sprachlosigkeit im 'Bürgerlichen Trauerspiel': Zum historischen Wandel dramatischer Motivationsformen," *Jahrbuch der deutschen Schiller-Gesellschaft* 27 (1983): 124. See also Gerhard Kaiser, "Krise der Familie: Eine Perspektive auf Lessings *Emilia Galotti* und Schillers *Kabale und Liebe*," *Recherches Germaniques* 14 (1984): 13-14 for a brief history of the *bürgerliche Trauerspiel*.

2 Ernst L. Stahl, "Emilia Galotti," *Das deutsche Drama* Bd. 1, ed. Benno von Wiese (Düsseldorf: Bagel, 1958) 103, refers to *bürgerliche Trauerspielen* as "vertiefte Familiendramen."

3 Hiebel 124.

4 See, for example, Fritz Martini, *Deutsche Literaturgeschichte* (Stuttgart: Kröner, 1984) 205.

5 Jochen Hörisch, "Die Tugend und der Weltlauf in Lessings bürgerlichen Trauerspielen," *Euphorion* 74 (1980): 194.

6 See Denis Jonnes, "*Solche Väter*: The Sentimental Family Paradigm in Lessing's Drama," *Lessing Yearbook* 12 (1980): 158.

7 Inge Stephan, "'So ist die Tugend ein Gespenst': Frauenbild und Tugendbegriff im bürgerlichen Trauerspiel bei Lessing und Schiller," *Lessing Yearbook* 17 (1985): 1-2.

8 Gotthold Ephraim Lessing, *Werke* vol. 1, ed. Wolfgang Stammler (Munich: Hanser, 1959) 313. (This volume hereafter referred to as Lessing, *Sara*).

9 H. Bornkamm, "Die innere Handlung in Lessings *Miß Sara Sampson*," *Euphorion* F. 3, 51 (1957): 385.

10 Jonnes 159 provides an interesting summary of the work: "Though Lessing's drama can be construed, on one level, as part of a struggle waged in the name of *Vernunft* and Enlightenment individualism, its deeper structure is more in the nature of a response to the crisis produced when each individual within a collectivity comes to deny the legitimacy of transcendent structures of authority (whether religious or political) or, in a more radical sense, the legitimacy of any authority beyond that established by each individual's power of reason."

11 Lessing, *Sara* 313.

12 Jonnes 160 writes even less sympathetic words about Mellefont: "The wooer or seducer, especially, more than simply a competitor of the father for the daughter, is a figuring of the rival, an embodiment of the egotistical, self-interested consciousness which the father encounters in the public sphere."

13 Lessing, *Sara* 314.

14 Jonnes 162 writes of this situation: "Sir William seems zealous in his affection for Sara."

15 Lessing, *Sara* 321.

16 Bornkamm 390.

17 Wolfram Mauser, "Lessings *Miss Sara Sampson*. Bürgerliches Trauerspiel als Ausdruck innerbürgerlichen Konflikts," *Lessing Yearbook* 7 (1975): 13, writes: "Der Widerspruch, in dem Sara am Beginn des Stückes steht und der sie in scharfe Konflikte führt, ist offenkundig.

Einerseits wagt sie die Flucht als Tat der Selbstverwirklichung, der persönlichen Würde und des Glücks . . . . Andererseits ist Sara den erstarrten, aber verinnerlichten Tugendnormen und den Gewissenszwängen eines festgefügten Glaubens so eng verhaftet, daß in der Konfliktsituation alle persönlichen Erwartungen zurückstehen und . . . die Stellung zum Vater zur alles überragenden Wertvorstellung wird."

18 Lessing, *Sara* 348.

19 Lessing, *Sara* 348.

20 See Hörisch 192 for an examination of this scene of reconciliation.

21 Lessing, *Sara* 393.

22 Lessing, *Sara* 393.

23 Peter Weber, *Das Menschenbild des bürgerlichen Trauerspiels* (Berlin: Rütten & Loening, 1970) 50.

24 Mauser 25 writes: "Indem sie [Sara und Mellefont] Schritte unternehmen, deren konsequente Verfolgung emanzipatorische Dimensionen annehmen konnte, verstoßen sie aber gegen Grundforderungen der herrschenden Morallehre und zugleich gegen elementare Interessen der Gesellschaft."

25 See Stephan 9.

26 See Bornkamm 388.

27 Frank G. Ryder, "*Emilia Galotti,*" *German Quarterly* 45 (1972): 329, writes for example: "The end of the play, indeed the whole play, cries out for logical explanation and finds none."

28 Gotthold Ephraim Lessing, *Werke* vol. 1, ed. Wolfgang Stammler, (Munich: Hanser, 1959) 557. (This volume hereafter referred to as Lessing, *Emilia*.)

29 Stephan 12 writes: "Odoardo ist . . . in erster Linie Tugendwächter und damit zugleich Herr über Leben und Tod der Tochter."
    John D. Poynter, "The Pearls of *Emilia Galotti,*" *Lessing Yearbook* 9 (1977): 86, expresses the same notion since he believes Odoardo must control his daughter's actions. He writes further: "Here is a parent who views the child so much a part of his own flesh that he is, in a sense, narcissistically involved with her. He endeavors to live through her, and to invest her with his own neurosis" (89). This statement is reminiscent of the phenomenon examined in chapter I that parents try to live through their children when the parents become older.

30 Lessing, *Emilia* 570.

31 Lessing, *Emilia* 572.

32 Leonard P. Wessell, "The Function of Odoardo in Lessing's *Emilia Galotti,*" *Germanic Review* 47 (1972): 251, writes: "Odoardo's avoidance of social activity is ultimately derived from his need to maintain his moral purity."

33 Poynter 89.

34 See Lessing, *Emilia* 572. Graf Appiani is of the same opinion and calls Odoardo: "Das Muster aller männlichen Tugend" (189).

35 Lessing, *Emilia* 574.

36 Wessell 248 writes that Odoardo's personality "involves: (1) an over-bearing demand for moral purity, (2) an extremely volatile, sponta-neous, emotional, and non-reflective tendency to act, and (3) yet paradoxically an inability to translate into action the contents and wants of his *reflective* consciousness." Wessell is supported in this assertion by Stahl who explains: ". . . Ehrgefühl und brausende Unbesonnenheit . . . Diese Eigenschaften bestimmen Odoardos tragisches Dilemma, das darin besteht, daß dieser sonst so entschlußfreudige Tatmensch bis zur Unfähigkeit paralysiert wird, um doch am Ende die unerhörte Tat aus unechtem Gefühl zu leisten" (110).

37 Lessing, *Emilia* 609.

38 See Wessell 258.

39 Lessing, *Emilia* 573. Ryder 336-7 explains that these words have been interpreted "(1) as evidence of the sensual attraction she [Emilia] already feels for the Prince, (2) as indicating awareness of potential vulnerability, perhaps slight, but still disturbing in the context of her father's moral standards, (3) as an expression of simple fear of the Prince, since no girl of her character would, on her wedding day, enter-tain thoughts of a liaison."

40 Lessing, *Emilia* 623. These words have been interpreted in various ways. Hörisch 191 sees Emilia's statement as an expression of her concern for the future-her passion may lead to a moral breakdown. Gerd Labroisse, "Emilia Galottis Wollen und Sollen," *Neophilologus* 56 (1972): 315, views Emilia's lines in much the same manner as Hörisch; however, he adds the notion that Emilia's concern for her possible passion "nur zur Bekräftigung ihres Entschlusses [zu sterben] dient, nicht aber der Grund davon ist."

   H. C. Hatfield, "Emilia's Guilt Once More," *Modern Language Notes* 71 (1956): 293, refers to this passage as "a means to an end, a way of gaining her aim." This interpretation seems to give a meaning to Emilia's words that Lessing did not intend. We have the statement "meine Sinne sind Sinne" and must accept it as such. To ascribe further meaning to these words that the text itself does not provide brings us away from a proper understanding of Emilia's character.

41 Labroisse 318 writes: "Das Verweigern jeder Verantwortung bestätigt die Notwendigkeit von Emilias Tod, bekräftigt die Richtigkeit der Entscheidung, die Tochter und Vater, vertrauend auf ihr vernünftiges Denken, getroffen hatten: Einem solchen Menschen ausgeliefert zu sein, ließ in der Tat keine Hoffnung zu."

G. A. Wells, "What is Wrong with *Emilia Galotti?" German Life and Letters* 37, April (1984): 164, explains in like manner that Emilia wants to die ". . . not because of Appiani's death, but because once she knows that she will not be allowed to escape from the Prince's presence, she realizes she will not be able to resist seduction by him." Wells goes on to write: "The intentions of the Prince and the intrigue of Marinelli merely trap Emilia in a situation which actuates tendencies in her and in her father that lead to tragedy" (172).

42 See Alois Wierlacher, "Das Haus der Freude oder Warum stirbt Emilia Galotti?" *Lessing Yearbook* 5 (1973): 147-62 for a close study of the effect of the Grimaldi house on Emilia. Here the author points out that this house is not a bordello, but rather a place in which Emilia has experienced uncontrolled passion previously.

43 See Stahl 106.

44 See Hiebel 124.

45 Jonnes 165.

46 Gerhard Kaiser attributes this guilt also to the fact that Odoardo lived apart from his family instead of being with them and acting as the "große Lehrer" (117). It would appear, however, that Odoardo has taught Emilia enough. See also Wessell 249.

47 See Stahl who writes well of the combination of "Ehrgefühl und brausenende Unbesonnenheit" in Odoardo's deed (110-see note 39 above for further quotation of this passage).

48 See Johannes Werner, *Gesellschaft in literarischer Form. H. L. Wagners "Kindermörderin" als Epochen- und Methodenparadigma* (Stuttgart: Klett, 1977): "Heinrich Leopold Wagner zählt zu den Vergessenen der deutschen Literatur" (5) and: "Zu unrecht . . . wurde Wagner vergessen, während manch ein Geringerer überlebte" (6).

Jürgen Haupt, "*Die Kindermörderin*. Ein bürgerliches Trauerspiel vom 18. Jahrhundert bis zur Gegenwart," *Orbis Litterarum*. 32 <4> (1977): 285, writes: Heinrich Leopold Wagner ist ein 'selbst unter Germanisten wenig, beim literarischen Publikum oft nicht einmal dem Namen nach bekannter Autor." See also Haupt 294 and:

Barbara Mabee, "Die Kindesmörderin in den Fesseln der bürgerlichen Moral: Wagners Evchen und Goethes Gretchen," *Women in German Yearbook* 3, ed. Marianne Burkhard and Edith Waldstein (London, New York and Lanham: University Press of America, 1986) 29-42.

49 Otto Mann, *Die Geschichte des deutschen Dramas* (Stuttgart; Alfred Kröner, 1969) 510. See also Haupt 291 and 294-5.

50 See Martini, *Literaturgeschichte* 223.

51 Werner 7. See also Georg Pilz, *Deutsche Kindesmord-Tragödien: Wagner, Goethe, Hebbel, Hauptmann* (Munich: Oldenbourg, 1982) 18 and 20 and Mabee 42.

52 See Wolfgang Beutin, et al, *Deutsche Literatur Geschichte von den Anfängen bis zur Gegenwart* (Stuttgart: Metzler, 1984) 135.
    See also Heinz-Dieter Weber, "Kindesmord als tragische Handlung," *Deutschunterricht* 28, Nr. 2 (1976) 76-78 for a brief examination of infanticide throughout history.

53 See Haupt 286.

54 Inge Stephan, Beutin, et al. 135, notes that Evchen as well as Gretchen in *Urfaust* killed their children "weil sie die gesellschaftliche Schande, die ein uneheliches Kind damals bedeutete, nicht ertragen können. Statt ihr zu entgehen, verfielen sie ihr in doppelter Hinsicht. Als uneheliche Mütter waren sie 'nur' verfemt und sozial deklassiert, als Kindsmörderinnen waren sie gesellschaftlich nicht mehr tragbar, sie wurden dem Schafott übergeben."

55 Heinrich Leopold Wagner, *Die Kindermörderin, Deutsche National-Literatur*, ed. Joseph Kürscher, vol. 80 *Stürmer und Dränger* 2. Teil, ed. H. Sauer (Berlin and Stuttgart: Spemann, n.d.) 295. (This volume hereafter referred to as Wagner, *Kindermörderin.*)

56 Wagner, *Kindermörderin* 298.

57 Wagner, *Kindermörderin* 300.

58 Wagner, *Kindermörderin* 306.

59 Wagner, *Kindermörderin* 307. See also Pilz 23.

60 See Wagner, *Kindermörderin* 308.

61 Heinz-Dieter Weber 78.

62 Wagner, *Kindermörderin* 325.

63 Heinz-Dieter Weber 89-90 writes: "Auch die Furcht vor dem Vater ist nicht eine Furcht vor seinem Zorn, sondern vor seiner Liebe . . . ; es ist die eigene innere Anerkennung der von ihm repräsentierten Normen, die bedrohlich wird. Nicht die äußeren Umstände führen zum unausweichlichen Konflikt, sondern die Tatsache, daß die in ihnen geltenden Normen von Evchen internalisiert wurden und in Geltung gehalten werden." Jürgen Haupt comments: "Zu mächtig sind die

Moral- und Justizschranken des Bürgertums, das repräsentiert wird
vom patriarchalisch und puritanisch auftrumpfenden Vater" (287) and:
"Die Vater-Figuren [im bürgerlichen Trauerspiel] repräsentieren
bürgerliche Würde und Familien-Ehre auch als 'Produzenten'
gegenüber dem genießenden Adel (Verführer-Figuren)." Wagner's
Evchen is aware of all these aspects. She says to von Gröningseck: "Sie
hielten Ihr Wort nicht, überließen mich meinem Schicksal, dem ganzen
Gewicht der Schande, die mich erwartet, dem Zorn meiner Anver-
wandten, der Wut meines Vaters, glaubst du, daß ich dies alles
abwarten würde? abwarten könnte?" (327).

64 Wagner, *Kindermörderin* 329. Pilz 41 writes of Evchen's concerns: "Da
Evchen aber gleichzeitig die Normen ihres Vaters als ihre eigenen
anerkennt und nicht als etwas, das ihr von außen aufgezwungen wurde,
ist ihr innerer Konflikt ohne Ausweg." See also 31.

65 Mabee 40 writes of Evchen's situation: "Die Tragik der Unfreiheit ihrer
Sinnlichkeit erfahren die verführten Mädchen bei Goethe und Wagner
im inneren Zwiespalt zwischen Gebundensein an ihre natürliche
Leidenschaft und an die Normen der Gesellschaft. Die resultierende
Verzweiflung und Melancholie über die Ausweglosigkeit führen bei
beiden Mädchen zum Kindesmord."

66 Wagner, *Kindermörderin* 333.

67 Haupt 293 (note 5) explains this situation: "Die Vater-Tochter-
Beziehung ist die entscheidende Konstellation des bürgerlichen
Trauerspiels. Autoritäre Verhaltensweisen wechseln mit 'empfind-
samen,' Zärtlichkeit schlägt um in Brutalität, wenn die Tochter
unerlaubt-der Vater hat absolute Gewalt-aus der Familie ausbricht."

68 It is significant to note that Evchen's mother died as a result of the
shame Evchen brought on the family (see Wagner, *Kindermörderin* 350).
This phenomenon can be found again in Hebbel's *Maria Magdalene*
(although the shame which kills the mother here is caused by the son's
arrest, not by the daughter) and in Ludwig Thoma's *Magdalena*.

69 Wagner, *Kindermörderin* 353.

70 Wagner, *Kindermörderin* 357.

71 Haupt 287 notes: "Fast freiwillig unterwerfen sich die Bürger-mädchen
den gesellschaftlichen Zwängen und christlichen Moralbegriffen, die sie
im 'Gewissen' verinnerlicht haben."

72 See Peter Michelsen, "Ordnung und Eigensinn: Über Schillers *Kabale
und Liebe*," *Jahrbuch des freien deutschen Hochstifts* (1984): 210.
    Fritz Martini, "Schillers *Kabale und Liebe*, Bemerkungen zur Inter-
pretation des 'Bürgerlichen Trauerspiels'," *Deutschunterricht* 4, Nr. 5
(1952): 23-25, sees the play as the presentation of the conflict between

generations. This is true for Ferdinand and his father, but Luise never really rejects her father's world.

73 Friedrich Schiller, *Sämtliche Werke* vol. 1, ed. Gerhard Fricke and Herbert G. Göpfert (Munich: Hanser, 1962) 757. (This volume hereafter referred to as Schiller, *Kabale*.)

74 Schiller, *Kabale* 758.

75 Martini, "Schillers *Kabale und Liebe*" 21-22. Michelsen 201 expresses the same notion when he writes: ". . . [Miller] ist der feste Vertreter einer von oben nach untern gegliederten Ordungswelt, die sich vor allem in seiner Rolle als 'Vater' spiegelt . . . ."

76 Schiller, *Kabale* 758-59.

77 Schiller, *Kabale* 801.

78 Schiller, *Kabale* 809. See Michelsen 203. Walter Müller-Seidel, "Das stumme Drama der Luise Millerin," *Goethe* 17 (1955): 96, notes: "Ihre Ahnungen lassen nicht darauf schliessen, daß sie die Unterschiede des Standes von vornherein als göttlich gesetzt erkennt. Wohl aber hat für sie die Bindung an den Vater-und nicht nur an ihren Vater-eine religiös verklärte Bedeutung."

79 Schiller, *Kabale* 839: Luise (*springt auf und eilt ihm [Miller] nach*). Halt! halt! O mein Vater!-Daß die Zärtlichkeit noch barbarischer zwingt als Tyrannenwut! -Was soll ich? Ich kann nicht! Was muß ich tun?
Miller. Wenn die Küsse deines Majors heißer brennen als die Trännen deines Vaters-stirb!
Luise (*nach einem qualvollen Kampfe mit einiger Festigkeit*). Vater! Hier ist meine Hand! Ich will-Gott! Gott! Was tu ich? Was will ich? Vater, ich schwöre-Wehe mir, wehe! Verbrecherin, wohin ich mich neige!-Vater, es sei!-Ferdinand-Gott sieht herab!-So zernicht ich sein letztes Gedächtnis. (*Sie zerreißt den Brief.*)
     Gerhard Kaiser 15 explains: "Es bleibt ihr nichts, als den Vater oder den Geliebten aufzugeben, eine Wahl, die zugunsten des Vaters, der Familie ausfällt."

80 Martini, "Schillers *Kabale und Liebe*" 30.

81 R. R. Heitner, "Luise Millerin and the Shock Motif in Schiller's Early Dramas," *Germanic Review* 41 (1966): 44. Martini, "Schillers *Kabale und Liebe*" 35, notes of Luise's inner development: "Die Luise, die jetzt der Unheil ahnende Vater vorfindet, ist nicht mehr nur ein ängstliches Mädchen, die gehorsame Tochter, das schlichte Bürgerkind, sondern ein Weib, das im Durchgang durch die tiefsten Schmerzen sich zur Hoheit einer seelischen Kraft wandelte, die endgültig dem Vater weit überlegen ist."

Chapter III

1 Rudolf Stiefel, *Grillparzers* Goldenes Vließ. *Ein dichterisches Bekenntnis* (Bern: Franke, 1959) 10, writes: "Für Grillparzer ist der Kindermord bloß Folge und Abschluß einer tragischen Entwicklung, die im Grunde schon durch den Vließraub entschieden ist."

2 See Stiefel 10.

3 Heinz Politzer, "Franz Grillparzer," *Deutsche Dichter des 19. Jahrhunderts*, ed. Benno von Wiese (Berlin: Schmidt, 1969) 272.
   Konrad Schaum, "Gesetz und Verwandlung in Grillparzers *Goldenem Vließ*," *Deutsche Vierteljahresschrift* 38 (1964): 79.

4 See E. E. Papst "Franz Grillparzer," *German Men of Letters*, ed. Alex Natan, vol. 1 (London: Wolff, 1961) 108.

5 August Sauer, ed. *Franz Grillparzer. Sämtliche Werke. Historisch-kritische Gesamtausgabe* part 2, vol. 9 *Tagebücher und literarische Skizzenhefte* (Vienna: Schroll, 1916) 49. See also Stiefel 138.

6 Franz Grillparzer, *Franz Grillparzer Sämtliche Werke, Ausgewählte Briefe, Gespräche, Berichte* 4 vols., ed. Peter Frank and Karl Pörnbacher, vol. 3 (Munich: Hanser, 1964) 1143. (This edition referred to as Grillparzer, *Werke*).

7 Grillparzer, *Werke* vol. 3 1009.

8 See W. E. Yates, *Grillparzer. A Critical Introduction* (Cambridge: Cambridge University Press, 1972) 85, who writes: ". . . we see the main characters of the work fashioning their own fate, from which they can never extricate themselves." See also 108.
   Papst 107 notes: "Driven out of a state of intact innocence, in which they are at one with the inner law of their being and the objective order of the world, his heroes and heroines enter a labyrinth of mental and moral delusion, in which they lose their intrinsic selves."
   Elenore Frey, "Spannung und Gleichgewicht in Grillparzers Welt," *Schweizerisches Monatsheft* 46 (1966/67): 371, writes: "so sieht sich Grillparzer immer wieder gezwungen, zwischen zwei Daseinsweisen-dem inneren und dem äußeren Leben-eine Wahl zu treffen, die er selber als sinnlos, unmöglich und unheilvoll erkennt."
   Dagmar C. G. Lorenz, *Grillparzer. Dichter des sozialen Konflikts.* (Vienna: Böhlau, 1986) 12, describes Grillparzer's works in general: "Konflikt-oft ohne Ausweg, ohne mildernden Kompromiß-, Auseinandersetzungen und Veränderungen, letztere nicht unbedingt zum Besseren, dies sind die Elemente, die Grillparzers Schaffen charakterisieren."
   Paul Böckmann, "Verkennen und Erkennen im Drama Grillparzers," *Festschrift Josef Quint*, ed. Hugo Moser, Rudolf Schützeichel, Karl

Stackmann (Bonn: Semmel, 1964) 39, also writes of this conflict: "Indem der Mensch sich handelnd von seiner Vergangenheit zu befreien sucht, gibt er ihr zugleich eine gesteigerte Wirksamkeit."

Konrad Schaum, "Grillparzers *Des Meeres und der Liebe Wellen*: Seelendrama und Kulturkritik," *Jahrbuch der Grillparzer-Gesellschaft* 11 (1974): 95-96, states: ". . . in allen Dramen überzeugt Grillparzer von der Unvermeidlichkeit der Begegnung mit den schicksalhaften und gestaltenden Kräften des Lebens."

9 See Frey 374 and Walter Naumann, *Grillparzer. Das dichterische Werk* (Stuttgart: Kohlhammer, 1956) 64.

10 Grillparzer, *Werke* vol. 3 286-7.   Schaum 78 writes: "Das Antike-Mythologische ist keine andere, romantisierte Welt, sondern ein zentraler, poetisch vereinfachter, sinnbildlicher Bereich, in dem sich die menschliche Situation der Gegenwart um so konkreter und überspannender abzeichnen kann." See also Böckmann 42.

11 Critics have interpreted this work in various ways.   Stiefel 116 writes: "Sein Argonautenzyklus ist nicht nur eine Liebes- und Künstler-tragödie, sondern ebensosehr ein religiöses Drama, in keiner anderen Dichtung stößt er so tief in die metaphysische Sphäre der 'letzten Dinge' vor." In just one sentence, Stiefel interprets the trilogy in three different ways.   Schaum 81 focuses on the notion that man is pulled away from his natural state of existence by uncontrollable forces and occurrences, while Politzer 130 describes the final portion clearly as "eine Ehetragödie im Sinne der unentrinnbaren Differenz zwischen den Geschlechtern." He concerns himself merely with the final portion of the trilogy and thereby fails to include in his examination factors significant for a complete understanding of the drama as an entity. Böckmann 49 writes at some length that just such an examination is necessary: "Zwar hat Grillparzer die Medeagestalt von Anfang an in den Mittelpunkt gerückt und zum Bindeglied zwischen den drei Stücken gemacht; aber es genügt nicht, sich nur am Medeandrama zu orientieren, als ginge es um die Tragödie einer verlassenen Frau. Wir mißverstehen das Werk, wenn wir es als einen Vorläufer moderner Ehetragödien in der Art Ibsens oder Strindbergs auffassen und nicht auf das Wechselspiel von Verbergen und Offenbarwerden der Schuld achten, das die ganze Trilogie durchwaltet." Thus Böckmann posits guilt as a principal theme of the work. Papst 109 notes that Grill-parzer's version of the Medea legend "is the first dramatic treatment . . . to make use of the earlier parts [. . .] and so lay bare the psychological process by which Medea is transformed from an untamed innocent, at one with herself and nature, into an otherwise wellnigh inconceivable figure of horror and guilt." See also Stiefel 10. Yates 84-85 comments that Grillparzer had originally intended to write only a *Medea*, but that subsequently he chose to depict "Medea's tragedy as the culmination of a whole series of events beginning with her father's capture of the Golden Fleece and murder of Phryxus."

See also Wolf Hartmut Friedrich, *Vorbild und Neugestaltung. Sechs Kapitel zur Geschichte der Tragödie* (Göttingen: Vandenhoeck & Ruprecht, 1967) 7-56 for an overview of major Medea works within world literature. Here Friedrich examines similarities primarily in plays by Euripides, Seneca, Wagner and Grillparzer, although he does list ten works in all, see page 9.

A subtopic of the marriage theme to which Stiefel refers is self-alienation, which Papst 109 sees depicted in the plays as well.

I. V. Morris, "Grillparzer's Individuality as a Dramatist," *Modern Language Quarterly* 18 (1957): 85, posits vanity as an important topic in the trilogy (and in *Des Meeres und der Liebe Wellen*).

Ernst Fischer, *Von Grillparzer zu Kafka. Sechs Essays* (Vienna: Globus, 1972) points to similarities between characteristics of Jason and Medea and Grillparzer's own biography and writes: "In der Arbeitspause fiel nicht nur die Erkenntnis Kants, sondern auch die Bekanntschaft mit einer Frau. Grillparzer verführte die Frau eines Freundes, ohne sie zu lieben. Er sah sich plötzlich in der Situation Jason-Medea und schrak davor zurück, das unmittelbar Erlebte dichterisch zu gestalten. Dann aber fand er die Kraft zu leidenschaftlicher Selbstanklage" (30) and: "Grillparzer nannte sich selber einen Menschen, 'der nur zwei Fremden und keine Heimat hat'" (32).

Several critics focus on the concept of fate. Schaum 81, for example maintains that throughout the work, fate is "die wirkende Kraft." Naumann 135 writes: "Der Aufbau der ganzen Trilogie dient dazu, zu zeigen, daß das Geschehene, das, was einer getan hat, für ihn das Schicksal bedeutet, dem er nicht entgehen kann."

Piero Rismondo, "Das 'zweite Gesicht' in Grillparzers *Das goldene Vließ*," *Jahrbuch der Grillparzer-Gesellschaft* 5 (1966): 141, comments: "So erweist sich Grillparzer auch in diesem Werk als ein Dichter des Schicksals, des geschichtlichen Schicksals, eines geschichtlichen Endes und Untergangs, in dem der Mensch sich zu bewähren hat." Fate is not understood in some outer, non-descript metaphysical sense, but rather hinges on the past experiences and actions of each person: all people, by virtue of their actions, bring about their own destinies.

Finally, the topic of self-realization in general terms is alluded to by a few critics. Matthias Brauckmann and Andrea Everwien, "Sehnsucht nach Integrität oder Wie die Seele wächst im Verzicht," *Gerettete Ordnung. Grillparzers Dramen*, ed. Bernhard Budde and Ulrich Schmidt (Frankfurt, Bern, New York, Paris: Lang, 1987) 65, maintain that the topic of *Das goldene Vließ* is "die Konfrontation von Medeas Freiheitsanspruch und der sozialen Bezogenheit moralischen Handelns." Schaum 80 writes: "Wie bei der überwiegenden Mehrzahl von Grillparzers Dramen, so gliedert sich auch die *Vließ*-Trilogie in ihrem Grundgefüge um Werdegänge einzelner Personen . . . ."

12   August Sauer and Reinhold Backmann, ed., *Franz Grillparzer Sämtliche Werke* part 1 vol. 10 *Gedichte. Erster Teil* (Vienna: Schroll, 1932) 56. See also Stiefel 118.

13   Grillparzer, *Werke* vol. 4 (1965) 370. See also Politzer 127.

14 Grillparzer, *Werke* vol. 4 760.

15 Grillparzer, *Werke* vol. 1 (1960) 798 (lines 27-28).
    This volume will subsequently be referred to as "Grillparzer, *Vließ*." All
    references to the text are taken from this edition and include page and
    line numbers.

16 Grillparzer, *Vließ* 799 (57).

17 Grillparzer, *Vließ* 801 (118-120).

18 Grillparzer, *Vließ* 801 (121-127).

19 Lorenz 69.

20 Grillparzer, *Vließ* 805 (249).

21 Grillparzer, *Vließ* 810 (381-385).

22 Grillparzer, *Vließ* 812 (497-499).

23 Grillparzer, *Vließ* 814-815 (497-499).

24 Grillparzer, *Vließ* 810 (391-392). Stiefel 120 writes of this murder: "Wie
    Kain den Bruder erschlägt Aietes den Gastfreund als einen Rivalen vor
    Gott."

25 See Edward McInnes, "Psychological Insight and Moral Awareness in
    Grillparzer's *Das goldene Vließ*," *Modern Language Review* 75 (1980): 578.
    Here he writes: "Right at the beginning of the trilogy Medea is aware
    of a conflict between the god's demands, as her father represents them,
    and her own sense of religious obligation."

26 Brauckmann and Everwien 85 write: "Die indirekte Instrumental-
    isierung der religiösen Instanz und des Gastrechts [im Mord an
    Phryxus] durch Aietes verletzt vor Medeas Augen das Normensystem
    der Barbaren. Indem der König gegen die Gastfreundschaft verstößt,
    zerstört er die von seiner Tochter hypostasierte Gemeinschaft-auch die
    familiäre."

27 Wiltraud Wick, "Innere Entwicklung der Charaktere in Grillparzers
    Drama," diss., Tübingen, 1951, 96-97, writes: "Mit der Erkenntnis des
    Verbrechens, das der Vater beging, dringt in das bereits durch Phryxus
    gestörte Gleichmass und Ebenmass ihres Wesens von aussen etwas ein,
    was ihre innere Sicherheit völlig erschüttert. Nicht erst durch Jason
    erfolgt die Störung; . . . ." Schaum 82 focuses on the idea of Medea's
    arrival at a new stage of development: "Die primitive Untat des
    habsüchtigen, barbarischen Vaters, die sie nicht gewollt, für die sie sich
    aber dennoch verantwortlich fühlt, reißt sie unversehens auf eine neue
    Stufe der Entwicklung: aus der ichbezogenen, willkürlichen Diana ist
    eine Seherin geworden, erfüllt von inneren Gewißheiten und geistigen
    Bindungen." Brauckmann and Everwien 60 attribute this sense of

separation to the objectification itself: "Die Instrumentalisierung des Einzelnen produziert den Zustand von Entfremdung, in welchem auch reale Gemeinschaft nicht möglich ist."

28 See Brauckmann and Everwien 65.

29 See Grillparzer, *Vlieβ* 819. The setting is described: "Kolchis. Wilde Gegend mit Felsen und Bäumen. Im Hintergrunde ein halbverfallener Turm, aus dessen oberstem Stockwerke ein schwaches Licht flimmert. Weiter zurück die Aussicht aufs Meer." Stiefel 129 writes of Medea's seclusion in the tower: "Medea kämpft auch um sie [die Selbstbegrenzung], aber aus hellsichtigem Wissen und Willen. Doch immer enger muß sie den Kreis um sich ziehen, wenn sie ihr Wesen rein behalten will. Nach dem Einbruch der Fremden verkriecht sie sich in ihren Turm, um ihre Einheit zu wahren."
Folma Hoesch, *Der Gestus des Zeigens. Wirklichkeitsauffassung und Darstellungsmittel in den Dramen Franz Grillparzers* (Bonn: Bouvier, 1972) 12, interprets the tower for Medea's self in much the same manner: "Sie [Medea] versucht [im 2. Teil], sich diesem Geschehen [dem Mord an Phryxus] zu entziehen und flieht in den Turm der Selbstbewahrung."

30 See Stiefel 128. Brauckmann and Everwien 64 explain the relationship between the individual and society when individuation is at work: "Selbstbestimmung, wie sie am Beispiel Medeas konkret wird, entbehrt jeder sozialen Bezüglichkeit-als ob Autonomie a priori in Opposition zur Gemeinschaft zu denken sei."
Lorenz 70 writes Medea "ist eine Fremde in ihrer Gesellschaft." Morris 86 understands Medea's rejection of and moving away from her father as "psychologically credible as the result of a terrible shock in one so naïve and buttoned-up as Medea is at first, but it can hardly be regarded as typical of mankind in general." Here Morris misses the point of generalizing Medea's rejection as being representative of typical adolescent behavior-see chapter I.

31 Grillparzer, *Vlieβ* 823 (95-96).

32 Wick 96 observes: "Die Neigung zu Phryxus rührt zunächst nur leise an die milderen Regungen, die in ihr schlummern. . . . Sie, die keinen anderen Lebenskreis kannte als das rauhe Kolchis, wird von der hellenischen Lichtgestalt getroffen wie ein dunkler Grund von jähen Sonnenstrahlen."

33 Grillparzer, *Vlieβ* 825 (178-182).

34 Grillparzer, *Vlieβ* 825 (189).

35 Grillparzer, *Vlieβ* 826 (218).

36 Brauckmann and Everwien 62.

37 Grillparzer, *Vlieβ* 834 (439-440). Compare this passage to the statement by Phryxus already quoted: "Halb Charis steht sie da und halb Mänade" (805, line 249).

38 See Grillparzer, *Vlieβ* 835 (478-483).

39 Grillparzer, *Vlieβ* 839 (558-559).

40 Grillparzer, *Vlieβ* 851 (906).

41 Grillparzer, *Vlieβ* 857 (1043).

42 Grillparzer, *Vlieβ* 862 (1169-1170).

43 Grillparzer, *Vlieβ* 863-864 (1208-1214). See Emil Staiger, *Spätzeit. Studien zur deutschen Literatur* (Zurich and Munich: Artemis, 1973) 213.

44 Grillparzer, *Vlieβ* 869 (1351-1354).

45 Grillparzer, *Vlieβ* 869-870 (1364-1378).

46 Hoesch 17 comments: "Die Wirklichkeit ihrer Liebe hat sich als stärker erwiesen als ihr Wille, als ihre Zugehörigkeit zu ihrem Volk, zu Vater und Bruder."

47 Wick 98 sees this phenomenon occuring after Jason's visit to the tower: ". . . sie steht nun in fragwürdiger Spannung zwischen zwei Polen des eigenen tieferen Seins, zweier Völker und Kulturen und schicksalhaften Menschentums überhaupt. . . . In dieser doppelten Gespaltenheit liegt der Kern der Tragik in Medeas Entwicklung."

48 Lorenz 76. McInnes 57 writes in a similar way: "She experiences love as a force which estranges her from herself, annuls her will, and drives her into a betrayal of the ties and loyalties which have sustained her from birth and shaped her sense of her identity."

49 See Stiefel 30 and Politzer 139. Indeed, the symbolism of the cave is very interesting and can add greatly to a fuller understanding of this scene. Caves were the birth places of such gods as Zeus and Hermes, according to Manfred Lurker. *Wörterbuch der Symbolik* (Stuttgart: Kröner, 1988) 314.

50 Grillparzer, *Vlieβ* 877 (1549-1550). See also Politzer 140.

51 Grillparzer, *Vlieβ* 912 (631). See Stiefel 16. He writes of this specific situation: "Medea ist dem Ruhelosen [Jason] bloß das Mittel zum größten Abenteuer, die Verkörperung des Vließes, das er erobern will" (27). Yates 90 observes that Jason uses Medea as "a mere tool" in his quest for the fleece.

  Christa Sutter Baker, "Unifying Patterns in Grillparzer's *Das goldene Vlieβ*," *Modern Language Notes* 89 (1974): 393, maintains: "In forcing her to help him obtain the fleece, he ensnares her free will."

52 Grillparzer, *Vließ* 886 (1732).

53 Grillparzer, *Vließ* 886 (1741).

54 Grillparzer, *Vließ* 886 (1742).

55 Grillparzer, *Vließ* 888 (1771-1772).

56 Rismondo 140.

57 T. C. Dunham, "Medea in Athens and Vienna," *Monatshefte* 38 (1946): 218, writes: "The burying of the chest and the golden fleece symbolizes her abandonment of the old and her determination henceforth to adapt herself to Hellenic customs and make herself more acceptable to Jason."

58 Hoesch 19.

59 Brauckmann and Everwien 96.

60 Grillparzer, *Werke* vol. 1 718. This reference and the two following concern *Sappho*, which is in the same volume as *Vließ*.

61 Grillparzer, *Werke* vol. 1 740.

62 Grillparzer, *Werke* 785. Wick 23 writes about the significance of clothing: ". . . das Motiv des Kleidertauschs [spielt] bei Grillparzer eine so bedeutende Rolle . . . in der sinnbildlichen Darstellung seelischer Wandlungserlebnisse. Er zeigt sich darin noch der Tradition des Jesuitendramas verhaftet."

63 A variety of interpretations have been given to the fleece itself. Yates 88 refers to it as "a sign of Medea's betrayal" when Jason displays it before Aietes at the conclusion of *Die Argonauten*. Böckmann 40 associates possession of the fleece with the symbolic "Schuldverflechtung des menschlichen Handelns," and alludes to the concept that by burying it, Medea attempts to free herself from her past in order to begin a new life among the Greeks. The connection of the fleece and guilt is also taken up by Naumann 114, although he adds the opposing concept of "Sühne" to his interpretation of the fleece's sumbolic nature. Stiefel 120 compares stealing the fleece with the biblical story of the fall of Adam and Eve. In this context, the fleece resembles the apple taken from the tree (as done by Jason); the tree is also guarded by a serpent. Moreover, in both traditions the desire for improvement (involving hubris) serves as the motivating force behind all action (see Stiefel 123). Stiefel 125 explains further that Jason returns with the fleece in a different mental state, he has died partially. This corresponds to the notion of the fall: "Der Sündenfall bedeutet den Verlust des Lebens um der Erkenntnis willen; die Austreibung aus dem Paradies ist ein Gang in den Tod." Finally Rismondo 136 refers to the fleece as "ein in die Wirklichkeit versetzter Traum," and explains further that in politi-

cal terms it represents the personification "einer imperialen Idee," more specifically "einer völkerüberspannenden 'Reichsidee'" (137).

64 Stiefel 44 writes of this: "Die Jagd nach diesem Idol wurde für Grillparzer zum Inbegriff aller menschlichen Abenteuer, des menschlichen Lebens und Strebens überhaupt. . . . Die Menschen kreisen um das Vließ wie die Gestirne um die Sonne." Here we see an example of the symbolic nature of literature for Grillparzer.   In this instance, we receive a "Bild der Wahrheit" (see note 15).

65 Grillparzer, *Vließ* 922 (924-925).

66 Hoesch 21.

67 Stiefel 24.

68 Grillparzer, *Vließ* 915 (716-718).

69 Grillparzer, *Vließ* 911 (587-588).

70 Grillparzer, *Vließ* 919 (877).

71 Grillparzer, *Vließ* 920 (892-896).

72 Grillparzer, *Vließ* 929 (1164-1165).

73 Grillparzer, *Vließ* 930 (1196).

74 Grillparzer, *Vließ* 947 (1743-1744).

75 See Grillparzer, *Vließ* 947 (172): "Liebend folgt ich, das Weib, dem Mann."

76 Grillparzer, *Vließ* 948 (1748).

77 See Grillparzer, *Vließ* 932-933 (1262-1279).

78 Grillparzer, *Vließ* 949 (1786-1795). See also Stiefel 41 and 146. Here he writes that murdering the children is "die einzige Möglichkeit Medeas, den Kindern ihr eigenes Schicksal zu ersparen" (146).

79 August Sauer, and Reinhold Bachmann, eds. *Franz Grillparzer. Sämtliche Werke. Historisch-kritische Gesamtausgabe* part 1, vol. 17 (Vienna: Schroll, 1931).   In his chapter comparing themes of various Medea dramas, Friedrich notes "Medeas Trennung von den Kindern hat also nicht erst Grillparzer erfunden . . ., aber er erst versetzt sie in die letzte, verzweifeltste Einsamkeit, läßt sie von allen, auch von den Kindern verraten werden . . ." (26). See also Friedrich 29.

80 Grillparzer, *Vließ* 945 (1684-1686).

81 Politzer 145 writes of the betrayal motif: "Erst . . . [Grillparzer] zeigt, daß der Kampf zwischen Medea und Kreusa schließlich um die Seele der Kinder geht und daß die leibliche Mutter im Begriffe steht, ihn zu verlieren."

82 See Friedrich 26.

83 Stiefel 41.

84 Stiefel 133.

85 Stiefel 132.

86 Wick 110 expresses much the same notion when she remarks: "Die Rachetat bedeutet also keine Rückkehr zum Kolchertum, eher eine Loslösung, eine Befreiung von jenen Mächten . . . . [Medea] erhebt sich innerlich zu einer Höhe, die jenseits von Kolchertum und Griechentum, von Hass und Liebe, von Wünschen und Hoffen, aber auch jenseits von allem sinnerfüllten Sein einsam emporragt."

87 Grillparzer, *Vlieβ* 968 (2366-2367).

88 Grillparzer, *Vlieβ* 968 (2373-2374).

89 Grillparzer, *Werke* vol. 1 248.

90 Friedrich Kaufmann, *German Dramatists of the 19th Century* (1940; Freeport, N.Y.: Books for Libraries Press, 1970) 80.

Chapter IV

1 Herbert Seidler, *Studien zu Grillparzer und Stifter* (Vienna, Cologne, Graz: Böhlau, 1970) 136.

2 W. E. Yates, *Grillparzer. A Critical Introduction* (Cambridge: Cambridge University Press, 1972) 166, writes of the psychological nature of the drama: "The whole emphasis in the play . . . is on 'psychology'-that is, on portrayal of character; and it achieves its dramatic power partly by the sympathetic portrayal of the heroine, who unsuspectingly brings herself to tragedy, but also by the precision and circumstantiality with which the development of the tragedy is shown."

Wiltraud Wick, "Innere Entwicklung der Charaktere in Grillparzers Drama," diss., Tübingen, 1951, 137 also maintains that the psychological perspective is of greatest importance: "Es geht dem Dichter auch in diesem Drama in erster Linie nicht um die Darstellung einer Idee, sondern um seelische Probleme und um metaphysische, soweit sie mit jenen im engsten Zusammenhang stehen."

Heinz Politzer, *Franz Grillparzer oder das abgründige Biedermeier* (Vienna, Munich, Zurich: Molden, 1972) 210, also alludes to the psychological aspect of the work: "Was in der Seele des Mädchens vorgeht, ist von den Gesetzen der Psychologie bestimmt, bis in einem Aufschwung, der ebenso folgerichtig wie unerwartet einsetzt, der Heldin tragische Statur verliehen wird."

In addition to the psychological reading, several critics have described the biographical aspects of the work. Raoul Auernheimer, *Franz Grillparzer. Der Dichter Österreichs.* (Vienna and Munich: Amalthea, 1972) 62 - 65, deals with the biographical aspect in great detail.

O. Paul Straubinger, *"Des Meeres und der Liebe Wellen* im Urteil der Zeit," *Grillparzer-Forum Forchtenstein* 4 (1968): 12-23, examines the biographical perspectives of this play extensively.   He writes, for example: "Schuldbewußt verflicht der Dichter unter dem Eindruck ihres Todes [Charlotte Paumgarttens] (16. September 1827) die Episode mit der Lampe in den dramatischen Höhepunkt der Handlung" (12). See also 13.

Grillparzer himself alludes to elements of his own life as they apply to the work [quoted in August Sauer and Reinhold Backmann, ed., *Franz Grillparzer. Historisch-kritische Gesamtausgabe* part I, vol. 19 (Vienna: Schroll, 1939)] "Im 3 [sic] Akt zu gebrauchen, wie damals Charlotte [von Paumgartten], als sie den ganzen Abend wortkarger und kälter gewesen war, als sonst, beim Weggehen, an der Haustür das Licht auf den Boden setzte, und sagte: ich muß mir die Arme freimachen, um dich zu küssen" (196).   "Hero etwas vom Gleichgewichte der S-z [Marie Smolk von Smolenitz]" (Sauer and Backmann pt. 1, vol. 19, p. 232). "Hero und Leander. Eine wunder-schöne Frau [Marie von Smolenitz] reizte mich, ihre Gestalt, wenn auch nicht ihr Wesen, durch alle diese Wechselfälle durchzuführen" [quoted in Peter Frank and Karl Pörnbacher, ed., Franz Grillparzer. *Sämtliche Werke. Ausgewählte Briefe, Gespräche, Berichte* vol. 4 (Munich: Hanser, 1965) 177.

Martin Kölling, "Verzagen an zerstörter Hoffnung," *Gerettete Ordnung. Grillparzers Dramen,* ed. Bernhard Budde and Ulrich Schmidt (Frankfurt am Main, Bern, New York, Paris: Lang, 1987) 151, mentions a possible political correlation between the work and Austria of Grillparzer's day.   He comments: "Für den aufmerksamen Zeitgenossen konnte kein Zweifel bestehen, daß dieses Stück den spezi-fisch österreichischen Alltag in kritischer Weise reflektierte."

Seidler 137 writes in broader terms of the socio-historic nature: "Grillparzer gestaltet immer wieder den Widerspruch zwischen der Unvollkommenheit und Brüchigkeit der menschlich-geschichtlichen Welt und der göttlichen Seinsordnung in der Gesamtschöpfung."

Bruce Thompson, *Franz Grillparzer,* Twayne's World Author Series 637 (Boston: Twayne Publishers, 1981) 65, identifies the action centering around Hero's collapse of resolution in the light of a "fall from grace." Thompson becomes more general when he writes: "It is the limitations of the ideal that Grillparzer is exposing in this play. . ." (66).

3   Franz Grillparzer, *Sämtliche Werke, Ausgewählte Briefe, Gespräche, Berichte* vol. 2, ed. Peter Frank and Karl Pörnbacher (Munich: Hanser, 1961) 17

(lines 200-206). All quotations from the text are taken from this edition and will be referred to as Grillparzer, *Meeres*. Each reference includes the page and line numbers. Politzer 214 comments on this passage: "Aus guten Gründen hat sie, was noch an kindlicher Neigung und töchterlichem Schutzbedürfnis in ihr verblieben ist, auf den Bruder des Vaters, den Priester übertragen."

4 Sauer and Backmann, *Franz Grillparzer* part 1, vol. 19, 198.

5 Sauer and Backmann, *Franz Grillparzer* part 1, vol. 19, 233.

6 Frank and Pörnbacher, *Franz Grillparzer* vol. 4, 641.

7 Politzer 223 notes, ". . . der väterliche Oheim [wird] zum Vollzugsorgan des Schicksals."

8 Grillparzer, *Meeres* 59 (1365).
   Konrad Schaum, "Grillparzers *Des Meeres und der Liebe Wellen*: Seelendrama und Kulturkritik," *Jahrbuch der Grillparzer-Gesellschaft* 11 (1974): 110, maintains: "Ob der Priester selbst es voll erfaßt oder nicht, die Haltung des Priesters ist nichts als Täuschung und Lüge, und es ist dieser Abgrund scheinbaren Rechts, in dem das Menschliche versinkt." See also Yates 175.

9 Politzer 226 remarks: "Ein Frauenwesen tritt vor uns hin, [. . .] Erweckerin, Schlafwandlerin, Vollstreckerin und Opfer eines seelisch-körperlichen Verhängnisses, der Leidenschaft . . ."

10 Grillparzer, *Meeres* 45 (997).

11 Grillparzer, *Meeres* 73 (1750-1753).

12 Grillparzer, *Meeres* 84 (2031-2032). See also Seidler 63.

13 Grillparzer, *Meeres* 23 (363-369).

14 Grillparzer, *Meeres* 19 (269). Yates 169 alludes to the symbolic nature of the dove for Hero when he associates Hero's stroking of the feathers with her stroking Leander's head. See also Thompson, *Franz Grillparzer* 67.

15 Grillparzer, *Meeres* 44 (982-986). See also Schaum 100.

16 Grillparzer, *Meeres* 82-83 (1996-1997). Several critics write about the fact that the Priest represents the inner, contemplative sphere of moral norms from which the conflict for Hero and Leander eventually stems.
   E. E. Papst, *Grillparzer*: Des Meeres und der Liebe Wellen (London: Arnold, 1967) 42, criticizes those who see the Priest merely as "the embodiment of an unnatural moral law." His law is not *unnatural* at all, for him (!), but it becomes so for Hero. The Priest's failure lies in his continuing attempt to impose this behavior on Hero. Here we see the unbending moral code typical of fathers, as expressed in chapter I.

Elsewhere Papst refers to the *vita contemplativa* as *Sammlung* when he writes: "In the last resort it is the Priest's function to uphold the true nature of *Sammlung* in all its visionary and mediatory aspirations, in the light of which Hero's conception of it verges on outright travesty" (44).

Thompson 66 expresses a similar notion: ". . . the priest is only acting in accordance with his conscience as the representative of what *he* regards as an ideal mode of existence."

17 Yates 176 describes the positive aspect of the laws when he writes: "But while he [the Priest] acts ruthlessly, the demanding code of duty he represents is essentially a positive one."

18 See Papst 44.

19 Papst notes that the conflict between Hero and the Priest begins in Act IV. Previously the conflict existed between Hero and Leander, see 41-42.

20 Critics disagree on this notion. Yates 175 writes, for example, that all the Priest's actions "are clearly determined by his unrelenting hope that he may still restore her [Hero's] equanimity and rescue her for her priestly office." Kölling 163 maintains: "Identität, welche die Liebeserfahrung hervorbringt und welche sich den verordneten Normen nicht mehr fügt, wird vom Oberpriester zerstört, um Hero wieder verfügbar zu machen."

21 Papst 42.

22 Grillparzer, *Meeres* 59 (1365-1366).

23 Grillparzer, *Meeres* 61 (1430-1435).

24 Papst 42.

25 Thompson, *Franz Grillparzer* 64. See also 66. Yates 175 also mentions this phenomenon: "Admittedly, the priest does not at this stage realize the depth of her involvement; his tragic limitation is that his own purity of devotion leads him consistently to underestimate the strength of her feelings for Leander. He has, however, seen her collapse . . ., and his continued severity shows at the very least an unattractive lack of imagination and sensitivity." This is, at best, a mild statement!

26 Yates 174.

27 Grillparzer, *Meeres* 13 (73-76). The Priest mentions this as well: "Du weißt, es war seit undenkbaren Zeiten / Begnadet von den Göttern unser Stamm / Mit Priesterehren, Zeichen und Orakeln, / Zu sprechen liebten sie durch unsern Mund" (16, lines 173-176).

28 Sauer and Backmann, *Franz Grillparzer* part 1, vol. 19, 191. Grillparzer writes further: "Sie hat bis zu ihrem Zusammentreffen mit Leander in

völliger Unbefangenheit gelebt. Von früher Jugend dem Tempeldienste gewidmet sagt das würdige, alles Gemeine ausschließende, reinliche, Gemütsruhe bewahrende desselben, ihrem aufs Rechte gestellten Sinne vorzugsweise zu. Die Priesterwürde war in ihrer Familie erblich, und sie rechnet sichs zum höchsten Glücke das hohe Vorrecht ihrer Ahnen in ihrer Person zu bewahren und fortzusetzen" (Sauer and Backmann, *Franz Grillparzer* part 1, vol. 19, 193).

29 Grillparzer, *Meeres* 14 (119-120).

30 No other critics deal with the dualism *vita activa* vs. *vita contemplativa* in these exact terms. Others do allude to this notion, however. Papst 12, for example, refers to the *vita contemplativa* as *Sammlung*. Kölling refers to the *vita contemplativa* as *Ordnung* and recognizes isolation as the price of order, see 153. Yates 166 adds to the necessity of isolation the facet of renunciation of sensuality. As a priestess, Hero "must forswear all earthly love; and such renunciation proves to be completely at odds with her true nature." Grillparzer himself focuses on the renunciation of love in his earliest diary entry dealing with the play: "Hero und Leander. Wie kein Mann sie rühren kann, und sie Priesterin der Venus wird" (Frank and Pörnbacher, *Franz Grillparzer* vol. 4, 356).

31 The seemingly complicated combination of Hero's escapist attitude coupled with her defective comprehension of her self-chosen existence is reflected in the comments of several critics. Yates 167, for example, explains that Hero chooses to become a priestess: "Her 'choice', in fact, is a piece of escapism, irresponsible because uncomprehending." Politzer 213-214 posits a similar notion concerning escapism: "In der Bindung an den reinen Diensten sucht das Mädchen die Lösung einer trüben häuslichen Situation. Ihr Entschluß ist auf Flucht, also auf Verneinung, gegründet, was niemals Gutes verspricht."
       Helmut Himmel, "Grillparzers Trauerspiel *Des Meeres und der Liebe Wellen*," *Literaturwissenschaftliches Jahrbuch* 14 (1973): 361, adds that Hero wants to avoid putting herself into a situation similar to her mother's: "Im I. Akt sieht sie in ihrem Priesterberuf einen Weg, der Dienstbarkeit zu entgehen, die die Frau dem Gatten unterwirft-wie sie es an ihrer Mutter sieht . . . ." Later he explains: "Die Hingabe an die Göttin soll sie vor der Hingabe an einen Menschen bewahren" (363).
       Finally Seidler 51 examines what Hero perceives will be the result of her escape into the priesthood: "Hero sieht den Frieden im Gegensatz zur abrupten, wirren Welt; nur in der Gleichförmigkeit ist stiller Selbstbesitz, *ihre* Lebensvoraussetzung gegeben."
       The notion of Hero's false perception of her existence as priestess is also extensively treated. Kölling 155, for example, writes: "Doch bereits im ersten Aufzug enthüllt das Stück diese falsche Vorstellung in den Ungereimtheiten von Heros Rede, wenn Hero ihre Identität im heiligen Bezirk zu finden glaubt, dessen Starrheit sie doch ahnt." Wick 128 also understands this phenomenon when comparing Hero, Medea and Sappho: "Wenn wir der Heldin dieses Dramas Sappho und Medea zur Seite stellen, so kommt ihr Entwicklungsgang in den Anfängen

mehr dem Sapphos gleich; denn die Einseitigkeit ihrer Existenz ist nicht Folge einer Naturbegebenheit wie Medeas Verwurzelung im kolchischen Boden, sondern das Ergebnis einer freien Wahl, einer Wahl allerdings, die die Bedingtheit der Seele übersieht oder vielmehr nicht kennt."

Bruce Thompson, *A Sense of Irony. An Examination of the Tragedies of Franz Grillparzer* (Bern: Lang, 1976) 73, writes: "during the first Act, therefore, it is suggested to the audience that Hero is entering the temple as Priestess for the wrong reasons. This is conveyed by her attitude to the ceremony, by her inadequate conception of what the office entails, and by her awareness of the fact that she is escaping from something of which she has only a limited knowledge and experience." See also Thompson, *Franz Grillparzer* 62 and 65.

Politzer 211 captures the notion of Hero's misperception when he states: "Hero nimmt ihre Priesterschaft nicht so sehr als eine Verbindlichkeit auf sich wie als Privileg in Anspruch."

Norbert Griesmayer, *Das Bild des Partners in Grillparzers Dramen* (Vienna, Stuttgart: Braumüller, 1972) 211, points to Hero's naivety: "Die Bilder sind vielmehr kindlich naiver Versuch Heros, eine Festigkeit anzunehmen, sich vor vielen Zügen einer Welt abzuschirmen, die einem tatsächlich noch völlig unsicheren Ich unverständlich und nur bedrohlich ist . . . ."

32   Wick 137 recognizes the improper nature of the priesthood for Hero: "Die Wurzel aller tragischen Verwicklungen liegt nicht in der Mißachtung der Gesetze, die das Priesteramt Hero vorschreibt, . . . sondern einmal in der Einrichtung der Welt selbst, aber mehr noch in der Tatsache, daß Hero aus ihrer Welt heraustritt und sich einem Dienste widmet, der ihrem Wesen nicht voll gerecht wird." The conflict does not stem from the fact that Hero improperly becomes a priestess, but rather from her failure to abide by the laws of the priesthood. This becomes the catalyst for the Priest's action. Hero is at a stage in life where she is trying to establish herself as an individual-she is at the threshold of individuation. Indeed, she makes the incorrect decision to become a priestess, incorrect because she regrets it just after it is too late to alter. Then she rejects the priesthood by acting against the priestly code of law. It is this final action which brings the Priest into opposition with Hero and Leander. Thus the tragic action does indeed depend on the rejection of the laws.

Thompson, *Sense of Irony* 74 notes: "The tragedy consists not in the fact that Hero's erotic feelings are at present subconscious, but that her potentialities for love have not yet been revealed to her."

33   Grillparzer, *Meeres* 21 (319-320).

34   Grillparzer, *Meeres* 15 (139). Papst 29 comments: "Thus, even before the tension within Hero is given specific form by her encounter with Leander, its presence is suggested in her character as seen through the eyes of those who know her."

35 Grillparzer, *Meeres* 28 (501).

36 Papst 27. See also Thompson, *Franz Grillparzer* 63.

37 Grillparzer, *Meeres* 28 (502). Seidler 51 notes: "In der Weihe spricht Hero nur Formeln: ihr ist das Priesterhafte keine persönliche Sache. Nur die innere Sicherheit sucht sie, die fühlt sie durch die wirre Welt bedroht."

38 Grillparzer, *Meeres* 35 (728-729).

39 Kölling 162 interprets this action as the indication of a "noch unbewußte Auflehnung," while Politzer 224 posits that the song itself is the reflection of inner emotion, specifically, love.

40 Grillparzer, *Meeres* 37 (767-768).

41 Grillparzer, *Meeres* 37 (786-789).

42 Seidler 53 posits that Hero believes she feels compassion for Leander: "Aber ihre Sprache verrät Tieferes: in der Eröffnung der Stelle durch das Leda-Motiv, in der Verdichtung der gefühlhaften Worte in den Anrufen an Leander, in der Art dieser Worte, die Freude, Glück, Hinneigung gestalten, endlich in der schlichten, aber bewegten Satzführung. Auch ihre Einstellung zur Welt ist geändert: sie hebt Leander aus der Außenwelt heraus und stellt ihn mit sich selbst ihr gegenüber, und sie erfaßt die Priesterwelt selbst nur mehr als Brauch und Gesetz, nicht mehr als Wunschbild."

43 Papst 29 remarks: "It is convenient, and appropriate to the structure of the play, to draw a broad distinction between two phases of action: a first phase of inner conflict located within Hero; and a second phase, in which the tension within Hero is resolved, but only through projection into the objective sphere of the outside world, where it produces a clash of wills between characters and culminates in her conflict with the Priest and its fateful consequences."

44 See Papst 39.

45 Grillparzer, *Meeres* 67 (1591-1593).

46 Griesmayer 211 alludes to this dual process when he writes: "Zugleich wird bei den Bildern Heros eine innere Widersprüchlichkeit und Unsicherheit sichtbar. Ihre Bilder, sowie die Leanders zeigen eine deutliche Isolierung und Gefährdung."

Walter Naumann, *Grillparzer. Das dichterische Werk* (Stuttgart: Kohlhammer, 1956) 69, writes: "Grillparzer sieht den Weg der Selbstgestaltung zwischen den Polen der Selbstbewahrung und der Selbstaufgabe, Symbol dieser Teilnahme ist die Liebe. . . ."

Yates 178 comments: "As surely as the priest knows that his standards are right for the priesthood, Hero knows that her love was right for her, she knows intuitively that for her, 'Ganzheit' cannot lie in priestly isolation but must lie in union with Leander." Griesmayer 208 perceives the general importance of love in the work: "Mit der Tragödie von Hero und Leander haben wir wieder ein Werk vor uns, bei dem das dramatische Geschehen wesentlich vom Raum der intimsten zwischen-menschlichen Beziehungen, vom Raum der Liebe, bestimmt ist."

47 Frank and Pörnbacher, *Franz Grillparzer* vol. 4, 356. See also Wick 134.

48 Grillparzer, *Meeres* 45 (1019-1020).

49 See Thompson, *Franz Grillparzer* 67 and Yates 170. Papst places the ceremonial jewelry on equal terms with the cloak in terms of symbolic value, see 35.

50 Grillparzer, *Meeres* 46 (1045-1048).

51 Grillparzer, *Meeres* 47 (1058-1061).

52 Papst 47 writes: "The action . . . falls . . . into exactly two equal halves. The invisible frontier between them runs with the mathematical precision of an equator through the 1060th of the play's 2120 lines."

53 Grillparzer, *Meeres* 51 (1185-1186).

54 See Grillparzer, *Meeres* 52-53 (1211-1229).

55 Thompson, *Franz Grillparzer* 64 refers to Grillparzer's diary entry quoted above (see note 47) when he writes: "It was Grillparzer's intention to depict her now [in Act IV] as a mature woman, whose sensuality has been aroused and who possesses a new self-assurance, oblivious to outside pressures . . . ." Yates 168 maintains: "In Act IV, the amorality of innocence has given way to a more mature amorality, that of devotion to love." See Politzer 224.

56 See Yates 173-174. He writes: "She is out of reach of that kind of creative self-possession which he [the Priest] teaches, but in her 'feeling of being a woman' she is now at least fully herself, and she stands in open dramatic conflict with him, spurning the duty and standards which he represents."

57 Grillparzer, *Meeres* 72 (1725-1733).

58 Kölling 163 summarizes this phenomenon simply by writing: "Mit der veränderten Einstellung zu sich selbst wandelt sich auch Heros Verhältnis zur Ordnung." Yates 166 also understands this point exactly when he writes that ". . . the dramatic conflict in *Des Meeres und der Liebe Wellen* is built on a disparity in standards which reveals itself only gradually, but which finally proves to be absolutely irreconcilable." Thompson, *Sense of Irony* 68 writes in a similar vein, stating that in this

play we are concerned "with a love which comes into conflict with the regulations of an institution." Kölling 147 describes the opposing "camps" in the following way: "Meeresstille und demütig kontemplativer Liebe als Symbolen der verordneten falschen Normen [. . .] stehen Hoffnung, Leidenschaft und Solidarität gegenüber."

Joachim Kaiser, "Grillparzers Dramatik," *Handbuch des deutschen Dramas,* ed. Walter Hinck (Düsseldorf: Bagel, 1980) 232, notes that Hero's character reflects an on-going change: "Das lebendige Wesen Hero konstituiert sich hier anders: aus immer neuen, verschiedenen, ja widersprüchlichen Reaktionsweisen, die unversehens zum Bilde einer bewegungsvollen Einheit konfigurieren." This change has reached its summit of expression in Act IV.

59 See Politzer 210 and Naumann 69.

60 Politzer 229.

61 Yates 173 writes: "All these deceptions are necessitated by, and are reminders of, the wrongfulness of her love ('wrongfulness' not in an absolute sense, but in relation to the vow to which she has committed herself)."

62 Grillparzer, *Meeres* 81 (1948-1950).

63 Papst 12.

64 Seidler 57 writes most convincingly of this concept and summarizes Hero's entire development: "Ursprünglich ist Heros Ziel die Welt der Sammlung, die ihr im Priestertum erreichbar scheint; die Welt des Alltags ist ihr fremd. Nun bricht aus der ihr fremden Welt die Macht der Liebe in ihr Leben ein und schafft eine neue Erlebniskonzentration in der Ausschließlichkeit der liebenden Hinwendung ans Du." Papst 38 writes of the unification of *Ich* and *Du* when describing the basis of the drama: ". . . the essence of her [Hero's] tragedy is precisely the loss of her self to that which is extrinsic, foreign, 'other'." Yates 176 also alludes to this concept: "Her love for Leander has become for her an authority far more forceful than that of the service to which she innocently dedicated herself." See also Thompson, *Franz Grillparzer* 64. He maintains that death comes because of "Hero's own complete identification with her lover."

65 Grillparzer, *Meeres* 85 (2051-2053).

66 See Papst 46.

67 Griesmayer 222. Papst 53 sees Hero's death in the same terms: ". . . Hero dies passively, not because she has found herself, but precisely because she has surrendered all her being to Leander." This surrender is the summit of Hero's individuation.

68 See Politzer 229.

69 Sauer and Backmann, *Franz Grillparzer* part 1, vol. 19, 233. A further note by Grillparzer demonstrates the Priest's defective understanding of Hero's nature when the Priest speaks of her in Act II as "sich selbstbewußt und klar" (Sauer and Backmann, *Franz Grillparzer* part 1, vol. 19, 233). The Priest, as we have seen, could not be farther from the truth in his statement.

70 Kölling 157 writes at some length about the notion of humane treatment: "Grillparzers Trauerspiel zeigt, wie wenig Hoffnung in den bewußten Anspruch auf Humanität gesetzt wird." He also notes, when comparing this play to Goethe's *Iphigenie*: "Auch ist das gemeinsame Merkmal aller Beziehungen nicht mehr gegenseitiger Respekt und sich entwickelndes Handeln [wie bei *Iphigenie*], sondern Über- und Unterordnung in allen Figurenrelationen" (158).

71 Naumann 97 writes: "Aber als, durch die Liebe, die dunklen Kräfte sie geweckt und gereift haben, ist es zu spät: denn diese Kräfte überwältigen sie mit ihrer Eigengesetzlichkeit, vernichten sie und lassen sie nicht zur Sammlung zurückkehren. Das ist die Tragik der Hero."

72 Frank and Pörnbacher, ed., *Franz Grillparzer* vol. 1 (1960) 248.

73 See Himmel 382.

74 See also Kölling 161.

Chapter V

1 See: Hartmut Reinhardt, "Hebbels Dramatik," *Handbuch des deutschen Dramas*, ed. Walter Hinck (Düsseldorf: Bagel, 198). 244-51.

Carol J. Ross, "Schiller and Hebbel: Ideas and Characters and the Portrayal of Women," diss., University of Toronto, 1974, 94-119.

Wolfgang Ritter, *Hebbels Psychologie und dramatische Charaktergestaltung*, Marburger Beiträge zur Germanistik 43 (Marburg: Elwert, 1973).

Mechthild Keller, "Anmerkungen zu Hebbels Dramentechnik: Motivation und Handlung," *Friedrich Hebbel: Neue Studien zu Werk und Wirkung*, ed. Hilmar Grundmann, Steinburger Studien 3 (Heide, West Germany: Boyen, 1982) 117-129.

Regina Fourie, "Friedrich Hebbels Dramentheorie. Eine kritische Darstellung," *Acta Germanica* 15 (1982): 41-51.

2 Friedrich Hebbel, *Werke*, vol. 1, ed. Gerhard Fricke, Werner Keller and Karl Pörnbacher (Munich: Hanser, 1963) 331. (All references to *Maria Magdalene* are taken from this edition and will be refered to as "Hebbel, *Maria Magdalene*." Subsequent references to other volumes of this edition will be referred to as "Hebbel, *Werke*" and will be followed by volume number.)

3 The word "Tod," or related words, could be the subject of an interesting study in itself.

See also Georg Pilz, *Deutsche Kindesmord-Tragödien: Wagner, Goethe, Hebbel, Hauptmann* (Munich: Oldenbourg, 1982) 71. He writes: "Die häufige Verwendung der Wörter 'sterben', und 'Tod' u. ä . . . trägt zudem dazu bei, daß das Todesmotiv im gesamten Drama unüberhörbar bleibt."

4 Hebbel, *Maria Magdalene* 331-332.

5 See Hebbel, *Maria Magdalene* 345-346. Here Anton states: "Mein Vater arbeitete sich, weil er sich Tag und Nacht keine Ruhe gönnte, schon in seinem dreißigsten Jahre zu Tode . . . ." See Pilz 77.

6 Hebbel, *Maria Magdalene* 333.

7 Hebbel, *Maria Magdalene* 334.

8 Hebbel, *Maria Magdalene* 334. At the end of this statement, Therese remarks: "Die Welt wird immer klüger, vielleicht kommt noch einmal die Zeit, wo einer sich schämen muß, wenn er nicht auf dem Seil tanzen kann!" Here we see an example of Hebbel's notion of the development of history, which plays an important role in his dramatic theory. The primary expression of this comes in Hebbel's "Mein Wort über das Drama" (Hebbel, *Werke*, vol. 3 (1965), 545-546):
"Das Drama stellt den Lebensprozeß an sich dar. Und zwar nicht bloß in dem Sinne, daß es uns das Leben in seiner ganzen Breite vorführt, was die epische Dichtung sich ja wohl auch zu tun erlaubt, sondern in dem Sinne, daß es uns das bedenkliche Verhältnis vergegenwärtigt, worin das aus dem ursprünglichen Nexus entlassene Individuum dem Ganzen, dessen Teil es trotz seiner unbegreiflichen Freiheit noch immer geblieben ist, gegenübersteht. Das Drama ist demnach, wie es sich für die höchste Kunstform schicken will, auf gleiche Weise ans Seiende, wie ans Werdende verwiesen: ans Seiende, indem es nicht müde werden darf, die ewige Wahrheit zu wiederholen, daß das Leben als Vereinzelung, die nicht Maß zu halten weiß, die Schuld nicht bloß zufällig erzeugt, sondern sie notwendig und wesentlich mit einschließt und bedingt; ans Werdende, indem es an immer neuen Stoffen, wie die wandelnde Zeit und ihr Niederschlag, die Geschichte, sie ihm entgegenbringt, darzutun hat, daß der Mensch, wie die Dinge um ihn her sich auch verändern mögen, seiner Natur und seinem Geschick nach ewig derselbe bleibt."
See also: Herbert Kaiser, *Friedrich Hebbel. Geschichtliche Interpretation des dramatischen Werks* (Munich: Fink, 1983) 53 and:
Peter Hagboldt, "Hebbel," *Monatshefte* 22 (1930): 204.
Reinhardt, "Hebbels Dramatik" 248, writes: "Geschichte gilt ihm [Hebbel] als universaler Entwicklungs- und Fortschrittsprozeß, in den die individuellen Handlungen so verflochten sind, daß ihr partikulares Wollen (und ihr tragisches Scheitern) einem höheren Zweck dient . . . ."
Closely related to the development of history is the notion of a time of change or crisis in history, as indicated by Therese's statement quoted above. Kaiser 53 writes of this concept: "Das 'bürgerliche

Trauerspiel in drei Akten' (1843) gestaltet den geschichtlichen Übergang von älteren, statischen zu neueren, dynamischen Lebensformen
um die Mitte des 19. Jahrhunderts als eine Umbruchsituation, die eine
furchtbare gesellschaftliche Vernichtungsmechanik hervorbringt."
See also: Sten G. Flygt, *Friedrich Hebbel*, Twayne's World Author
Series 56 (New York: Twayne Publishers, 1968) 68; Reinhardt,
"Hebbels Dramatik" 248; and Ross 102.

9 It is interesting to compare this dream with, for example, Adam's dream
   in Kleist's *Der zerbrochene Krug*, which foretells what happens in that
   play. The importance of dreams is also expressed in Hebbel's *Trauerspiel in Sicilien*, Hebbel, *Werke*, vol. 1, 398 (lines 265-66): "Was die
   bedeuten, / Steht nicht im Traumbuch."

10 Hebbel, *Maria Magdalene* 335.

11 Hebbel, *Maria Magdalene* 336.

12 Hebbel, *Maria Magdalene* 367.

13 See Hebbel, *Maria Magdalene* 365. Here Klara explains:

    "O frag noch, was alles zusammenkommt, um ein armes Mädchen
    verrückt zu machen. Spott und Hohn von allen Seiten, als du auf die
    Akademie gezogen warst und nichts mehr von dir hören ließest. Die
    denkt noch an den!-Die glaubt, daß Kindereien ernsthaft gemeint
    waren!-Erhält sie Briefe?-Und dann die Mutter! Halte dich zu deinesgleichen! Hochmut tut nimmer gut! Der Leonhard ist doch recht brav,
    alle wundern sich, daß du ihn über die Achsel ansiehst. Dazu mein
    eignes Herz. Hat er dich vergessen, zeig ihm, daß auch du-o Gott!"

14 Hebbel, *Maria Magdalene* 338.

15 Hebbel, *Maria Magdalene* 340.

16 Hebbel, *Maria Magdalene* 341.

17 Klaus Ziegler, *Mensch und Welt in der Tragödie Friedrich Hebbels*
    (Darmstadt: Wissenschaftliche Buchgesellschaft, 1966) 104, comments:
    "So erscheint Anton als Personifikation und aktiver Hauptexponent
    jener anonymen Gesellschaft, die Klaras Denken, Handeln und Schicksal bestimmt; aber zugleich ist er auch wiederum willenlos getriebenes,
    sklavisches Objekt der Gesellschaft." See also Pilz 76 and 77.
       Ross 151 writes: "It is the society with its specific tradition, beliefs,
    and attitudes which destroys Klara, but these attitudes are most
    pronounced in the character of Meister Anton."
       Benno von Wiese, *Die deutsche Tragödie von Lessing bis Hebbel*
    (Hamburg: Hoffmann & Campe, 1955) 610, describes Anton as "der
    starre, eigensinnige, unbelehrbare und bei aller Moral durchaus selbstgerechte Vater, die Spitze eines Systems der patriarchalischen Bevormundung." See also 619.

Several other critics refer to Anton as the representative of society. See: Herbert Kraft, *Poesie der Idee. Die tragische Dichtung Friedrich Hebbels* (Tübingen: Niemayer, 1971) 111;
Ludger Lütkehaus, *Hebbel. Gegenwartsdarstellung. Verdinglichungsproblematik. Gesellschaftskritik* (Heidelberg: Winter, 1976) 71, and Flygt 69.

18 von Wiese 611-12.

19 Wolfgang Wittkowski, "Klara und Mariamne. Kleinstädterin und Königin," *Friedrich Hebbel. Neue Studien zu Werk und Wirkung,* ed. Hilmar Grundmann, Steinburger Studien 3 (Heide, West Germany: Boyen, 1982) 156, writes, Meister Anton ". . . stilisiert sich auf der Bühne der sozialen Öffentlichkeit zum tragisch-heroischen Opfer letztlich seiner einzigartigen und unerreichten Kodextreue."

20 Hebbel, *Maria Magdalene* 380.

21 Hebbel, *Maria Magdalene* 348.

22 Hebbel, *Maria Magdalene* 359-360.

23 Hebbel, *Maria Magdalene* 342. (See passage quoted at note 86 for the citation of Klara's version of the Lord's Prayer.)

24 Hebbel, *Maria Magdalene* 352.

25 Hebbel, *Maria Magdalene* 355.

26 Hebbel, *Maria Magdalene* 348.

27 Hebbel, *Maria Magdalene* 340.

28 See Manfred Lurker, *Wörterbuch der Symbolik* (Stuttgart: Kröner, 1988) 792.

29 Lurker 792-793.

30 See Lurker 793.

31 Lurker 793.
C. G. Jung, *The Basic Writings of C. G. Jung,* ed. Violet S. deLaszlo (New York: Modern Library, 1959) 302, writes that water "is the commonest symbol for the unconscious." This develops an interesting correlation with Klara's suicide as a return to the unconscious (see summary of chapter V).

32 See also: John Fetzer, "Water Imagery in *Maria Magdalena*," *German Quarterly* 43 (1970): 715-719 for an interesting examination of how *Wasser* and *Brunnen* are repeated as a preparation for Klara's suicide.

33 Anton's fixation with honor and dishonor is treated by many authors.
    Flygt 71, for example, writes that Anton "drives himself and his family
    to conform to the minutiae of middle-class conventions in order not to
    be the object of pity or scorn. The one thing which he cannot endure is
    to be disgraced, dishonored in the eyes of his own middle class."
    Ross 151 expresses how this extreme fixation dominates Anton,
    explaining that judgment of society and the effects of shame are more
    important to him than "the destruction of his children," ultimately
    resulting from his unchanging attitude. Ross' use of the plural with
    regard to children, however, is confusing since Karl is not destroyed,
    but rather escapes from the situation. See Herbert Kraft 111-114 for a
    discussion of Karl's figure. Kraft concludes by stating: "Zwar ist Karl
    nicht der Garant einer neuen Welt, aber seine Existenz bedeutet Hoff-
    nung auf ihre Möglichkeit" (114). The notion that Karl's leaving brings
    hope seems problematic. Karl has an escapist attitude; how will this
    possibly alter and improve the world situation? Karl runs away from
    his problems and unpleasant life. This does not appear as a construc-
    tive possibility.
       Hartmut Reinhardt, "Friedrich Hebbel: *Maria Magdalena*," *Deutsche
    Dramen*, ed. Harro Müller-Michaels, vol. 1 (Königstein: Athenäum,
    1981) 179-180, also points to the destructive consequence of Anton's
    world view when he remarks: "Indem Meister Anton auf ehrenhafter
    Reputation besteht und um jeden Preis die Schande vermeiden wissen
    will, liefert er sich-und die Familie-um der forcierten Innebewahrung
    willen gerade der undurchschauten Abhängigkeit von Außen aus, stößt
    er die Tochter in ihr tragisches Schicksal hinein." He also notes: "Der
    Tod der Tochter scheint ihm innerlich nicht so zuzusetzen wie der
    Gedanke, daß die Familie nun erst recht ins Gerede kommt, also die
    Furcht vor dem Gerede" (178).
       See also Mary Garland, *Hebbel's Prose Tragedies* (Cambridge:
    Cambridge University Press, 1973) 161. She writes: ". . . Anton aims at
    no more-and no less-than his name: his life's reward shall be judged
    solely by his honest name."
       Lütkehaus 75 also mentions Anton's emphasis on honor: "Die
    menschlich-gesellschaftlichen Interaktionen, die sich auf dieser Basis
    ergeben, stehen unter dem Diktat eines Ehrbegriffs, der bekanntlich
    die öffentliche Ehre, die Reputation meint, der aber nur unzureichend
    erfaßt wird, wenn man sich darauf beschränkt, seine Veräußerlichung
    und Strenge zu inkriminieren." See also Keller 119 und von Wiese 613.

34 Hebbel, *Maria Magdalene* 352. Kraft 108 remarks about this oath: "Mit
    dem erzwungenen Eid Klaras hat am Ende des ersten Akts die Entar-
    tung der bürgerlichen Sittlichkeit ins Äußerliche ihren vollen Ausdruck
    gefunden."
       Keller 120 comments: "Das für Meister Anton lebenerhaltende
    Sich-Anklammern   an   Klaras   gegenwärtige   und   zukünftige
    Unbescholtenheit schärft sein Gespür für die Gefährdung des letzten
    Halts.   Darum muß Klaras verzweifelte Reaktion auf Leonhards
    Verlöbnisbruch einen Verdacht in ihm erregen, dem er nur dadurch

zu begegnen weiß, daß er der Unglücklichen den folgenschweren Schwur abverlangt."

35 Lütkehaus 78 perceives this objectification issue when he writes: "Klara soll sein, was auch Karl sein sollte: Mittel gesellschaftlicher Selbst-darstellung und Selbstrechtfertigung, Objekt eines krankhaften Ehr-Geizes, der sich zwar pflichtgemäß und moralisch versteht, primär aber sublimierter Aggressivität entspringt . . . ." See also 77 and 79.

36 Hebbel, *Maria Magdalene* 340.

37 Hebbel, *Maria Magdalene* 345.

38 Hebbel, *Maria Magdalene* 345.

39 Several authors comment on Leonhard's fixation with the dowry: Kaiser 57 notes: "Sein Interesse an Klara ist weder menschlich begrün-det (er liebt sie nicht) noch gesellschaftlich (er folgt keinem Rollend-ruck), sondern rein egoistisch-materiell."
    See also: Birgit Fenner, *Friedrich Hebbel zwischen Hegel und Freud* (Stuttgart: Klett-Cotta, 1979) 167; Flygt 70 and 71; and:
    Joachim Müller, "Stilkritische Beobachtungen an Hebbels Geschlechter-Dialogen," *Friedrich Hebbel. Neue Studien zu Werk und Wirkung*, ed. Hilmar Grundmann, Steinburger Studien 3 (Heide, West Germany: Boyen, 1982) 135.

40 Kaiser 55. See also Pilz 78.

41 Hebbel, *Maria Magdalene* 371.

42 Hebbel, *Maria Magdalene* 351.

43 See Hebbel, *Maria Magdalene* 339. Here Leonhard states: "Die Zeit benutz ich dazu, der kleinen buckligten Nichte des Bürgermeisters, die so viel bei dem Alten gilt, die seine rechte Hand ist, wie der Gerichts-diener die linke, den Hof zu machen. Versteh mich recht! Ich sagte ihr selbst nichts Angenehmes, ausgenommen ein Kompliment über ihre Haare, die bekanntlich rot sind, ich sagte ihr nur einiges, das ihr wohlgefiel, über dich [Klara]! . . . Warum sollt ichs verschweigen? Geschah es doch in der besten Absicht!"

44 Reinhardt, "Friedrich Hebbel" 174 writes: "Der Eid, den er Klara abgepreßt hat, steht nun unter einer Bedingung, die ihre Lage ausweg-los machen wird: Bräche sie ihren Eid, so triebe sie den Vater in den Tod."

45 Hebbel, *Maria Magdalene* 366-367.

46 Hebbel, *Maria Magdalene* 368.

47 Reinhardt, "Friedrich Hebbel" 176. Garland 178 writes in a similar vein: "But Hebbel also causes Leonhard to use the very word which

drives Klara to her doom, 'schwören', exploiting it to achieve yet another climax combining symbolic character illumination with tragic paradox."

48 Garland 178.

49 Reinhardt, "Friedrich Hebbel" 174 mentions the similarity between *Maria Magdalene* and *Kabale und Liebe* concerning the oath.

See also Ladislas Löb, "Domestic Tragedy-Realism and the Middle Classes," *The German Theatre*, ed. Ronald Haymen (London: Wolff, 1975) 75.

50 The topic of Klara's adherence to her father's code is often treated in cirtical analyses of *Maria Magdalene*. See, for example, Flygt 75. See also Benno von Wiese 610. Here he describes Klara as "die an die sittlichen Vorstellungen ihres Vaters wehrlos gebundene Tochter." Pilz 75 writes: "Klara erscheint . . . als Opfer, das von allen Seiten umstellt ist und das nur zu reagieren vermag im Sinne des mörderischen Zwanges einer zur absoluten Norm erhobenen kleinbürgerlichen Moral."

Rolf Högel, "Zur Frage der Identität des Helden in Hebbels Dramen," *Hebbel-Jahrbuch* (1974): 150, points out that by failing to flee from her parent's home, as Karl plans to do by going to sea, she demonstrates her firm entrenchment in the "Beschränktheit der klein-bürgerlichen Lebensverhältnisse."

Edward McInnes, *German Social Drama 1840 - 1900: From Hebbel to Hauptmann* (Stuttgart: Heinz, 1976), makes many enlightening state-ments about this work and the *bürgerliche Trauerspiele* in general. He writes, for example: "Underlying the awareness of destructive social divisions in all these plays there is a recognition of a severe aleination between parent and child which has its root in a shared dependence upon communally enforced standards and desires" (25). But his view of Klara's adherence to bourgeois standards, to which he alludes in the passage just quoted, becomes inconsistent. He comments: "There is no doubt that Klara herself in her concern to avert the danger which threatens her father sees her whole life as finally released from the pressures of communally accepted attitudes" (31). He writes further that by virtue of the awareness she has of the danger to her father, "she acknowledges an imperative which annuls all worldly consideration" (31). These two statements indicate that Klara no longer views "accepted attitudes" and "worldly consideration" as important. Finally, however, he makes an observation that best expresses the situation in Hebbel's drama: ". . . the apprehension of the inward development of the heroine . . . is encompassed throughout by a qualifying awareness of her continuing (if indefinable) susceptibility to the pressures of this destructive milieu" (32). Thus, McInnes finally admits that Klara continues to be affected by the standards of the society in which she exists. Had Klara truly freed herself from the "communally accepted attitudes," as McInnes suggests elsewhere, either she would not have hesitated to swear the oath to Leonhard or she would have continued to exist on her own, no matter what the consequences would have been for her father. But this is clearly *not* the case.

51 See Reinhardt, "Friedrich Hebbel" 184-185.

52 Reinhardt, "Friedrich Hebbel" 180 notes that Klara's progressive movement toward death is marked by her contemplation of Anton's promise of suicide and his concept of honor. See also Garland's discussion 161 and 188 of Anton's oath. She writes: "The misuse by Anton of the legal practice of the oath in an issue of life and death, prevails most conspiciously over repressed emotions of love and compassion" (188).

53 See Garland 188.

54 Garland 214.

55 Hebbel, *Maria Magdalene* 361.

56 Hebbel, *Maria Magdalene* 363.

57 Hebbel, *Maria Magdalene* 366.

58 This observation is also presented by Joachim Müller 137. He comments, Friedrich's "'Darüber kann kein Mann weg' . . . demonstriert die auch für einen wahrhaft Liebenden unüberwindbare Barriere kläglicher kleinbürgerlicher Moral." See also Pilz 70, 73 and 79.
   Reinhardt, "Friedrich Hebbel" 181 remarks in a similar fashion: "Nicht primär der männliche Geschlechtsegoismus verrät sich darin als vielmehr die Befangenheit im bürgerlichen Reputationsgedenken gemäß dem Ehren-Schanden-Schema, dessen Forderung Priorität vor der Liebe erhält, die Mann und Frau verbinden."

59 See Hebbel, *Maria Magdalene* 355.

60 Högel 150 notes: "In diesem Drama . . . ist der dramatische Vorgang identisch mit Klaras schrittweisem Vorrücken auf einem Wege, dessen Richtung, seitliche Begrenzungen und Ende ihr von den Verhaltensweisen des Vaters, Leonhards und des Sekretärs gesetzt werden."

61 Hebbel, *Maria Magdalene* 366.

62 Keller 121 notes: "Das Versagen des Sekretärs und die wiederholte Absage Leonhards, sorgfältig motiviert auch sie, bringen das unausweichliche Entweder-Oder, das Klaras Entscheidung fordert, schonungslos zum Bewußtsein. Nur mit dem Selbstmord des Vaters könnte sie sich ihr eigenes Leben erkaufen; da dieser Weg für sie ungangbar ist, bleibt nur der in den Tod." This statement is certainly correct; however, Keller overlooks the fact that the father's suicide would also bring guilt to Klara. She believes that only through her own death can she preserve her father's moral innocence.

63 Hebbel, *Maria Magdalene* 372. Reinhardt, "Friedrich Hebbel" 181, writes of this: "Selbstmord und Kindesmord können, obwohl frevel-haft, für sie nicht gegen den Frevel aufkommen, den der Vatertod bedeuten würde, weil sie sich unter den durch den Doppelschwur geschaffenen Bedingungen den Selbstmord des Vaters als Mord zurechnen müßte."

64 See Hebbel, *Maria Magdalene* 377. See also Kraft 119 where he notes: "Sie stirbt, weil sie für ihren Vater sterben muß."

65 See Wittkowski 156. He writes: "Wenn sie den Selbst- und Kinder-mord weniger schwer wiegen läßt als den Vatermord, dann regiert da . . . die allzu bewußte Logik der Selbstlosigkeit. Sie ist im 18. Jahrhundert und bis tief ins 19. hinein der höchste sittliche Wert."

66 Kraft 119 comments: "Was sie tut, ist von der Rücksicht auf ihren Vater bestimmt, den die Schande erdrücken würde . . ."

67 See Kraft 119.

68 Kaiser 53 explains the hopeless nature of Klara's situation: "Erst durch das Ineinanderwirken der beiden Motivzusammenhänge der Verführung (Bindung an Leonhard) und des Juwelendiebstahls (Auslieferung an den Ehrbegriff des Vaters) wird ihre Lage ausweglos . . . ."
    Ziegler 103 describes Klara's situation and suicide by stating: "Das Ergebnis des Selbstmordes ist nur die sichtbare Offenbarung des allem zeitlichen Handlungswechsel bereits vorgegeben, durch ihn nur bestätigten, nicht gewandelten Zustandes der Not . . . ."

69 Hebbel, *Werke*, vol. 3, 546.
    See also Wolfgang Liepe, "Zum Problem der Schuld bei Hebbel," *Hebbel in neuer Sicht*, ed. Helmut Kreuzer (Stuttgart: Kohlhammer, 1969) 42-58.

70 See Hagboldt 202; Reinhardt, "Hebbels Dramatik" 247; and Keller 118.

71 See note 8 for citation of the corresponding passage from Hebbel's "Mein Wort über das Drama."

72 Hebbel, *Werke*, vol. 4 (1966), 666 [3158]. All references to the diaries are from this volume. The references will be referred to as "Hebbel, *Tage-bücher*" and will be followed by page and citation number.) Ritter 46 defines the notion of *Maßlosigkeit* more exactly as hubris.

73 Ross 100. See also Fourie 45.

74 Ross 100.

75 Ritter 46. See also Hebbel, *Tagebücher* 176 [915] and 599 [2901].

76 Hagboldt 202 explains: "Just as life is a separation of the individual from the eternal source of all existence, so death is a reunion with this source. Death is a sacrifice which every individual must make to the Idea." See also Ross 101 and Keller 118. Keller writes: "Die mit der conditio humana vorgegebene Verschuldung des Menschen kann nur durch dessen Untergang gesühnt werden . . . ."

77 Hebbel, *Tagebücher* 666-667 [3158]. (This is the continuation of the entry quoted in note 72.)

78 Hebbel, *Tagebücher* 340 [1827]. See also Ritter 46.

79 Hebbel, *Maria Magdalene* 382. Löb 80 explains: "Although Meister Anton is said to be capable of generosity, his conduct is bitterly inhuman. Love, for him, must yield to financial security; prayer must be accompanied by life-denying gloom; sensitivity must hide behind aggression."

Benno von Wiese 621 notes: "Eingesperrt in seine enge, moralische Selbstgerechtigkeit, rollt er alle sittlichen Probleme nur von der Beschränktheit seiner allzu fixierten, für absolut gehaltenen Position auf." See also Kaiser 59 and Keller 119.

80 Hebbel, *Tagebücher* 605 [2926].

81 See Hebbel, *Tagebücher* 304 [1611]: "Einen Menschen zum bloßen Mittel herabzuwürdigen: ärgste Sünde."

82 Hebbel, *Maria Magdalene* 381. Keller 120 notes that "Allen dramatis personae gemeinsam ist, daß sie ihr Selbstverständnis aus ihrem Ehrverständnis herleiten . . . ."

83 Hebbel, *Tagebücher* 604-605 [2926]. The concept "guilt of all, guilt of none" is widely discussed in the secondary literature. Högel 151 writes: "Aus Sorge um ihr öffentliches Aussehen versagen sie [Anton, Leonhard, Friedrich] Klara jede Hilfe, jede Rettung aus dem 'Korridor', innerhalb dessen sie sich auf die Entscheidung zwischen dem eigenen Freitod und dem Selbstmord des Vaters zubeugt." To this extent, all three men are guilty.

Hansgünther Heyme and Peter Kleinschmidt, "Hebbel und das heutige Theater," *Handbuch des deutschen Dramas*, ed. Walter Hinck (Düsseldorf: Bagel, 1980) 256, note: "Keiner ist recht eigentlich nur Täter, alle sind auch Opfer . . . ." See also Kaiser 61.

84 Kaiser 62.

85 This criticism is echoed by Ziegler 106, who describes society as a "Verhängnis, . . . Niederin und Feindin menschlicher Innerlichkeit, Freiheit, Wesenhaftigkeit, . . . unbarmherzig[e] Jägerin der menschlichen Kreatur . . . ." Benno von Wiese 614 also levels sharp criticism against society when he comments: "Denn es sind die banalen Verhältnisse, die Bindung an gesellschaftliche Normen, die das

Menschentum ruinieren, nicht aber das Böse in jener bisher von
Hebbel gedichteten gegantischen Übersteigerung." See also 612.
   Hilmar Grundmann, "Hebbels Gesellschaftsbegriff: Die eigentliche
Ursache für seine Modernität," *Hebbel-Jahrbuch* (1984): 89, concludes:
"Das Ganze ist maßlos, und zwar in der Hinsicht, daß es jeden
Anspruch auf ein Minimum an Individualität bereits im Ansatz
unmöglich macht. . . Die tragische Isolierung wurzelt nicht nur im
Individuellen, sondern ebenso im Sozialen."

86   Hebbel, *Maria Magdalene* 378.

87   Hebbel, *Maria Magdalene* 381-382.

88   Högel 153 writes about Klara's humanity: "Das Drama zeigt selbst, daß
     Hebbel alles tut, um, eigene schwere Erlebnisse verarbeitend, in Klara
     ein Mädchen zu gestalten, dem auch der nicht vergebungsbereite
     Zuschauer menschliche Größe zuerkennen muß."

89   von Wiese 614 writes: "In ihrer Gebundenheit an die väterliche
     gesellschaftliche Denkform lebt trotz allem eine höhere, menschliche
     Sittlichkeit des Duldens, die für Hebbel die Idee des Weibes verkör-
     pert, und von hier aus wächst Klara über die Düsterkeit der gehetzten,
     wehrlos preisgegebenen Kreatur hinaus und zeigt etwas von dem Adel
     reiner Menschlichkeit, den sie selbst kaum zu leben wagt, und der
     dennoch der einzige, wenn auch unendlich schwache, tröstende
     Schimmer in der Unmenschlichkeit dieser bürgerlichen Welt ist."

90   See note 31.

91   See J. D. Wright, "Hebbel's Klara. The Victim of a Division in Alle-
     giance and Purpose," *Monatshefte* 38 (1946): 304.

92   See Gero von Wilpert, *Sachwörterbuch der Literatur* (Stuttgart: Kröner,
     1979) 25-26.

Chapter VI

1   Ernst Alker, *Die deutsche Literatur im 19. Jahrhundert* (Stuttgart: Kröner,
    1981) 702.

2   See Gerhard Schulz, "Gerhart Hauptmanns dramatisches Werk," *Hand-
    buch des deutschen Dramas*, ed. Walter Hink (Düsseldorf: Bagel, 1980)
    314.

3   Hans Joachim Schrimpf, "Hauptmann: Rose Bernd," *Das deutsche
    Drama vom Barock bis zur Gegenwart*, ed. Benno von Wiese (Düsseldorf:
    Bagel, 1960) 172. He states more exhaustively that for Hauptmann in
    general, "Aus diesen Elementarantrieben [Haß und Liebe in allen
    zwischenmenschlichen Beziehungen, zwischen den Gesellschaftsk-
    lassen, den Geschlechtern und in der Familie, . . . Hunger, Angst und

Machtantrieb, Geschlechtstrieb, Vaterschaft und Mutterinstinkt, . . . Sehnsucht nach einem ganzen und undemütigen Dasein, nach erdentbundener Schwerelosigkeit], die durch den Menschen hindurch- und über ihn hinweghandeln, denen er kaum mehr als Subjekt gegenüberzutreten vermag, sondern die ihn nur als Objekt durch Dasein stoßen und vor sich hertreiben;* . . . alles irdische Leid [entspringt]" (172).

Schulz 319 states that Hauptmann has been defined as the "Dichter menschlichen Leids schlechthin, das verbunden war mit aller menschlichen Existenz. Die zu Leid und Tragik führenden Ursachen lagen bei solcher Betrachtungsweise nicht im gesellschaftlichen Sein des Menschen begründet, sondern gehörten schon zu seiner besonderen Zwischenstellung zwischen Tier und Gott, die ihn als *homo sapiens* vor allen Naturwesen auszeichnete."

4 See Georg Pilz, *Deutsche Kindesmord-Tragödien: Wagner, Goethe, Hebbel, Hauptmann* (Munich: Oldenbourg, 1982) 95.

5 See Jean Jofen, *Das letzte Geheimnis. Eine psychologische Studie über die Brüder Gerhart und Carl Hauptmann* (Bern: Franke, 1972) 79.

   Schulz 320 notes: "Tatsächlich wird sein dramatisches Werk vor allem von Familienkonflikten bestimmt."

6 See Schulz 317.

7 Schulz 317 writes of this phenomenon: "Nirgends wird die Abhängigkeit des Menschen von seinem 'Milieu' und seiner Herkunft rascher und deutlicher faßbar als in seiner Sprache."

8 See Schrimpf 173. See also Schulz's entire article (311-326) in which the basic elements of Hauptmann's dramas are explained in greater detail.

9 Gerhart Hauptmann, *Das gesammelte Werk* Erste Abteilung, vol. 4 (Berlin: Suhrkamp, 1943) 243-44. This volume will hereafter be referred to as Hauptmann, *Rose*.

   Wolfgang Blutzlaff, "Die Enthüllungstechnik in Hauptmanns *Rose Bernd*," *Deutschunterricht* 13 IV (1961): 63, notes: "Daß Hauptmann sich mit der Spiegelung der Vergewaltigungsszene im Dialog begnügt, kann als Beispiel dafür dienen, wie falsch es ist, ihn schlechtweg zum Naturalisten zu stempeln, der die ungeschminkte Wirklichkeit auch in ihren gräßlichen Erscheinungen wiedergibt." See also Schrimpf 174.

   Heidemarie Liselotte Thornton, "The Situation of Women in Gerhart Hauptmann's Early Naturalistic Works," diss., Vanderbilt University, 1981, 91, points to the fact that *Rose Bernd* is not a strongly naturalistic drama.

10 See Warren R. Maurer, *Gerhart Hauptmann*, Twayne's World Author Series 670 (Boston: Twayne Publishers, 1982) 97.

   See Peter Sprengel, *Gerhart Hauptmann: Epoche-Werk-Wirkung* (Munich: Beck, 1984) 129.

See Peter Sprengel, *Die Wirklichkeit der Mythen. Untersuchungen zum Werk Gerhart Hauptmanns aufgrund des handschriftlichen Nachlasses* (Berlin: Schmidt, 1972) 284-5. See also Schrimpf 166 and Pilz 89.

11   See Sprengel, *Wirklichkeit* 284 and Pilz 89.

12   Maurer 101 writes: "The fate of Rose Bernd may, therefore, have helped Hauptmann allay his sense of guilt toward Marie by reassuring him that, as opposed to his alter ego Flamm, he had behaved decently."

13   See Sprengel, *Hauptmann* 137, Sprengel, *Wirklichkeit* 285 and Pilz 96.

14   Schrimpf 175-6. See also 168. Here Schrimpf writes of the father-figures: "Es ist die 'rauhe Tugend', was sie durchgängig charakterisiert, tugendhaft und bis zur Selbstzerstörung redlich, gottesfürchtig, kirchenfromm und standesbewußt führen sie in ihrer Familie ein strenges häusliches Regiment, das nicht frei ist von patriarchalischer Tyrannis."

15   See Rudolf Mittler, *Theorie und Praxis des sozialen Dramas bei Gerhart Hauptmann* (Hildesheim, Zurich, New York: Olms, 1985) 234. He comments on "Die Wohlanständigkeit:" "Beschränkt und gefordert wird sie von Vater Bernd, der darin immer einen negativen Fixpunkt von Roses Entscheidungs- und Handlungsmächtigkeit darstellt."

16   Hauptmann, *Rose* 199.

17   See Maurer 99 and Sprengel, *Wirklichkeit* 286.

18   Hauptmann, *Rose* 210.

19   Hauptmann, *Rose* 214.

20   Hauptmann, *Rose* 219.

21   Hauptmann, *Rose* 221.

22   Hauptmann, *Rose* 257.

23   Hauptmann, *Rose* 274.

24   See Eberhard Hilscher, *Gerhart Hauptmann* (Berlin: Verlag der Nation, 1969) 264.

25   Hauptmann, *Rose* 222.

26   Hauptmann, *Rose* 230.

27   See Hauptmann, *Rose* 208.

28   Hauptmann, *Rose* 272.

29 Hauptmann, *Rose* 275.

30 Hauptmann, *Rose* 278.

31 Hauptmann, *Rose* 279.

32 Ladislas Löb, "Domestic Tragedy-Realism and the Middle Classes," *The German Theatre*, ed. Ronald Haymen (London: Wolff, 1975) 84, writes of Bernd: ". . . his greed, his narrow-mindedness, his effete pietism and his self-defeating search for respectability indicate the extent to which former middle-class values are now regarded as vices."

Thornton 97 comments on Bernd in a similar fashion: "Old Bernd's reaction [at the conclusion of the drama] is not that of a Christian with compassion and understanding, much less that of a father towards his daughter, but rather that of a narrow-minded bigot who cannot go beyond the letter of the law."

33 Butzlaff 63 points out: "Bernd erfährt alles auf einmal, die Folge ist, daß am Endes des V. Aktes für ihn eine Welt zusammenbricht." See also 62.

34 Jofen 196 maintains that "es immer der Vater ist, der das Unglück veranlaßt und herbeiführt . . . ."

35 See Schurz 324.

36 See Schurz 323. Sprengel, *Hauptmann* 136 writes: "Das Bild der Hetz-jagd ist . . . ein bei Hauptmann häufig wiederkehrender Ausdruck des tragischen Verhängnisses . . . . In *Rose Bernd* erhält es spezifische Funk-tion: als Sinnbild des Verhältnisses der Frau zu den Männern wird es zur dominierenden metaphorischen Struktur des Dramas."

37 See Hauptmann, *Rose* 212. The description of the setting for Act II begins, "Die große Wohnstube im Hause des Erbscholtiseibesitzers Flamm. Der große, niedrige Raum, der zu ebner Erde liegt, hat eine Tür nach rechts in den Hausflur. Eine zweite Tür in der Hinterwand verbindet das große Zimmer mit einem kleineren, das Herr Flamm seine Jagdkammer nennt. Es sind darin Vorrichtungen zur Anferti-gung von Patronen; Kleider und Gewehre hängen an der Wand, ausgestopfte Vögel, die man bemerkt, wenn die Tür geöffnet wird, und der standesamtliche Aktenschrank." See also Sprengel, *Hauptmann* 136.

38 Hauptmann, *Rose* 196.

39 See Hauptmann, *Rose* 196-7. See also Thornton 98.

40 Hauptmann, *Rose* 197.

41 Hauptmann, *Rose* 195.

42 See Jofen 33, where he remarks: "Nicht nur die Stellung der Frau, sondern auch die Stellung des Mannes macht die Verbindung unmöglich."

Thornton 98 describes the impossibility of divorce in Hauptmann's day: "Divorce at that time was still considered a social scandal and was, therefore[,] a rarity."

Mittler 234 comments: "Die Liebe [Roses] zu Flamm richtet sich gegen die Wertorientierung der Wohlanständigkeit, die aber letztlich voll gültig bleibt."

43 Hauptmann, *Rose* 223.

44 Hauptmann, *Rose* 223.

45 Hauptmann, *Rose* 240.

46 Hauptmann, *Rose* 259.

47 See Pilz 105.

48 Hauptmann, *Rose* 265. Thornton 99 describes Flamm's treatment of Rose: "Instead of trying to understand Rose's situation, Flamm can only consider what has happened as it pertains to him." To this extent we perceive Flamm's egocentricity.

49 See Hauptmann, *Rose* 202.

50 See Schrimpf 175.

51 Hauptmann, *Rose* 203.

52 Schrimpf 180 writes: "Es ist eins der verhängnisvollen Zusammentreffen des Stücks, daß Streckmann gerade die Abschiedsszene der Liebenden belauscht und darauf seine erpresserische Drohung gründet. Nun hat er Rose in der Hand, denn er hat die Macht, ihre Verbindung mit Keil zu zerstören, und sie ist ihm wehrlos ausgeliefert."

53 Hauptmann, *Rose* 206.

54 Hauptmann, *Rose* 245.

55 Hauptmann, *Rose* 247.

56 Karl Holl, *Gerhart Hauptmann. His Life and Work 1889-1912* (1913 Chicago: McClurg, 1973) 32-33.

57 Schrimpf 180. Schrimpf 177-8 also notes: "Die auswählende und Akzente setzende Verknüpfung der Ereignisse zur fortschreitenden Handlung und eine sorgfältige Vorbereitung und Motivierung der einzelnen Handlungsschritte dienen hier der Vergegenwärtigung eines tödlichen Netzes, das sich mit jeder willentlichen oder abgepraßten Bewegung der Personen noch gegen ihren Willen immer enger

zusammenzieht und dem Gesamtgeschehen den Charakter unaus-
weichlicher Notwendigkeit verleiht."

Maurer 98 remarks: "Having established his fateful constellation of
forces in the first act, Hauptmann slowly but inexorably introduces
circumstance after circumstance that closes the snare around his
heroine."

Mittler 231 observes: ". . . es wurden ihr [Rose] immer neue Bedingungen gesetzt, nach denen sie ihr Handeln ausrichten mußte;
umgekehrt: ihrem Handeln lag kein eigener positiver Plan zugrunde,
es realisierte keine individuelle Absicht oder einen selbst gesetzten
Zweck, sondern es erscheint als immer erneuerte notwendige Reaktion
auf äußerlich gesetzte Anforderungen."

58 See Schrimpf 174, Thornton 102 and Mittler 234-5.

59 Hauptmann, *Rose* 196 and 197.

60 Hauptmann, *Rose* 207.

61 Hauptmann, *Rose* 243.

62 Hauptmann, *Rose* 256.

63 See Hauptmann, *Rose* 269.

64 Holl 32. See also Mittler 232 and 236. He writes 233: ". . . sie erfüllt
die gesellschaftlichen Erwartungen an den anständigen Lebenswandel
eines jungen Mädchens. Dabei ist der wesentliche Punkt der, daß sie
diese gesellschaftlichen Erwartungen selbst an sich stellt, sie als ihren
eigenen Maßstab an ihr Handeln anlegt und alle Umstände, in denen
sie sich befindet, danach beurteilt."
Schrimpf 176 comments: "Rose ist seelisch unabtrennbar an dieses
Vaterhaus gebunden," and: "Wie in den älteren Dramen steht Rose
unter dem Druck und der Drohung des väterlichen Tugendrigorismus"
(176).

65 Hauptmann, *Rose* 272. Thornton 100 comments: "Rose is utterly alone
in her suffering and fear."

66 Sprengel, *Hauptmann* 134 writes that the fourth act shows "die
Zerstörung der Hoffnungen, die das verständnisvolle Eingehen Frau
Flamms auf Roses wortloses Geständnis der Schwangerschaft
ursprünglich erweckt hatte." This contributes to Rose's isolation. See
also Thornton 99-100.

67 Hilscher 263. Schrimpf 181 notes: "Es folgt-im vierten und fünften
Akt-was kommen muß: die gänzliche Vereinsammung Roses, die
unerreichbare Verdüsterung ihres Leidens, das im Kindesmord
gipfelt."
Pilz 100 also comments on Rose's isolation: "Die besondere Tragik
ihrer Situation besteht nun darin, daß sie durch ihr Verhältnis zu

Flamm in doppeltem Sinne schuldig wird: sie hintergeht den Mann, dem sie aus dem Gefühl der Verpflichtung für den Vater die Ehe versprochen hat, und die ohnehin leidgeprüfte Frau des Geliebten, die sie seit früher Kindheit kennt und die ihr in mütterlicher Fürsorge zugetan ist. Roses wachsende Vereinsamung ist durch diese Ausgangs-situation wesentlich mitbedingt."

See also Barbara Mabee, "Die Kindesmörderin in den Fesseln der bürgerlichen Moral: Wagners Evchen und Goethes Gretchen," *Women in German Yearbook* 3, ed. Marianne Burkhard and Edith Waldstein (London, New York, Lanham: University Press of America, 1986) 36, where she explains the motif of isolation in infanticide dramas.

68 Hauptmann, *Rose* 265.

69 Hauptmann, *Rose* 266. See also Mabee 31 where she points out that the fear of shame becomes over and over the primary reason for infanti-cide.

70 See Butzlaff 69.

71 See Hilscher 263.

72 Pilz 94 writes: "Streckmanns erneut angefachter Sexualneid, die daraus erwachsende scharfe und lautstark geführte Auseinandersetzung mit Rose, die Vater und Bräutigam sowie die Landarbeiter und Mägde auf den Plan ruft, der Umschlag in direkte Aggression, Keils Verletzung und die fatale Beschimpfung Roses-all dies spielt sich mit atembe-raubender Geschwindigkeit ab und übersteigt Roses Verfassungsvermö-gen."

73 Hauptmann, *Rose* 280.

74 Hauptmann, *Rose* 280.

75 Hilscher 264. Thornton 96 writes of Rose: ". . . in her hour of need she receives little compassion and understanding."

76 Pilz's entire book deals with the topic. See also Hilscher 264, Maurer 100, Sprengel, *Hauptmann* 131, Schrimpf 166-170.
    See Otto Mann, *Die Geschichte des deutschen Dramas* (Stuttgart: Kröner, 1969) 510.

77 Schurz 324.

78 Hauptmann, *Rose* 283.

79 Hauptmann, *Rose* 284.

80 Mann 510. See Mabee 30. Here she expresses that insanity is a common theme in infanticide dramas.

81 Hauptmann, *Rose* 284. Pilz 95 writes: "Ihr [Rose] bleibt die letzte grausame Enthüllung überlassen: der Mord an ihrem Kind, den sie in totaler Verlassenheit von Gott und den Menschen begangen hat, um dem neugeborenen Lebenswesen die Martern zu sparen, die sie selbst hat erleiden müssen." See also Hilscher 264.

82 Sprengel, *Wirklichkeit* 288 writes: "Mutterliebe steht letzten Endes noch hinter der Kindstötung."
   Thornton maintains the same notion when she comments on infanticide as "an expression of Rose's mother instinct, albeit, a perverted one." See also 100 and 105.

83 Butzlaff 68 writes, for example: "Alle fünf Personen, d. h. Streckmann, Flamm, Frau Flamm, August und Bernd, werden auf die Probe gestellt. In dem Augenblick, in dem ihnen bisher Verborgenes und für sie, mit Ausnahme von Streckmann, Unangenehmes über Rose bekannt wird, stehen sie in einer Grenzsituation. Sie müssen entscheiden zwischen öffentlicher Moral und Eigennützigkeit auf der einen, von engen Gesetzen freier, selbstloser Menschlichkeit auf der anderen Seite." His condemnation of Flamm and Bernd reads: "Flamm und Bernd versagen im entscheidenden Augenblick, Flamm aus Gründen persönlicher Eitelkeit und Eifersucht, auch aus mangelndem Vertrauen Rose gegenüber, Bernd, weil er ohne schlechten Willen in seiner Wortgläubigkeit und Kirchentreue nicht mehr zu wahrer Barmherzigkeit fähig ist" (68). See also Sprengel, *Wirklichkeit* 286 and Schrimpf 169.
   Schurz 316-7 writes: "Das Drama blieb immerhin Denkvorgang, also Artikulation von bisher Unartikuliertem und damit letzten Endes eben doch der Versuch, der Wirklichkeit größere Transparenz abzugewinnen, sie verständlich und damit humaner zu machen."

84 Hauptmann, *Rose* 198.

85 Hauptmann, *Rose* 224-5.

86 Hauptmann, *Rose* 226.

87 Hauptmann, *Rose* 266.

88 This aspect of Frau Flamm's character is often described by critics. See Butzlaff 69, Maurer 98, Pilz 103.
   Hilscher 265 writes: "Die kranke Frau Flamm bringt für das verschüchterte, ratsuchende Mädchen gütiges Verständnis auf, behandelt sie mit feinem Takt und verspricht ihr Beistand in der schweren Stunde."
   Schrimpf 176 comments: "Frau Flamm, wenig älter als ihr Mann, [ist] durch Verlust ihres einzigen Kindes und jahrelanges Siechtum im Leiden und Erfahren gereift, von einer ganz weltlichen, naturhaften Güte und diesseitig-praktischen Humanität bestimmt."

89 Sprengel, *Hauptmann* 137, writes: "Der rigorosen Verurteilung jeder außerehelichen Beziehung durch den bibeltreuen Bernd . . . steht Frau

Flamms programmatische Aufwertung der Mutterschaft gegenüber, eine Aufwertung, die sich ursprünglich ausdrücklich auf die ledige Mutter bezog." See also Sprengel, *Wirklichkeit* 287.

90 See Mittler 238. See also Schrimpf 181.

91 Schrimpf 184 notes of this phenomenon: "Es ist nun abermals ein Ereignis tragisch-ironischer Gegenläufigkeit, daß Keil-durch den Verlust seines Auges-gerade in dem Augenblick fühlender, hellsichtiger und offener für die Verzweifelung Rose Bernds wird . . . ."

92 Hauptmann, *Rose* 274. See Pilz 102.

93 See Hauptmann, *Rose* 255-6: "Gottes Wege sein wunderbar! Und wie a een'n heimsucht, darf man nich murren. Im Gegenteil, ma soll sich freun. Und sehn Se, Frau Flamm, so geht mirsch beinahe jetze. Mir is recht! Um so besser, je schlimmer 's kommt. Um so mehr wächst der Schatz in der Ewigkeit."

94 See Hauptmann, *Rose* 281. The corresponding statement in Friedrich Hebbel, *Maria Magdalene* in *Hebbels Werke* vol. 1, ed. Gerhard Fricke, Werner Keller and Karl Pörnbacher (Munich: Hanser, 1963) 381, reads: ". . . du hättest mir das Kopfschütteln und Achselzucken der Pharisäer um mich her nicht erspart . . . "

95 Hauptmann, *Rose* 284.

96 Hilscher 265 comments: "Zu menschlicher Größe wächst schließlich August Keil empor. Anfangs erscheint er als einfältiger Frömmler, der sich ein abgeschiedenes, stilles Leben wünscht. . . . Allmählich ahnt er Roses Zustand, und als die Katastrophe eintritt, steht er tapfer zu ihr . . . ." Pilz 103 remarks: "Doch ist ihm [Keil] völlig zu Recht das letzte Wort in der Tragödie überlassen, da er der einzige ist, der die Abgründe des Leids, durch die Rose hindurchgegangen ist, ahnt."

97 See Pilz 102.

98 Sprengel, *Wirklichkeit* 286 remarks: "Im Schlußakt . . . ist es . . . gerade August, der aus verwandter Leidenserfahrung heraus einfühlsame Worte des Verständnisses vorfindet, in hoffnungsloser Verspätung freilich."

99 Schulz 325.

100 Gerhart Hauptmann, *Das gesammelte Werk* Erste Abteilung, vol. 17 (Berlin: Suhrkamp, 1943) 232.

Bibliography

Primary Literature

Grillparzer, Franz. *Sämtliche Werke*. Ed. Peter Frank and Karl Pörnbacher. 4 vols. Munich: Hanser, 1960-1965.

___. *Sämtliche Werke*. *Historisch-kritische Gesamtausgabe*. Ed. August Sauer (and Reinhold Backmann). 43 vols. Vienna: Schroll, 1901-1948.

Hauptmann, Gerhart. *Das gesammelte Werk*. Ed. E. R. Weiss. 17 vols. Berlin: Suhrkamp, 1942.

Hebbel, Friedrich. *Werke*. Ed. Gerhard Fricke, Werner Keller and Karl Pörnbächer. 5 vols. Munich: Hanser, 1963-1966.

Jung, C. G. *The Basic Writings of C. G. Jung*. Ed. Violet S. DeLaszlo. New York: Modern Library, 1959.

___. *The Collected Works of C. G. Jung* Trans. R. F. C. Hall. 19 vols. Bollingen Series 20. New York: Pantheon, 1966. Vol. 7.

___. *The Collected Works of C. G. Jung* Trans. R. F. C. Hall. 19 vols. Bollingen Series 20. Princeton: Princeton University Press. Vol. 9.

Lessing, Gotthold Ephriam. *Gesammelte Werke*. Ed. Wolfgang Stammler. 2 vols. Munich: Hanser, 1959.

Schiller, Friedrich. *Sämtliche Werke*. Ed. Gerhard Fricke and Herbert G. Göpfert. 5 vols. Munich: Hanser, 1960-1962.

Wagner, Heinrich Leopold. *Die Kindermörderin*. In *Deutsche National-Literatur. Historisch-kritische Ausgabe.* Vol. 80 *Stürmer und Dränger II.* Ed. A. Sauer. Berlin, Stuttgart: Spemann, n.d. 283-357.

Secondary Literature

Alker, Ernst. *Die deutsche Literatur im 19. Jahrhundert.* Stuttgart: Kröner, 1981.

Angress, R. K. "The Generations in Emilia Galotti." *Germanic Review* 43 (1968): 15-23.

Anshen, Ruth Nanda. "The Conservation of Family Values." *The Family: Its Function and Destiny.* Ed. Ruth Nanda Anshen. New York: Harper, 1959. 511-522.

Auernheimer, Raoul. *Franz Grillparzer. Der Dichter Österreichs.* Vienna: Amalthea, 1972.

Baker, Christa Sutter. "Unifying Imagery Patterns in Grillparzer's *Das goldene Vlies.*" *Modern Language Notes* 89 (1974): 392-403.

Benveniste, Emile. *Indo-European Language and Society.* Trans. Elizabeth Palmer. London: Faber and Faber, 1973.

Beutin, Wolfgang, et. al. *Deutsche Literatur Geschichte von den Anfängen bis zur Gegenwart.* Stuttgart: Metzler, 1984.

Böckmann, Paul. "Verkennen und Erkennen im Drama Grillparzers." *Festschrift Josef Quint.* Ed. Hugo Moser, Rudolf Schützeichel, Karl Stackmann. Bonn: Semmel, 1964. 39-55.

Bornkamm, H. "Die innere Handlung in Lessings *Miß Sara Sampson.*" *Euphorion* 51 III (1957): 385-97.

Brauckmann, Matthias, and Andrea Everwien. "Sehnsucht nach Integrität oder Wie die Seele wächst im Verzicht."

Gerettete Ordnung. Grillparzers Dramen. Ed. Bernhard Budde and Ulrich Schmidt. Frankfurt, Bern, New York, Paris: Lang, 1987. 58-105.

Brüggemann, Fr. "Der Kampf um die bürgerliche Welt- und Lebensanschauung in der deutschen Literatur des 18. Jahrhunderts." *Deutsche Vierteljahresschrift* 3 (1925): 94-127.

Burkhard, Marianne, and Edith Waldstein, eds. *Feminist Studies and German Culture.* Lanham, MD: University Presses of America, 1986.

Butlzaff, Wolfgang. "Die Enthüllungstechnik in Hauptmanns *Rose Bernd.*" *Deutschunterricht* 13, No. 4 (1961): 59-70.

Cocalis, Susan L. "Der Vormund will Vormund sein: Zur Problematik der weiblichen Unmündigkeit im 18. Jahrhundert." *Amsterdamer Beiträge zur neueren Germanistik.* Vol. 10. *Gestaltet und Gestaltend. Frauen in der deutschen Literatur.* Ed. Marianne Burkhard. Amsterdam: Rodopi, 1980. 33-55.

Coser, Rose Laub. "Authority and Structural Ambivalence in the Middle-Class Family." *The Family. Its Structures and Functions.* Ed. Rose Laub Coser. New York: St. Martin, 1974. 362-73.

Davis, Kingsley. "The Sociology of Parent-Youth Conflict." *The Family. Its Structures and Functions.* Ed. Rose Laub Coser. New York: St. Martin, 1974. 446-59.

Drewitz, Ingeborg, ed. *The German Women's Movement.* Bonn: Hohnwacht, 1983.

Dunham, T. C. "*Medea* in Athens and Vienna." *Monatshefte* 38 (1946): 217-25.

Fenner, Birgit. *Friedrich Hebbel zwischen Hegel und Freud.* Stuttgart: Klett-Cotta, 1979.

Fetzer, John. "Water Imagery in *Maria Magdalena*." *German Quarterly* 43 (1970): 715-19.

Fischer, Ernst. *Von Grillparzer zu Kafka. Sechs Essays*. Vienna: Globus, 1972.

Fischer, Walter. *Hebbel. Maria Magdalena*. Frankfurt am Main: Diesterweg, 1967.

Flygt, Sten G. *Friedrich Hebbel*. Twayne's World Authors Series 56. New York: Twayne Publishers, 1968.

Friedrich, Wolf Hartmut. *Vorbild und Neugestaltung. Sechs Kapitel zur Geschichte der Tragödie*. Göttingen: Vandenhoeck & Ruprecht, 1967.

Fourie, Regine. "Friedrich Hebbels Dramentheorie: Eine kritische Darstellung." *Acta Germanica* 15 (1982): 41-51.

Frey, Elenore. "Spannung und Gleichgewicht in Grillparzers Welt." *Schweizerisches Monatsheft* 46 (1966/67): 371-87.

Galle, Roland. "Hegels Dramentheorie und ihre Wirkung." *Handbuch des deutschen Dramas*. Ed. Walter Hinck. Düsseldorf: Bagel, 1980. 259-72.

Garland, Mary. *Hebbel's Prose Tragedies*. Cambridge: Cambridge University Press, 1973.

Gilbert, Lucy and Paula Webster. *Bound by Love: The Sweet Trap of Daughterhood*. Boston: Beacon, 1982.

Greif, Esther Blank. "Fathers, Children, and Moral Development." *The Role of the Father in Child Development*. Ed. Michael Lamb. New York: Wiley, 1976. 219-36.

Griesmayer, Norbert. *Das Bild des Partners in Grillparzers Dramen*. Vienna: Wilhelm Braumüller, 1972.

Grundmann, Hilmar, ed. *Friedrich Hebbel. Neue Studien zu Werk und Wirkung.* Heide, West Germany: Westholsteinische Verlagsanstalt Boyen, 1982.

Grundmann, Hilmar. "Hebbels Gesellschaftsbegriff: Die eigentliche Ursache für seine Modernität." *Hebbel-Jahrbuch* (1984): 85-102.

Guthke, Karl S. *Gerhart Hauptmann: Weltbild im Werk.* Munich: Franke, 1980.

Hagboldt, Peter. "Hebbel." *Monatshefte* 22 (1930): 199-204.

Harrison, R. B. "The Fall and Redemption of Man in Schiller's *Kabale und Liebe.*" *German Life and Letters* 35 I (1981): 5-13.

Hatfield, H. C. "Emilia's Guilt Once More." *Modern Language Notes* 71 (1956): 287-96.

Haudry, Jean. *Les Indo-Européens.* Paris: Presses Universitaires de France, 1981.

Haupt, Jürgen. "*Die Kindermörderin.* Ein bürgerliches Trauerspiel vom 18. Jahrhundert bis zur Gegenwart." *Orbis Litterarum.* 32, No. 4 (1977): 285-301.

Heitner, R. R. "Luise Millerin and the Shock Motif in Schiller's Early Dramas." *Germanic Review* 41 (1966): 27-44.

Heyme, Hansgünther, and Peter Kleinschmidt. "Hebbel und das heutige Theater." *Handbuch des deutschen Dramas.* Ed. Walter Hinck. Düsseldorf: Bagel: 1980. 252-58.

Hiebel, Hans Helmut. "Mißverstehen und Sprachlosigkeit im 'Bürgerlichen Trauerspiel': Zum historischen Wandel dramatischer Motivationsformen." *Jahrbuch der deutschen Schiller-Gesellschaft* 27 (1983): 124-53.

Hilscher, Eberhard. *Gerhart Hauptmann*. Berlin: Verlag der Nation, 1969.

Himmel, Helmut. "Grillparzers Trauerspiel *Des Meeres und der Liebe Wellen*." *Literaturwissenschaftliches Jahrbuch* 14 (1973): 359-93.

Hoesch, Folma. *Der Gestus des Zeigens. Wirklichkeitsauffassung und Darstellungsmittel in den Dramen Franz Grillparzers*. Bonn: Bouvier, 1972.

Högel, Rolf K. "'Ort: eine mittlere Stadt'. The Setting of Hebbel's *Maria Magdalene*." *Modern Language Notes* 87 (1972): 763-68.

___. "Zur Frage der Identität des Helden in Hebbels Dramen. Eine Studie zur interpersonellen Struktur der Hebbelschen Dramen." *Hebbel-Jahrbuch* (1974): 139-66.

Holl, Karl. *Gerhart Hauptmann. His Life and Work 1889-1912*. 1913. Chicago: McClurg, 1973.

Hörisch, Jochen. "Die Tugend und der Weltlauf in Lessings bürgerlichen Trauerspielen." *Euphorion* 74 (1980): 186-97.

Horkheimer, Max. "Authoritarianism and the Family." *The Family: Its Function and Destiny*. Ed. Ruth Nanda Anshen. New York: Harper, 1959. 381-98.

Ingen, Ferdinand van. "Tugend bei Lessing. Bemerkungen zu *Miß Sara Sampson*." *Amsterdamer Beiträge zur neueren Germanistik* 1 (1972): 43-73.

Janson, Deborah. "The Emancipation Which Enslaved." *New German Review* 1 (1985): 15-27.

Jofen, Jean. *Das letzte Geheimnis. Eine psychologische Studie über die Brüder Gerhart und Carl Hauptmann*. Bern: Franke, 1972.

Jonnes, Dennis. "Solche Väter: The Sentimental Family Paradigm in Lessing's Drama." *Lessing Yearbook* 12 (1980): 157-74.

Kaiser, Gerhard. "Krise der Familie: Eine Perspektive auf Lessings *Emilia Galotti* und Schillers *Kabale und Liebe.*" *Recherches Germaniques* 14 (1984): 7-22.

Kaiser, Herbert. *Friedrich Hebbel. Geschichtliche Interpretation des dramatischen Werks.* Munich: Fink, 1983.

Kaiser, Joachim. "Grillparzers Dramatik." *Handbuch des deutschen Dramas.* Ed. Walter Hinck. Düsseldorf: Bagel, 1979. 229-43.

Kaufmann, Friedrich Wilhelm. *German Dramatists of the 19th Century.* 1940. Freeport, NY: Books for Libraries Press, 1970.

Keller, Mechthild. "Anmerkungen zu Hebbels Dramentechnik: Motivation und Handlung." *Friedrich Hebbel. Neue Studien zu Werk und Wirkung.* Ed. Hilmar Grundmann. Heide, West Germany: Boyen, 1982. 117-29.

Kluge, Friedrich, and Alfred Götze. *Etymologisches Wörterbuch der deutschen Sprache.* Berlin: de Gruyter, 1948.

Kölling, Martin. "Verzagen an zerstörter Hoffnung." *Gerettete Ordnung. Grillparzers Dramen.* Ed. Bernhard Budde and Ulrich Schmidt. Frankfurt am Main, Bern, New York, Paris: Lang, 1987. 147-64.

Kraft, Herbert. *Poesie der Idee. Die tragische Dichtung Friedrich Hebbels.* Tübingen: Niemeyer, 1971.

Kreuzer, Helmut. *Hebbel in neuer Sicht.* Stuttgart, Berlin, Cologne, Mainz: Kohlhammer, 1969.

Labroisse, Gerd. "Emilia Galottis Wollen und Sollen." *Neophilologus* 56 (1972): 311-23.

Lamb, Michael E.	"The Changing Roles of Fathers." *The Father's Role: Applied Perspectives.* Ed. Michael E. Lamb. New York: Wiley, 1986.

Lewis, Michael, and Marsh Weinraub. "The Father's Role in the Child's Social Network." *The Role of the Father in Child Development.* Ed. Michael Lamb. New York: Wiley, 1976. 157-84.

Liepe, Wolfgang.	"Zum Problem der Schuld bei Hebbel." *Hebbel in neuer Sicht.* Ed. Helmut Kreuzer. Stuttgart: Kohlhammer, 1969. 42-58.

Löb, Ladislaus. "Domestic Tragedy: Realism and the Middle Classes." *German Theatre: A Symposium.* London: Wolff; N. Y.: Barnes and Noble, 1975. 59-86.

Lorenz, Dagmar C. G. *Grillparzer. Dichter des sozialen Konflikts.* Vienna: Böhlau, 1986.

Lucarini, Spartaco. *The Difficult Role of a Father.* Trans. Hugh Moran. New York: New York City Press, 1979.

Lurker, Manfred. *Wörterbuch der Symbolik.* Stuttgart: Kröner, 1988.

Lütkehaus, Ludger. *Hebbel: Gegenwartsdarstellung, Verdinglichungsproblematik, Gesellschaftskritik.* Heidelberg: Winter, 1976.

Lynn, D. B. *The Father: His Role in Child Development.* Monterey: Brooks/Cole, 1974.

McInnes, Edward. *The Development of German Social Drama 1840-1900: From Hebbel to Hauptmann.* Stuttgart: Heinz, 1976.

___. *"Maria Magdalena* and the Bürgerliches Trauerspiel." *Orbis Litterarum* 28 (1973): 46-67.

___. "Psychological Insight and Moral Awareness in Grillparzer's *Das goldene Vlieβ*." *Modern Language Review* 75 (1980): 575-82.

Mackay, Wade C. *Fathering Behaviors. The Dynamics of the Man-Child Bond*. New York: Plenum, 1985.

Malinowski, Bronislaw. "Parenthood, the Basis of Social Structure." *The Family. Its Structures and Functions*. Ed. Rose Laub Coser. New York: St. Martin, 1974. 51-63.

Mann, Otto. *Die Geschichte des deutschen Dramas*. Stuttgart: Kröner, 1969.

Marone, Nicky. *How to Father a Successful Daughter*. New York: McGraw-Hill, 1988.

Martini, Fritz. *Deutsche Literaturgeschichte*. Stuttgart: Kröner, 1984.

Martini, Fritz. "Schillers *Kabale und Liebe*. Bemerkungen zur Interpretation des 'Bürgerlichen Trauerspiels'." *Deutschunterricht* 4, No. 5 (1952): 18-39.

Maurer, Warren R. *Gerhart Hauptmann*. Twayne's World Author Series 670. Boston: Twayne Publishers, 1982.

Mauser, Wolfram. "Lessings *Miss Sara Sampson*. Bürgerliches Trauerspiel als Ausdruck innerbürgerlichen Konflikts." *Lessing Yearbook* 7 (1975): 7-27.

Michelsen, Peter. "Ordnung und Eigensinn: Über Schillers *Kabale und Liebe*." *Jahrbuch des freien deutschen Hochstifts* (1984): 198-222.

Minder, Robert. "Le père et l'image de l'autorité dans la vie et la litterature allemandes." *La Revue des lettres modernes* (Paris) 1, No. 2 (1954): 1-15.

Mittler, Rudolf. *Theorie und Praxis des sozialen Dramas bei Gerhart Hauptmann.* Hildesheim, Zurich, New York: Olms, 1985.

Mitterauer, Michael, and Reinhard Sieder. *The European Family.* Chicago: University of Chicago Press, 1982.

Morris, I. V. "Grillparzer's Individuality as a Dramatist." *Modern Language Quarterly* 18 (1957): 83-99.

Müller, Joachim. "Stilkritische Beobachtungen an Hebbels Geschlechter-Dialogen." *Friedrich Hebbel. Neue Studien zu Werk und Wirkung.* Ed. Hilmar Grundmann. Heide, West Germany: Boyen, 1982. 131-146.

Müller-Seidel, Walter. "Das stumme Drama der Luise Millerin." *Goethe* 17 (1955): 91-103.

Nash, John. "Historical and Social Changes in the Perception of the Role of the Father." *The Role of the Father in Child Development.* Ed. Michael Lamb. New York: Wiley, 1976. 65-87.

Naumann, Walter. *Franz Grillparzer. Das dichterische Werk.* Stuttgart: Kohlhammer, 1956.

Nickel, Horst, and Ellen M. T. Köcher. "West Germany and the German-Speaking Countries." *The Father's Role.* Ed. Michael E. Lamb. Hillsdale, N. J.: Erlbaum, 1987. 89-114.

Papst, E. E. "Franz Grillparzer." *German Men of Letters.* Ed. Alex Natan. Vol. 1. London: Wolff, 1961. 99-120.

Papst, E. E. *Grillparzer. Des Meeres und der Liebe Wellen.* London: Arnold, 1967.

Parsons, Talcott. "The Social Structure of the Family." *The Family: Its Function and Destiny.* Ed. Ruth Nanda Anshen. New York: Harper, 1959. 241-274.

Pilz, Georg. *Deutsche Kindesmord-Tragödien: Wagner, Goethe, Hebbel, Hauptmann.* Munich: Oldenbourg, 1982.

Politzer, Heinz. *Franz Grillparzer oder Das abgründige Biedermeier.* Vienna: Molden, 1972.

___. "Franz Grillparzer." *Deutsche Dichter des 19. Jahrhunderts.* Ed. Benno von Wiese. Berlin: Erich Schmidt, 1969. 272-302.

___. "Der Schein von Heros Lampe." *Modern Language Notes* 72 (1957): 432-37.

Pols, Werner. *Deutsche Sozialgeschichte 1815-70.* Munich: Beck, 1979.

Powel, Barbara. *How to Raise a Successful Daughter.* Chicago: Nelson-Hall, 1979.

Poynter, John D. "The Pearls of *Emilia Galotti.*" *Lessing Yearbook* 9 (1977): 81-95.

Reinhardt, Hartmut. "Friedrich Hebbel: *Maria Magdalena.*" *Deutsche Dramen.* Ed. Harro Müller-Michaels. Vol. 1. Königstein: Athenäum, 1981. 171-99.

___. "Hebbels Dramatik." *Handbuch des deutschen Dramas.* Ed. Walter Hinck. Düsseldorf: Bagel, 1980. 244-51.

Rismondo, Piero. "Das 'zweite Gesicht' in Grillparzers *Das goldene Vließ.*" *Jahrbuch der Grillparzer-Gesellschaft* 5 (1966): 129-41.

Ritter, Wolfgang. *Hebbels Psychologie und dramatische Charaktergestaltung.* Marburger Beiträge zur Germanistik 43. Marburg: Elwert, 1973.

Robinson, Bryan E., and Robert L. Barret. *The Developing Father. Emerging Roles in Contemporary Society.* New York: Guilford, 1986.

Ross, Carol Jean. "Schiller and Hebbel: Characters and Ideas and the Portrayal of Women." Diss. University of Toronto, 1974.

Ryder, Frank G. "Emilia Galotti." *German Quarterly* 45 (1972): 329-47.

Sabean, David. "Verwandtschaft und Familie in einem württembergischen Dorf 1500 bis 1870: einige methodische Überlegungen." *Sozialgeschichte der Familie in der Neuzeit Europas.* Ed. Werner Conze. Stuttgart: Klett, 1976. 231-46.

Schantzky, B. E. "Genre Painting and the German Tragedy of Common Life." *Modern Language Review* 54 (1959): 358-67.

Schaum, Konrad. "Gesetz und Verwandlung in Grillparzers *Goldenem Vließ.*" *Deutsche Vierteljahresschrift* 38 (1964): 388-423.

___. "Grillparzers *Des Meeres und der Liebe Wellen.* Seelendrama und Kulturkritik." *Jahrbuch der Grillparzer-Gesellschaft* 11 (1974): 95-114.

___. "Universale und zeitlose Aspekte in Grillparzers *Goldenem Vließ.*" *Colloquia Germanica* 12 (1979): 77-93.

Schneider, Heinrich. "Emilia Galotti's Tragic Guilt." *Modern Language Notes* 71 (1956): 353-55.

Schrecker, Paul. "The Family: Conveyance of Tradition." *The Family: Its Function and Destiny.* Ed. Ruth Nanda Anshen. New York: Harper, 1959. 488-510.

Schrimpf, Hans Joachim. "Hauptmann: Rose Bernd." *Das deutsche Drama vom Barock bis zur Gegenwart.* Ed. Benno von Wiese. Vol. II. Düsseldorf: Bagel, 1960. 166-85.

Schulz, Gerhard. "Gerhart Hauptmanns dramatisches Werk." *Handbuch des deutschen Dramas.* Ed. Walter Hinck. Düsseldorf: Bagel, 1980. 311-26.

Seidler, Herbert. *Studien zu Grillparzer und Stifter.* Wiener Arbeiten zur deutschen Literatur. Vienna, Cologne, Graz: Böhlau, 1970.

Shepard, Flola L. "Hebbel's *Gedanken-Lasten* in the *Maria Magdalene.*" *Journal of English and Germanic Philology* 30 (1931): 80-86.

Sprengel, Peter. *Gerhart Hauptmann: Epoche-Werk-Wirkung.* Munich: Beck, 1984.

___. *Die Wirklichkeit der Mythen. Untersuchungen zum Werk Gerhart Hauptmanns aufgrund des handschriftlichen Nachlasses.* Berlin: Schmidt, 1972.

Stahl, E. L. "Emilia Galotti." *Das deutsche Drama.* Ed. Benno von Wiese. Vol I. Düsseldorf: Bagel, 1958. 101-12.

Staiger, Emil. *Spätzeit.* Zurich, Munich: Artemis, 1973.

Stephan, Inge. "'So ist die Tugend ein Gespenst': Frauenbild und Tugendbegriff im bürgerlichen Trauerspiel bei Lessing und Schiller." *Lessing Yearbook* 17 (1985): 1-20.

Stern, Martin. "Das zentrale Symbol in Friedrich Hebbels *Maria Magdalene.*" *Hebbel in neuer Sicht.* Ed. Helmut Kreuzer. Stuttgart: Kohlhammer, 1969. 228-46.

Stiefel. Rudolf. *Grillparzers* Das goldene Vließ. *Ein dichterisches Bekenntnis.* Bern: Francke, 1959.

Straubinger, Paul. "*Des Meeres und der Liebe Wellen* im Urteil der Zeit." *Grillparzer-Forum Forchtenstein* 4 (1968): 12-23.

Thompson, Bruce. *Franz Grillparzer.* Twayne's World Author Series 637. Boston: Twayne Publishers, 1981.

___. *A Sense of Irony. An Examination of the Tragedies of Franz Grillparzer.* Bern: Lang, 1976.

Thornton, Heidemarie Liselotte. "The Situation of Women in Gerhart Hauptmann's Early Naturalistic Works." Diss. Vanderbilt University, 1981.

van Stockum, T. C. "Grillparzers Medea-Trilogie *Das goldene Vließ* (1818-1820) und ihre antiken Vorbilder." *Neophilologus* 47 (1963): 120-25.

Weber, Heinz-Dieter. "Kindesmord als tragische Handlung." *Deutschunterricht* 28, No. 2 (1976): 75-97.

Weber, Peter. *Das Menschenbild des bürgerlichen Trauerspiels.* Berlin: Rütten & Loening, 1970.

Weber-Kellermann, Ingeborg. *Die deutsche Familie. Versuch einer Sozialgeschichte.* Frankfurt am Main: Suhrkamp, 1974.

Weinraub, Marsha. "Fatherhood: The Myth of the Second-Class Parent." *Mother/Child, Father/Child Relationships.* Ed. Joseph H. Stevens, Jr., and Marilyn Mathews. Washington, DC: National Association for the Education of Young Children, 1978. 109-133.

Wells, G. A. "What is Wrong with *Emilia Galotti*?." *German Life and Letters* 37 (1984): 163-173.

Werner, Johannes. *Gesellschaft in literarischer Form. H. L. Wagners* Kindermörderin *als Epochen- und Methodenparadigma.* Stuttgart: Klett, 1977.

Wessell, Leonard P. "The Function of Odoardo in Lessing's *Emilia Galotti.*" *Germanic Review* 47 (1972): 243-58.

Wick, Wiltraud. "Innere Entwicklung der Charaktere in Grillparzers Drama." Diss. Tübingen, 1951.

Wierlacher, Alois. "Das Haus der Freude oder Warum stirbt Emilia Galotti?" *Lessing Yearbook* 5 (1973): 147-62.

Wiese, Benno von. *Die deutsche Tragödie von Lessing bis Hebbel.* Hamburg: Hoffmann & Campe, 1955.

Wilpert, Gero von. *Sachwörterbuch der Literatur.* Stuttgart: Kröner, 1979.

Wittkowski, Wolfgang. "Klara und Mariamne. Kleinstädterin und Königin." *Friedrich Hebbel. Neue Studien zu Werk und Wirkung.* Ed. Hilmar Grundmann. Heide, West Germany: Boyen, 1982. 147-58.

Wright, J. D. "Hebbels Klara. The Victim of a Division in Allegiance and Purpose." *Monatshefte* 38 (1946): 304-316.

Yates, W. E. *Grillparzer. A Critical Introduction.* Cambridge: Cambridge University Press, 1972.

Ziegler, Klaus. *Mensch und Welt in der Tragödie Friedrich Hebbels.* Darmstadt: Wissenschaftliche Buchgesellschaft, 1966.

North American Studies
in Nineteenth-Century German Literature

is a series of monographs on post-Romantic literature of the nineteenth century in the German-speaking lands. The series endeavors to embrace studies in criticism, in literary history, in the interdependence with other national literatures, and in the social and political dimensions of literature. Our aim is to offer contributions by American scholars to the renovation of literary history, the reformation of the canon, the rediscovery of once significant authors, the reevaluation of texts and their contexts, and a renewed understanding and appreciation of a body of literature of acknowledged international importance in the nineteenth century.

Jeffrey Sammons
Yale University